Weight
Conversion Table

Kilograms	Pounds
0—7 kg	0—16 lbs
6—9.5 kg	14—21 lbs
9—12.5 kg	20—28 lbs
11.5—15 kg	26—33 lbs
14—18 kg	31—40 lbs
16.5—21.5 kg	37—48 lbs
20—24.5 kg	45—55 lbs
23—29 kg	52—64 lbs
28—36 kg	62—80 lbs
34—43 kg	75—95 lbs

Clothing Size
Conversion Chart

Japanese size	Height in inches
60 cm	0–26"
70 cm	26–30"
80 cm	30–34"
90 cm	34–38"
100 cm	38–42"
110 cm	42–46"
120 cm	46–50"
130 cm	50–53"
140 cm	53–57"
150 cm	57–61"

Washing Instructions

Symbol	Description
↻↻	Gentle wring or spin dry
弱 40°C	Machine washable (max. water temperature shown)
エンソサラシ	Can use bleach
	Drip dry in the shade
	Use press cloth between iron and fabric
ドライ	Dry clean only
手洗イ 30°C	Hand washable (max. water temperature shown)
高	Iron (with high temperature)
中	Iron (with medium temperature)
低	Iron (with low temperature)
✕	"X" over any symbol means that it should not be done

Japan for Kids

Japan for Kids:
The Ultimate Guide for Parents and Their Children

Diane Wiltshire Kanagawa
Jeanne Huey Erickson

KODANSHA INTERNATIONAL
Tokyo • New York • London

Interior art by Akio Harada
Jacket art by Renee-Naomi, age 5

Distributed in the United States by Kodansha America, Inc.,
575 Lexington Avenue, New York, N.Y. 10022, and in the
United Kingdom and continental Europe by Kodansha
Europe Ltd., 95 Aldwych, London WC2B 4JF. Published by
Kodansha International Ltd., 17-14 Otowa 1-chome,
Bunkyo-ku, Tokyo 112-8652, and Kodansha America, Inc.

99 00 01   10 9 8 7 6

ISBN 4-7700-1531-3

Library of Congress Cataloging-in-Publication Data

Kanagawa, Diane Wiltshire, 1955-
  Japan for kids : the ultimate guide for parents and their
  children / Diane Wiltshire Kanagawa and Jeanne Huey
  Erickson.—1st ed.
      p.   cm.
  Includes index.
  ISBN 4-7700-1531-3
  1. Child rearing—Japan.   2. Mothers—Travel—Japan.
  3. Children—Japan.   4. Americans—Japan.   5. Europeans
  —Japan. I. Erickson, Jeanne Huey, 1962-   II. Title.
HQ769.K29 1992   92-978
649'.1'0952—dc20   CIP

CONTENTS

FOREWORD

RYOKO DOZONO, M.D., Ph.D.

When I first heard that Diane and Jeanne were writing a parents' guide to Japan, I was elated. As a mother of young children myself, I knew that I could look forward to some pertinent and practical help on all aspects of parenting.

As a gynecologist catering largely to the foreign community, I realized how valuable a book like this would be to English-speaking residents of Japan. Every day I encounter parents who are desperate for information and advice on a variety of topics. "Where can I find extra-large maternity clothes?" "Which international preschool would be best for my child?" "Do you know a magician for my son's birthday party?" One can find this information in Japan but it is time-consuming to track down. The life of a parent is busy enough, especially for those residing in a foreign country. A manual with all of these tips and inside scoops is much needed.

I was impressed with the authors' dedication to this project. Over two years were spent exploring parks and zoos, schools, and toy stores and checking out numerous tips from other parents. Jeanne and Diane jokingly remarked that their market research for this book took place every day of their lives as the parents of five young children between them.

During the writing of the book, I marveled at their creativity and their enthusiasm, but especially at their attitude toward Japan. Always looking at the positive aspect of every situation, they remind many of us of what a wonderful place Japan is to live with young children. The cultural gap of East and West is bridged by *Japan for Kids*. As I read through the original drafts of this book, I realized that this was a definitive source book for all parents, whatever their nationality. Nowhere else is there such a comprehensive listing on such a wide range of subjects geared to make parenting in Japan easier and more enjoyable. What fun it is to view parenting in Japan through the eyes of these two energetic American mothers.

INTRODUCTION

Are the characters on "Sesame Street" more familiar to you than many of your relatives? Do your wildest fantasies involve an uninterrupted night's sleep? Does the rattle in your glove compartment turn out to be crayons and Cheerios? If you answered yes to any of the above, then perhaps you live in a home with children. So do we. Our combined experiences as parents in Japan run the gamut from childbirth in a Japanese hospital to finding the right elementary school for a six-year-old. This is a book of information we have gathered in the process. Sometimes we learned the hard way—have you ever paid U.S.$65 for a child's haircut?! Sometimes new friends shared their secrets.

There is no doubt that life with young children can be challenging, if not overwhelming at times. A posting or long vacation to a foreign land such as Japan can send even the most experienced parent into a panic. In this book, you will find innovative ideas and suggestions for dealing with everything from the high cost of living to the language barrier. We have found that a little advance planning can make all the difference. Whether you are preparing for a new baby in the family or your initial move to Japan, knowing what to bring or where to buy it here can make adjusting to your new life-style infinitely easier.

After a combined total of thirteen years in this country and five children of various ages between us, we feel qualified to say that Japan is a terrific place to raise children. The Japanese have a special place in their hearts for children, and this is reflected in their cultural traditions as well as in their tolerance for the typical two-year-old.

We hope that *Japan for Kids* will give you the courage and confidence to enjoy life with your children in this wonderful country. We urge you to take advantage of the exciting possibilities awaiting you. After you survive the initial adjustment period, you will find your family's life forever enriched by the time spent in Japan.

1
Getting
out
and about

J apan is a land of contrasts, from sleepy hillside villages to the sprawling concrete expanses of the major cities. This country offers an endless variety of things to do and interesting places to visit and, at first sight, a veritable nest of routes and transport systems which can make getting out and about a frustrating and time-consuming ordeal. A language problem and a couple of screaming kids do not make your task any easier. However, with a little planning and flexibility it is possible to run errands, do the shopping, and visit friends without taking all day or spending a fortune on cab fares. How you choose to travel to any one place may differ from day to day depending on the traffic, weather, time, and budget considerations, not to mention your energy level. With these factors in mind, take time to consider your options carefully.

If you walk to the train with the baby in the stroller, you then have to carry the stroller and your child up and down the stairs in the train stations. Should you drive to the department store on a Saturday to pick up one item if you have to sit in your car for forty-five minutes waiting for a space in the parking garage? If you take the bus, you could be home by the time you get the car parked. Being well prepared and knowing your options—a bus route near your home, a good corner to get a cab, the back-street short-cuts—will prove invaluable.

THINGS TO TAKE ALONG

Never leave home without a few of the necessities your small children might need. Diapers, wipes, zip-lock bags, and a change of clothes are standard fare for diaper bags worldwide. In Japan, however, you need to add a few items to the list that you may not usually carry. For example, small packs of tissue are a must as many public toilets do not provide toilet paper or paper towels.

In the summer heat and humidity, you will see many Japanese carrying a handkerchief (*hankachii*) to wipe their brow. A *hankachii* is great in the summer, particularly those made of absorbent gauze and toweling and year-round they can be used for cleaning up hands and faces after eating or washing while on the move. Kid-sized handkerchiefs, decorated with cartoon characters, are available in addition to designer versions for Mom and Dad.

For cold weather, the Japanese have a wonderful gadget for warming the kids' hands and bodies. Called *tsukaisute kairo,* these hot packs are handy for outdoor outings. They are sold in packages of ten or so and range from the size of a child's hand to the size of an adult's hand. They can be found in most drugstores, where they are prominently displayed during the winter months. To activate the packs, take them out of the plastic and rub them between your hands. After about five minutes, they will be warm and can then be tucked into coat pockets or under clothing, or held in the hand. They will stay warm for four to twelve hours and are especially useful when traveling outdoors in winter or for trips to the zoo or amusement park. Do not get caught as we once did, watching the afternoon parade at Tokyo Disneyland while our hands froze because we had underestimated the cold. All the Japanese children sitting on the curb had these little hot packs; we finally had to buy gloves for our children at ¥2,000 a pair!

FOOD FOR ON-THE-GO

A few snacks can go a long way toward keeping the kids happy while traveling. Although the Japanese consider it impolite to eat in the train, bus, or taxi, young children are usually exceptions. If you find yourself in a tight spot and need to give the children a little something to keep them going, try to snack as neatly as possible and always clean up your mess, even if it is just a few crumbs. Older children should sit on a bench at a bus stop or on the train platform for snacking. On the Shinkansen (Japan's superexpress railway line) or other long-distance trains, eating is acceptable and tables are provided.

For travel or school meals, Japanese children pack their lunch or snacks in a small box. Lacking the handle by which Western lunch boxes are carried, these containers are carried in drawstring bags or wrapped in square cloths and carried by the knot. This portable meal is called an *obento*, and it is a custom that has been practiced for centuries by the Japanese. Special *obento* equipment is available that includes matching carrying bags or cloths, matching *obento* boxes, pint-sized thermos flasks and mugs, and matching cutlery and chopstick sets. Some thermoses even come with a pop-up straw. Children get thirsty in the strangest of places, and a small thermos of water tucked in the diaper bag can come in handy when on the road.

To go with the *obento* boxes there are matching *oshibori* sets. These are small washcloths that fit in a plastic cylinder or zippered bag. When you leave the house in the morning, dampen the washcloth, close it in the cylinder or bag and it will stay wet all day long for cleaning up after play or meals. Just do not forget to wash it, or you will find a moldy *oshibori* on your next outing.

Some of the best-quality *obento* boxes for children are found at the Sanrio shops in department stores (see chap. 2). Sanrio is a large company that manufactures children's goods featuring cartoon characters, such as Hello Kitty and the Runabouts, in an amazing array of designs from stuffed animals to stickers to underwear to *obento* boxes. You will be surprised what the kids will eat when the food is appealingly arranged in one of these boxes!

Filling the *obento* box can be fun for everyone. Besides the usual nutritious snacks such as crackers and peanut butter, cheese cubes, and apple slices, there is a whole new snack world to explore in the Japanese supermarket.

Osembe are Japanese rice crackers, and they come in every shape, flavor, and size imaginable. Most grocery stores have an entire aisle filled with different kinds of rice crackers, from festive, seasonal crackers to the standard peanut or *nori* (seaweed) mixture. Most kids enjoy these snacks, which are also sold in individually wrapped packages.

Those parents who like to sneak nutrition into their children's snacks should try a small, round cracker called a *tamago boru* (literally, "egg ball"). This popular snack is full of calcium and dissolves in the mouth, making it suitable for even babies. *Tamago boru* come in large bags filled with single-serving packs decorated with bright cartoons. Most stores also carry large bags of alphabet or animal crackers that are low in sugar and inexpensive.

Besides *osembe*, you might want to introduce your child to "good-for-you" Japanese treats such as dried seaweed, or *nori* strips. These come in individual packs, just right for slipping into your bag. Be aware, however, that the *nori* sometimes sticks to the teeth or the roof of the mouth. One of our toddlers was stared at because the bits of *nori* stuck to his teeth made them look black. Another interesting snack choice is strips of dried squid (*saki ika*). Many children love the salty flavor and chewy texture. For an unusual taste sensation, try the strips of squid with cheese sandwiched in between.

In the refrigerated section of your supermarket, you will find small cartons of juice, milk, and yogurt. They range in size from tiny (three swallows) to the average drink-box size (200 ml). To identify the contents, it is usually safe to look for a picture of a fruit on the carton or to judge by the color of the carton—red for apple, orange for orange, etc. Many of these drink cartons are decorated with cartoon characters that appeal to children. When looking for milk, if you can find a carton with a picture of a cow—take it, it is most likely what you want. The brown-colored cartons usually contain chocolate or coffee drink variations. Plastic bottles of *yakuruto*, a sweet yogurt-based drink popular with children, are also sold.

In addition to food, a small surprise or wrapped package to open en route can go a long way toward keeping the kids occupied on public transportation or while you maneuver through rush-hour traffic. We fill our purses and glove compartments with hand-sized pinball games, sticker books, finger puppets, and small pencil and crayon sets. For distracting the kids during a long trip, some good children's cassette tapes and books are helpful. If you want these in your native tongue at a reasonable price, bring them with you or order from home (see the Mail-Order Books and Toys From Abroad section in chap. 4).

TRANSPORTATION

Before discussing the specifics of traveling around Japan, there are a few general guidelines for safety that the foreigner should be aware of.

First, never leave your house without identification of some sort. By law, you should have your alien registration card (or passport if you are not a resident) with you at all times.

Second, your children should also have some form of identification on them, especially for day trips or visits to crowded places. Chances are that your child would have no way to communicate with the authorities if he or she was separated from you. We put our *meishi* (name card) in our older children's pockets and pin a plastic laminated card on the baby's back. There are also I.D. bracelets, necklaces, and tags available from mail-order sources. The Right Start Catalog mentioned in chapter 3 has I.D. tags to lace onto your child's shoes. Another company, K.I.Dentification, makes fabric belts and bracelets that close with Velcro and have a place for you to write your child's name, address, telephone number, and other necessary information. They will mail overseas, and you can get a catalog by writing to them at 909 Marina Village Pkwy. #232, Alameda, California 94501, USA.

Third, when traveling away from home, always carry a copy of your insurance card and a reasonable amount of cash—¥20,000 or so—in case emergency medical care is needed. If you have Japanese National Health Insurance or company insurance, the hospital will want your policy number; if you have private insurance, you will have to pay cash for treatment.

RIDING THE RAILS

The quickest way to travel around the cities is by train and subway. Most children find the ride exciting, and you will not need to do too much in the way of distracting them. Besides being quick, the trains are clean, safe, and on time. You will see Japanese schoolchildren as young as six and seven riding the train alone. Throughout Japan, public transportation (subways and buses) is free for children up to the age of six, and children from six to twelve ride for half fare.

Certain times of the day should be avoided when traveling with small children on the train. There really are men whose job it is to stand and shove passengers onto the train before the doors close! Needless to say, a child could be injured or at least seriously frightened in the crush. On the train, no allowances are made for a little person to breathe or see out the window. When caught in this situation with a three-year-old, one friend lifted his child up and held her over his head for the duration of the ride. It worked, but we do not recommend it for daily travel. The exact time of this rush is different for each train station and line and is one of those things that you have to learn from experience.

A good subway and train map including JR and other private lines will be a lifesaver, but the best way to learn to ride with ease is to do it often. During non-rush-hour times, the other passengers will smile and coo at your young children. If you have a stroller or a sleeping child, often someone will offer you their seat or help in some way. A complete stranger once took a friend's heavy stroller and bags all the way up three flights of station stairs so that she could carry her tired and grumpy two-year-old.

You can buy a train or subway pass (*teiki*) at any station. Passes are sold for one route only, so unless you ride a regular route often, they may not be worth buying. One way to avoid the crush at the ticket machines is to buy *kaisuken*—books of eleven tickets for the price of ten.

A couple of things to remember: The "silver" seats at one end of the train car are reserved for elderly or handicapped passengers. If your children want to kneel on the seat to look out the window, make sure they slip their shoes off and place them on the floor with the toes pointing out, as Japanese children do. Also, be careful when boarding the train as the gap between the train and the platform can be dangerously wide at times.

LONGER TRAIN TRIPS

For information on all JR services, including the Shinkansen, you can call Infoline Service in English at (03) 3423-0111, Monday through Friday from 10:00 A.M. to 6:00 P.M. You can get transportation as well as tourist information in English through the toll-free "Travel Phones," which operate from 9:00 A.M. to 5:00 P.M. For eastern Japan, call 0120-222800; for western Japan call 0120-444800.

Reservations cannot be made through Infoline Service or the Travel Phones. To reserve seats on the Shinkansen or any other long-distance train, such as a resort-bound train, you will need to call a travel agent or go to the station from which you want to leave.

In general, reserved seats are not available on local trains, though some trains have a first-class car, called a Green Car, where seats can be reserved. Seats on resort trains must be reserved, and the fare includes the bus ride from the station to the resort.

The Shinkansen is an experience that should not be missed while in Japan. From the age of six, children must have their own seat, and they travel at half fare in economy and reserved seats until age twelve. If you have a child under six, you may buy a children's ticket or hold the child in your lap. If you happen to be traveling during an off time, say, the middle of the week or midday, there will often be empty seats nearby that your small child can occupy if you did not reserve one.

Besides nonreserved and reserved seating (both of which are available in smoking and nonsmoking cars), each Shinkansen has a first-class car, the Green Car, where each person, including small children, must have their own seat and pay full fare. There are also four types of private compartments available. Not all types may be available on every train; it depends on where and when you are traveling. These compartments are nice if you are traveling with children, and, as in first class, every person in the compartment pays full fare.

The ride on the Shinkansen is smooth, and the cars are clean, spacious, and quiet. Bathrooms are plentiful, trays unfold in front of each seat to hold snacks or coloring books, and shades pull down to keep the sun out of sleepy eyes. Children can be made quite comfortable, especially if they have their own seat.

BY BUS

The bus can come in handy after a long day out with the kids, especially if there is a stop near your house. As with a cab, the bus can be a great help for that 10-minute walk from the station with the kids. Also, bus routes cover many places that the subway lines do not, so on special outings the bus may be your only alternative. Buses run as efficiently as they can considering they have to maneuver through traffic.

If you have your stroller with you, a balancing act worthy of a juggler is required to manhandle stroller and baby onto the bus and to hold them both while riding. You must take the baby out of the stroller to board the bus and so a stroller that folds up easily with one hand is useful. The rush-hour crowd on the bus can be a crush, so use your judgment when riding with children.

There are many bus companies in Japan, all of which are privately owned. If you want to ride the bus regularly on a particular route, you will need to find the end of the line for that bus (either end; usually a train or subway station) and go there. That is where you will find an office with a map (*chizu*) of the route and regular passes for sale. A pass is good for one bus and one route only.

CATCHING A CAB

Taxi cabs are the most expensive way to travel within a city; the meter just keeps ticking while you keep sitting. Cabs are best when you have a short distance to go—time it so you can get out just before the meter turns past the first fare—or when you encounter adverse circumstances: you are caught in the rain without an umbrella, you bought too much, the kids will not walk another step.

Japan's cabs are probably the cleanest and safest in the world. The drivers take pride in their cars, and you are expected to respect them as you would your own, maybe even more. Some rules for riding a cab are "understood." First, the back door on the left side of the cab pops open automatically, so keep children away from the door's range, and do not try to open it yourself. Second, you will notice that there are white covers on the seats and that the driver wears white gloves. This is a clean car. Do not let your child walk across the seat or put his feet on it in any way; if necessary, slip his shoes off upon entering the car. Place the stroller with its dirty wheels on the floor of the car. Be courteous and friendly to the driver, and he will do his best to get you where you need to go.

When giving directions to a driver there are a few Japanese words that everyone should know. If the place you are going to is not well known and you do not have a map, give him the name of an obvious landmark nearby. Once you have the driver going in the right direction, you can tell him where to turn or go straight. A bit more vocabulary would come in handy, but if you are desperate, use these words:

Right: *migi*

Left: *hidari*

Straight: *massugu*

Stop here: *tomatte kudasai* ("Stop" and "O.K." also work well.)

For those who frequently take cabs, or who are sometimes caught without any money, cab tickets are available in Tokyo. No more madly counting your change to see if you can afford to ride all of the way home. The cab coupons are available at Takashimaya or Mitsukoshi department stores in Tokyo or the Daimaru Department Store next to Tokyo Station. These coupons are available in various amounts and can be used for any cab company.

DRIVING A CAR

If you are a foreigner and drive a car in Japan, congratulations. You have entered a new phase of tolerance testing. You probably know that driving on the freeway with a screaming child in the back seat can be hair-raising. Just wait until you are moving at three kilometers per hour in traffic with a screaming child in the back seat. It is not always that bad, but making adequate preparations beforehand will save you a headache or two.

You may be able to drive for a limited amount of time with a license from your home country or an International Driver's License, but if you are a resident of Japan, you should have a Japanese license. If you do not speak Japanese, you may want to take a Japanese-speaking person with you to the licensing bureau, although the English forms are quite easy to fill out. If you do not have a license from your home country, you must take the same driver's test as the Japanese. The test is available in English, but it is very extensive and attendance at a driving school is required to pass. The cost for the driving school is exorbitant, so it is really not worth the time and expense involved. If possible, try and get your driver's license before you leave your home country. To apply for a Japanese license, you will need your passport, alien registration card, one photo (2.4 cm by 3 cm), a valid license from your home country, and ¥3,000. It is important to note that you must have at least three months experience in your home country before you can apply for a Japanese license. To find the licensing bureau nearest you, call the head office in Tokyo at (03) 3474-1374, or write 1-12-5 Higashi Oi, Shinagawa-ku, Tokyo.

In Japan, all passengers must wear seat belts "while riding in a car furnished with seat belts." The safest place for children to ride is in the back seat, and if they are young, they should be in a special infant or toddler car seat. Many good brands of car seats are available in department and children's stores (see chaps. 2 and 3). See-through shades for car windows are a must for protecting children's eyes—they can be ordered through the Perfectly Safe catalog listed in chapter 3.

Before you drive, it is important to get the English-language book *Rules of the Road*. Published by the Japan Automobile Federation (JAF), it can be purchased for a small fee. JAF is an organization similar to the American Automobile Association (AAA) in the United States. For a nominal yearly fee, they provide a number of helpful services should anything happen to your car while on the road. JAF's head office is at 1-21-5 Ebisu Nishi, Shibuya-ku, Tokyo, phone (03) 3463-0111. Offices are also located throughout Japan and can be reached in the following cities at these numbers: Yokohama, (045) 8437110; Osaka, (06) 534-0111; Kobe, (078) 303-0111; and Kyoto, (075) 682-0111.

As you may have noticed, most cities in Japan were not "laid out by the crows." There is not much modern logic in the layout of the streets; there is no street numbering system; and only the major streets have names. As a result, your road map will become your best friend. Try to find one in English that has street names, block numbers, and as much detail as possible. Since you will be using the map often (even taxi drivers use maps to find their way around Tokyo) buy some clear adhesive film and cover both sides of the map. This way it can be easily rolled up and will not disintegrate or get mutilated in the glove compartment. For Tokyo residents, one good choice is *Tokyo, A Bilingual Atlas* (Kodansha, 1987), which is a city map in book form.

Getting lost from time to time while driving is a natural state of affairs in Japan. New arrivals are often told that the average time spent finding one's way after getting lost is one hour. When you have to travel to a new location for an important appointment, consider taking a practice run the day before, if possible. You'll find there are not too many cars on the road before 7:00 A.M., so use the time to practice learning shortcuts and back streets. Shortly after moving here, one friend got so tired of driving around trying to find his way home that he gave up, hailed a cab, gave the cabbie his *meishi* and money for the fare, and then followed the taxi home in his own car.

BIKING IT

Throughout Japan, parents and their children run errands, buy groceries, go on outings—all by bicycle, and often on the same bicycle. One of the most amazing sights for newcomers to Japan is the petite Japanese mother riding her bike with a child on the front and a child on the back. Most lightweight touring bikes cannot carry the load, but the bikes sold in Japan are made specifically for this kind of travel. The child bike seats available here allow a child to ride in the front (great for balance and control of the child) or on the back of the bike. These seats do not have the high back for support found on the seats in the United States. For those molded seats with chest straps or for character seats, such as Cookie Monster, you will have to order from overseas or bring one with you. See the Perfectly Safe mail-order catalog in chapter 3 to order these seats from the United States.

If you want to ride a bike in Japan, it is best to buy it here. You can buy a new bike from your neighborhood bike shop or a used one through the newspaper or bulletin boards where foreigners sell used items.

After you buy your bike, you are required to register it if you plan to park it in any of the bike parking areas and to protect your loss in case it is stolen. To register your bike, take it to the local *koban*, or police box. The police will check it for safety regulations (i.e., brakes in good condition, adequate light for riding at night) and then put a sticker on it to show that it has been registered. At the same time, it is a good idea to have them put your name, address, and phone number on the bike in Japanese. Also, be sure to write down your registration number at home as you will need it if the bike is lost or stolen. If you buy a bike here, the shop that sold it will register it for you. If you do buy your bike from a local shop, chances are that they will take a personal interest in your bike's maintenance and up-keep. One friend who rides her bike everywhere says that each time she rides by the shop where she bought her bike, they run out and stop her so that they can check the tires!

We have not found any hard and fast rules as to where or how you can park your bike. Every once in a while, the neighborhood police will round up all bikes that are questionably parked. Friends who ride often say this occurs every three or four months. If your bike is not where you left it, go to the nearest *koban* to report that it is missing. Most large train stations have a bike lot nearby. Department stores usually have lots around to the side or at the back. If someone does not like where you have parked, they will let you know. However, when in doubt, park with others—sometimes there is safety in numbers.

It is a good idea to lock your bike when you leave it for any length of time. Despite the relative safety of Japan, bikes are stolen, and foreign bikes may be more likely to be taken. A strong chain or bar lock is best. Most Japanese bikes have a wheel lock that allows you to lock the front wheel with the turn of a key. Even though you may keep one key permanently in the lock, do not lose the other one. A friend had a prankster remove his key once, leaving him with a locked wheel.

Most cyclists in Japan do not wear helmets, nor do their children. This does not mean that biking is less dangerous in Japan than anywhere else. Cyclists, especially young children, should always wear a helmet. Bike helmets are available in some stores, but for the most part they are made of styrofoam and are not as advanced as the molded plastic type readily found in the United States. If you have difficulty finding a safe, top-quality helmet, you will have to order from overseas or contact one of the following outlets in Japan. The demand for these helmets up to this point has been low, so many stores do not stock them.

The sturdy Bell brand of bike helmets is one of the best in the United States, and there is a distributor in Osaka. Maruchu and Co., Ltd., does not handle any retail business, but they will direct you to the nearest supplier of Bell bike helmets in your area. Contact them at Matsuri Bldg. 6 F, 13-16 Ichijodori, Sakai-shi, Osaka-fu, (0722) 23-1401. Another good brand of helmet, O.G.K., can be purchased from the Osaka Grip Mfg. Co., Ltd. For the retailer nearest you, write to 5-27-2 Takaida Hondori, Higashiosaka-shi, Osaka-fu, or call (06) 782 4353–6.

There are two bike accessories popular in Japan that we have found to be especially helpful in the cold weather. "Handle warmers" are mitts that attach to the bike handles, eliminating the need for gloves on a cold or windy day. Another must for cycling in windy weather is a bike wind-shield. This clear plastic shield, which fits on the front of the bicycle, protects a child sitting on a front bike seat from the cold wind.

For the most part, bicycles travel on the sidewalk. This is safer for the cyclist, but not as fast as riding on the open road in a bike lane. The sidewalks are crowded, and you must stop and start a lot. This is one reason why women here ride ladies' bikes and not the men's type with a crossbar. It is illegal to ride a bike on which you cannot touch the ground with your toes when mounted (this is one of the things that the police check when registering your bike).

On a road without sidewalks bikes also travel inside the guardrail or white line. This is where pedestrians walk, too, and if there are a lot of poles and people on the road, you will be doing a lot of starting and stopping here as well. A word of advice from one experienced biker is to practice measuring how long it takes you to meet an approaching object. When pedestrians are approaching and there is a pole in the way, you need to be able to judge when to slow down, ring your bell, stop, or get off your bike.

For information about rules for cyclists, see the same JAF publication, *Rules of the Road,* as mentioned in the section on driving.

See chapter 5 for recreational cycling facilities in Tokyo for adults and courses just for children.

WALKING
One of the nicest things about living in Japan is the chance you have to walk to stores, to parks, or to just stroll in the sunshine. Japan is full of people walking, and in the cities there are side streets and paths just for pedestrians and bikes. The rule at crosswalks is that, if a pedestrian puts out his hand to signal he wants to cross, cars are to stop. This practice is not foolproof, but it gives you some idea of the respect traditionally granted to pedestrians by most drivers.

Major streets usually have ample sidewalks, and those that do not will have a white painted line or a guardrail. One of the main things to watch for when walking, especially with children, is bicycles. They often approach at a brisk speed, so it is best to hold your child's hand on the sidewalk.

The easiest way to walk any distance with small children is with a good stroller (see chap. 3). You will not see many Japanese children over the age of two or three in a stroller, but we never let that stop us from putting our older preschoolers in a stroller whenever they were tired. No complaints about heat, sore feet, or whatever, and they can snack or just enjoy the sights as you go along. One word about sore feet: Avoid them by wearing comfortable walking shoes. A good pair of walking or running shoes (preferably from another country for size and economic reasons) are a valuable investment for you and your children.

For a leisurely walk to the park or corner store, there are small trikes and pedal cars that a three- or four-year-old can ride while you walk. A special feature of some of these trikes and cars is a steering handle that allows Mom or Dad to push from behind as the child rides (see chap. 3).

AIRPLANE TRIPS

Even if you view long airplane trips with thrill rather than trepidation, you will probably feel daunted by the prospect of flying for hours and hours with an infant or young child. Throughout the years, we have survived long plane rides with and without spouses, with newborns and two-year-olds. We hope some of our experiences will make your own travel a little less harried.

As soon as you know your travel date, reserve your seat on the plane. When traveling with children, most people feel that the best seats on the plane are either in front of the bulkhead or on a row near the front of the middle section. If possible, request that your travel agent book you on a flight that is not too full.

Infants can often fit in a bassinet provided by the airline that attaches to the wall in front of the bulkhead seat. The size of the bassinet will depend on the airline you are flying with; some bassinets are padded and large enough for a six-month-old, while others are little more than cardboard boxes that can barely hold a six-week-old. An infant can also spend some time in a front carrier, which frees Mom or Dad's hands to read or eat a meal. The front carriers made by Tot Tenders (see the overseas baby equipment catalogs section in chap. 3) hold the baby facing outward, making sitting for long periods comfortable for all involved. This company also makes a specially designed carrier for twins.

Toddlers and older children will probably prefer the middle rows where the armrests can be removed. They are not removable in most bulkhead seats, which makes it impossible for a child to lie across any empty seats.

We have quite a few friends who give their children a mild over-the-counter sedative, such as Dramamine or Benadryl, before boarding. Both of these medications combat air sickness and may cause drowsiness. The only drawback is that the medicine may also have the opposite effect. You should ask your pediatrician for advice if you are thinking about using such drugs.

When traveling with more than one young child, you will need a sturdy, light-weight stroller that folds up easily. Also, for an infant, a front or back carrier is a must if you are traveling alone. We pile as many bags as possible on the stroller, sometimes even strapping the carry-on luggage in the seat. Whenever our preschooler feels like riding, he sits on top of the heap. Of course, this system is a problem when going through security clearance. Their rules require you to empty the stroller, which means you have to unload all the bags and then put them back on again.

If your stroller is a narrow model that will fit down the aisle of the plane, go ahead and push it right onto the plane and to your seat. Some parents prefer to board with the kids when the preboarding message is announced. This enables you to get settled without blocking the aisles, and you can claim overhead storage space and blankets and pillows. The drawback of early boarding is the extra time you then have to spend on the plane.

In our carry-on bags we pack a change of clothes for everyone—even Mom—in case of air sickness or spills. Cups with lids and straws or spouts are a must when traveling with small children. Put any drinks that they serve on the plane into these cups to minimize spills. For cleanups, it is helpful to have a wet washcloth or two in a zip-lock bag. In separate plastic bags, put diaper-changing supplies and a mini first-aid kit containing acetimenophen, band-aids, and lots of tissues. A small spray can of mineral water is soothing for dry faces and is a quick way to clean sticky hands. There are also some new antibacterial wipes on the market that come in handy for wiping off the toilet seat or children's hands before they eat. It is also good to take disposable bibs, or clothespins to make bibs out of a napkin, as well as slipper socks for everyone to wear during the flight.

Apart from carry-on luggage and all of the essentials that make a trip go smoother, we recommend a system that has saved our sanity many times. If your children are old enough, let them each carry a backpack full of small games and toys. You can also give each of them their own bag filled with gaily-wrapped surprises and treats that can be opened at intervals during the trip. Even the best-behaved children will become bored and restless on a long plane ride, so it is better to have too many surprises than not enough. Remember, the plane could always be delayed, and once you arrive at your destination you still have to go through immigration, wait for luggage, go through customs, and, if you are coming into Japan through Narita, you will most likely have to ride in a bus or taxi for an hour or more to reach your home.

When you are ready to pack the goodies to keep the kids busy, remember that they do not have to be expensive items. Be on the lookout for small toys, stickers, markers, and pads, and stock up when you find them. Sometimes we even use old toys that our children have not played with for a while. Wrap them all in gift paper before the flight, and you have instant "presents." Wrapping is not necessary, but for very young children it does add to the excitement.

A few companies in the United States offer customized travel packs for children. Two of our favorites are Sealed With A Kiss, and Between You And Me. Sealed With A Kiss offers a travel package of eight or more imaginative games to keep kids busy. They mail only within the United States, and they accept VISA, MasterCard, and American Express. Write to 6709 Tildenwood Lane, Rockville, Maryland 20852, USA. Between You And Me features a Toddler Travel Pack full of toys and accessories suitable for children under three years of age. They also sell a Travel Activity Pack, which is a backpack full of toys and activities tailored to your child's age. They will mail overseas, and they accept VISA and MasterCard. Write to Fran Weaver, 3419 Tony Drive, San Diego, California 92122, USA, or call (619) 455-9370.

If you have a nursing infant with you, you can rest assured in the knowledge that breastfeeding often during the long flight will be the most comforting thing for your baby. For infants, sucking is the best way to relieve ear pain due to changes to in cabin air pressure. Remember to drink plenty of fluids and to wear comfortable clothes that allow for discreet breastfeeding. You may want to book a window seat for extra privacy.

If you have a child in diapers, make sure that you take plenty with you. Airlines often stock diapers, but you should not count on their supply. Although we are proponents of cloth diapers, disposables are invaluable when traveling long distances. For easy changes, dress children who are still in diapers in clothes that unsnap at the crotch. Soft, comfortable clothes are important for everyone, and we usually dress our children in sweat suits with T-shirts underneath to accommodate temperature changes.

No matter how your child is dressed, changing diapers is a bit of a hassle on an airplane. Some airlines have installed changing tables in the bathrooms, while other airlines still leave you to change the baby on the toilet lid. It is wise to bring a plastic pad for diaper changes; and if you have a row of seats to yourself and need to change a wet diaper, just do so on the seat. Passengers in the bulkhead seats can try using the floor space. Bring small plastic bags for soiled diapers, or use the airsick bags in the seat pockets. Be sure to ask the flight attendant where you should dispose of them.

You may want to bring a portable potty seat for young children. The company Children-On-The-Go makes an incredibly small folding seat that slips into a plastic case for easy storage. See the One Step Ahead catalog in chapter 3 for this product.

For older children it is a good idea to take along a small thermos of water for each child. The best kind are the ones with the pop-up straw that even the youngest child can operate by himself without spilling. Sucking on the straw can help relieve ear-aches from pressure changes, and the water helps to ward off dehydration. In addition to water, you may also want to pack small cartons of fruit juice and some favorite snacks, such as Cheerios, apple slices, and peanut butter crackers. For picky eaters, it helps to have sandwiches and snacks that can be eaten in place of airline food. On flights to and from Japan, you can often order an *obento* meal, or you can ask for the special kids' meal. Both of these consist of foods that kids usually like, and they are most often served cold. This means that you can conveniently save part of the meal for the child to eat later if he is sleeping or not hungry when the meal is served.

Last but not least, jet lag is an inevitable part of international flights. There are many books, diet plans, and remedies on the market to combat jet lag, but for young children the only strategy we have found that works is patience. Let them sleep when they are tired and eat when they are hungry, and eventually everyone will be back on schedule.

Now That You Are International

Traveling abroad can be a great adventure for the entire family. It is nice to keep a record of trips for children, and one way to do this is to have a travel book for each child. The Sanrio shops (see chaps. 2 and 4) have cute "travel" books, or you could purchase a plain autograph book at a stationery store. On the airplane, ask a flight attendant, or perhaps the pilot if he is available, to sign the child's book. Having a memento of a flight is an educational way to remember different routes and destinations.

A helpful book for families-on-the-go is the Family Travel Guides Catalogue. Published by Carousel Press, this catalog offers a thorough selection of English-language books about worldwide travel with children of all ages. The catalog also carries games, atlases, and activities geared toward the traveling family. To get a copy, write to Family Travel Guides Catalog, P.O. Box 6061, Albany, California 94706, USA. For book orders, VISA and MasterCard are accepted.

Also for traveling families, a company called Rascals in Paradise offers a variety of trips and tour packages with both U.S. and international destinations for parents and children. For a brochure, write to them at 650 Fifth Street #505, San Francisco, California 94107, USA, or call (415) 978-9800.

Families living abroad may want to take advantage of some of the home exchange programs that cater to families traveling and vacationing abroad. For those with young children, staying in someone's home can be less stressful and less expensive than an extended stay in a hotel. The following programs offer your family a chance to exchange friendships and culture with families all over the world.

International Home Exchange Service

Intervac U.S., P.O. Box 3975, San Francisco, California 94119, USA

The Exchange Book, issued by the International Home Exchange Service three times a year, lists over 7,000 exchange opportunities in more than twenty countries. Subscribers are free to contact any party listed to arrange a mutually agreeable house or apartment swap.

Servas International

Regenburgsgade 11, Aarhus C, DK-8000, Denmark
☎ (45) 86-190319

Servas is an international cooperative system of travelers and volunteer hosts which was established to help build world peace, goodwill, and understanding by providing opportunities for contacts between persons of different cultures and backgrounds. Hosts (mostly individuals and families plus some community groups) provide information about themselves for listing in a national host directory. Approved Servas travelers choose the hosts they wish to contact about possible visits (usually for two nights) to share life in the hosts' homes and communities. Servas charges travelers a small fee. No money changes hands between travelers and hosts. Servas is a nonprofit, interracial, and interfaith organization with consultative status as a nongovernmental organization in the United Nations. For more information or to join, call Kunio Tanaka at (03) 3721-1507 or Ms. Kimura at (0427) 25-9143. You can also contact the Servas Japan coordinator at 3-13-15, Denenchofu, Ota-ku, Tokyo 145, or write to the headquarters in Denmark.

a
Shopping
around
Town

The service lavished upon the customer in Japan can make shopping a heady experience for even the most jaded shopper. From the moment you enter the store and encounter the ranks of bowing salespeople chorusing "*irrashaimase*" (May I help you?), your wish is their command, right down to the intricate wrapping of even the smallest package. In Japan, the customer is king, and this can mean a lot to busy parents shopping with active children.

DEPARTMENT STORES

You and your entire family could spend several days comfortably ensconced in any of Japan's state-of-the-art department stores. There is nothing like these stores anywhere else in the world. Some of them have better facilities for children than others, but all of them are fun and easy to visit with the kids. Our listings cover stores and floors of particular interest to parents and young children. For a more complete rundown on the adult sections of Tokyo department stores, read *Born to Shop, Tokyo*, by Suzy Gershman and Judith Thomas (Bantam Books, 1987). Renovations are continually taking place in the major stores, so there is usually something new and exciting to discover each time you visit. Each store has a different personality, but you will be happy to know that almost all of them have that wonderful Japanese invention, the Baby Room. Forget the times you had to pretend to try on clothes in department stores just so you could breastfeed your baby in privacy. Never again will you experience the hassle of finding a place to change a dirty diaper in the middle of a mall. We thought we had found paradise the first time we stumbled upon the rows of clean changing tables, vending machines dispensing diapers and Gerber juice, hot water for mixing formula, and private booths with comfortable chairs for mothers to feed their babies. And there's more! These department stores provide an infinite number of services for parents and children. Whether it's an electric breast pump you want to rent or a beloved toy that needs repair, the department store is a good place to look for help. If you have a lot of shopping to do, consider using the babysitting service available at some of the major stores. You must call ahead for reservations, but it is worth looking into. All department stores are open on Saturdays and Sundays and closed one day during the week. It can make you crazy trying to remember which day which branch of which store is closed, so keep a record in your wallet.

Upon entering a department store, ask at the information counter for an English information brochure, which is available at some of the larger stores. Also check to see if there are any special sales that day. In many department stores, the next to the top floor is the bargain space, and we have run into great sales on everything from used kimonos to children's potties. Fortunately, all department stores accept major credit cards; many stores also offer their own credit card to customers. You can pick up an application form for store credit cards at the general information desk or at the foreign customers' service desk if they have one. If you didn't bring your stroller, ask at the information counter for one of their complimentary "baby cars." The supply is limited; on crowded weekends it's best to bring your own.

On the children's floor, inquire about a membership club for kids. Registration is usually free and will entitle you to invitations to special sales as well as other bonuses throughout the year. Even if there isn't a children's club, ask to be put on the mailing list for the sales of children's clothing that are held several times a year. If you find a brand of clothing that you especially like, try to get on that particular mailing list as well. We have a few favorite designers whose clothes are so expensive that we can only afford to buy them at sale prices. Most designers of children's clothing have sales at the end of each season. It is easier to get on these lists if you are a regular customer, but each designer has his or her own policy about these invitations—don't be afraid to ask at the counter.

A word about children's fashions in Japan. Japanese designers are noted for their originality and the quality of their adult clothes; the same holds true for their trendy and colorful collections of children's wear. Many of the designer names you will see on children's clothing are those of Japanese designers. Some are world-famous designers of adult clothes who

29

sell a line of children's wear in Japan; others are imported from Paris, London, or Milan. Wherever they are from, you can be sure that children's wear purchased in Japan will be the best in design and quality. Almost all of the clothes that you buy here will be sized according to the Japanese system. Refer to the chart below for translating Japanese sizes into Western sizes.

Japanese size	Height in inches	Weight in kilograms and pounds	
60 cm	0–26″	0–7 kg	0–16 lbs
70 cm	26–30″	6–9.5 kg	14–21 lbs
80 cm	30–34″	9–12.5 kg	20–28 lbs
90 cm	34–38″	1.5–15 kg	26–33 lbs
100 cm	38–42″	14–18 kg	31–40 lbs
110 cm	42–46″	16.5–21.5 kg	37–48 lbs
120 cm	46–50″	20–24.5 kg	45–55 lbs
130 cm	50–53″	23–29 kg	52–64 lbs
140 cm	53–57″	28–36 kg	62–80 lbs
150 cm	57–61″	34–43 kg	75–95 lbs

Many stores offer a free delivery service, although, depending on where you live and the time of year, it may take a few days. If you need an item repaired that was purchased at the store, there is usually only a small fee, if any. We had a Combi stroller repaired for ¥450 once. Even though we had not purchased it at the store that repaired it, they accommodated us because they carry that brand. Getting in touch with the manufacturer directly can also bring results—one friend found a broken Combi stroller in the garbage and, after contacting Combi, was sent a pack of nuts and bolts to fix it—for free.

When you get hungry, don't forget the restaurant floor that can be found in most stores. There is often a children's restaurant on the children's floor, so be sure to look around there first if you have the kids with you. Even at the adult restaurants, kiddie meals, complete with kid-sized utensils and a treat, are usually available. The food sections in the basement are the perfect place to pick up dinner on your way home. The deli selections are terrific—everything from fried chicken to won ton soup—plus the prices are often reduced at the end of the day.

Department store pet shops are always fun for the kids to visit. Some stores have puppies and kittens in addition to the usual assortment of birds, turtles, and fish. A few places have rooftop play areas, and many have beer gardens on the roof in the warmer months.

While in Japan, try to visit a few, if not all, of the major department stores. Don't forget to take visiting friends and relatives on a grand tour from basement to rooftop, for a unique Japanese experience. We're sure they'll agree that there is nothing like it back home!

Check the listings below to find out what special features each store offers. A detailed description is given of a number of department stores that have a lot to offer children. Although only the main branch of a particular department store is described here, the image of the store and the types of services available at other branches are similar despite the different location.

Isetan Department Store

3-14-1 Shinjuku, Shinjuku-ku, Tokyo　東京都新宿区新宿 3-14-1
☎ (03) 3352-1111
🚆 Shinjuku Station (east exit), JR Yamanote, JR Chuo, JR Sobu, Marunouchi, Toei Shinjuku, Keio, Odakyu lines; or Shinjuku Sanchome Station, Marunouchi, Toei Shinjuku lines
Hours: 10:00 A.M. to 7:00 P.M. Closed on Wednesdays

Isetan spares no expense when it comes to appearance or customer satisfaction and service. From the foreign customer club to the sports club to the travel agency, this company's aim is to become involved in all aspects of its customers' lives. If you are a foreigner, they suggest you join the foreign customer club to receive information on sales and events. Information is mailed out in English each month. Isetan has branch stores in Kichijoji, Tachikawa, Matsudo (Chiba), Urawa (Saitama), Niigata, and Shizuoka.

Isetan in Shinjuku is hard to miss. If you take the train, go out the east exit of JR Shinjuku Station and turn right. If you drive, it is easy to find on Meiji Dori. The store boasts 1,000 parking places in its two garages.

Maternity/Newborn

The sixth floor of the Isetan store in Shinjuku houses maternity, newborn, and children's wear. For new and expectant mothers, Isetan has a special club called the "Stork Club." At the club, members can read books, watch videos, and listen to tapes regarding products they will need and also receive guidance on delivery and nursing of newborn babies. Members are notified of special sales for two years after their children are born. A checklist is available—in English at the Foreign Customers' Service Counter—that covers all the items mothers may need for a newborn. Maternity fashions are by Norikoike, Baby It's You, Blanc d'oeuf, and many more Japanese designers. Newborn fashions are by Baby Dior and other top designers. Both manual and electric breast pumps are sold.

Facilities for Babies

On the seventh floor near Eat Paradise is a bathroom with a private toilet and sink large enough for a mother, toddler, and newborn to share. On the sixth floor, there is a bathroom made especially for children, with small-scale sinks and toilets. The "Newborn Baby Corner" is a quiet, spacious area that has baby beds, comfortable chairs, and a nursing room. There are vending machines for disposable diapers, juice, and baby food.

Kids' Fashion and Toys

For kids, the sixth floor is a haven of toys and fun. Parents will find all their favorite children's brands here in abundance. There is a large Sanrio shop and a Dickory Farm restaurant for special children's meals. On this floor, Isetan holds its toy hospital on the first and third Sunday of every month. Repair periods range from the same day to two to three weeks. During long holidays such as spring vacation, Golden Week, and summer vacation, the store holds toy fairs and special events for kids and parents at the sales corner on the fifth floor and on the roof. Check their newsletter for information.

Play Areas

Children will enjoy visiting the pet store and play area on the roof. The usual ¥100 rides are here, and the video games are under shelter in case of rain. On the sixth floor and throughout the store, there are videos for kids to watch while you shop. Of course, in the toy department there are enough toys on display to entertain the kids for an hour or more.

What's to Eat?

Not only is there the Dickory Farm restaurant on the sixth floor, but there is also a wide choice of food available on the seventh floor. From pasta to sushi, fancy to family, you will find something to suit your taste here. For a quick snack, don't forget the food samples in the basement.

Matsuya Department Store

3-6-1 Ginza, Chuo-ku, Tokyo　東京都中央区銀座 3-6-1
☎ (03) 3567-1211
🚃 Ginza Station (A12 exit), Ginza, Marunouchi, Hibiya lines
Hours: 10:00 A.M. to 7:00 P.M. Closed on Tuesdays.

If you are shopping in Ginza, head to Matsuya for the best facilities in the area for babies and children. Matsuya has a young and trendy image, and the store has kept up with the competition with its recent renovations. Although it is not as large as some of the other stores, it is extremely well organized. Matsuya's foreign customer service program is called International Corporate Services, or Cai-Caisho. For information in English, call (03) 5565-3031/2.

Matsuya has two stores in Tokyo, in Ginza and Asakusa. To get to Matsuya in Ginza, take the A12 (Matsuya) exit at Ginza Station. If you drive, there is garage parking at Matsuya, and often meter spaces are available on nearby streets.

Maternity/Newborn

On the sixth floor near the Baby Room is the newborn gift area. This relatively new section contains a lovely selection of infant wear and special gifts. Maternity wear is also in this area with brand names such as Baby It's You and Comme Ca Du Mode.

Facilities for Babies

The Baby Room on the sixth floor has clean, padded changing tables. There are vending machines here for juice and milk. A private booth with stools, but no comfortable chairs, is available for nursing mothers.

Kids' Fashion and Toys

The emphasis at Matsuya is on trendiness with creations by Japanese designers at the forefront. Kenzo is here—his coats and sweaters for kids are soooo stylish—along with some of the Japanese and European designers you'll see at other stores. The boutiques are arranged in an orderly fashion, not too far from the toy section, so you can let the kids play but still keep an eye on them as you browse.

Big discount sales and semi-bargain sales are held twice a year. Apply for invitations on the sixth floor. Matsuya does not have a babysitting service or a children's club, but they do stage a model train show every year during the summer vacation, which is a fun outing for the kids.

Play Areas

In the middle of the toy section there is an "island" full of new gadgets and games displayed on a low table for the children to enjoy. In one corner, near the children's clothing section, is a play area full of wooden blocks and some climbing equipment. Small stools for parents surround the area, which is a great place to turn the kids loose for a while. Just remember to take their shoes off before they enter the play area.

The rooftop level houses a pet shop and Playland, which is open every day from 10:00 A.M. to 7:00 P.M., except in rainy weather. There are a dozen or so ¥100 rides here, in addition to an outdoor cafe and snack bar. There is a covered area with numerous video games that is open even on rainy days.

What's to Eat?

If the kids start whining for a snack, you can buy a pack of cheese sticks at the Sanrio shop on the sixth floor. For meals, try the restaurants on B2 and the eighth floor and don't forget the snack bar on the rooftop in nice weather.

Mitsukoshi Department Store

1-4-1 Muromachi, Nihombashi, Chuo-ku, Tokyo　東京都中央区日本橋室町 1–4–1
☎ (03) 3241-3311
Mitsukoshimae Station, Ginza, Hanzomon lines
Hours: 10:00 A.M. to 7:00 P.M. Closed on Mondays.

We usually take visitors to the Nihombashi main branch of Mitsukoshi for the ultimate Japanese welcoming act. At 10:00 A.M., when the store opens, you will hear music played on a huge pipe organ in the middle of the store. This serenade is accompanied by hundreds of employees lined up at the entrance, bowing a welcome to every customer who enters. The performance only lasts a few minutes so be sure to arrive early.

Mitsukoshi prides itself on its well-qualified staff. Nutritionists are on hand to give advice in the baby goods department, shoe fitters sell children's shoes, and toy consultants handle the toys. The concept is meant to ensure safety, high quality, and luxury in all of their products. Mitsukoshi has always had a more "elite" image than other stores, and one of the most obvious differences is their tendency to carry more formal, traditional clothing, especially in the children's wear department. This is where you can find an Eton suit for your four-year-old son's preschool graduation.

The Mitsukoshi store in Ginza is smaller than their flagship store, but it has a Sanrio shop and a nice selection of children's clothes and toys.

There are six branches in the greater Tokyo area, located in Nihombashi, Shinjuku, Ginza, Ikebukuro, Yokohama, and Chiba. Other branches are in Osaka, Osaka Hirakata, Hiroshima, and Kobe.

The Nihombashi store is easy to find. At Mitsukoshimae Station there is a subway-level entrance into the store, and if you exit onto the street, the store is directly in front of you.

Maternity/Newborn

Mitsukoshi carries standard infant wear and gifts for new babies. Maternity wear is by Mitsuko Tachibana, Mitsukoshi Original, and Mezzo Forte, to name a few. Free seminars on pregnancy and delivery are given several times a year at the baby consultation room on the fourth floor. Certified doctors give free counseling on breast-feeding, between 1:30 P.M. and 4:30 P.M. every Saturday.

Facilities for Babies

The Baby Room on the fourth floor is equipped with changing tables, a baby swing, and two private rooms with comfortable chairs for breast-feeding mothers.

Kids' Fashion and Toys

The clothing department on the fourth floor is quite spacious. The entire floor was renovated in 1990 to reflect Mitsukoshi's new concept in children's fashion. The main theme of the children's floor is "noble European style creating an elegant children's world." The tendency is toward fancy, formal clothes for children, with European designer names being the most prominent. Here is the largest selection in town of suits for little boys, in sizes as small as eighteen months. Party dresses, coats, and fancy shoes are available in all sizes for girls. The toy section is spread over a large area, with a small space set aside for children to play with new products and display toys. Kids can also try out the tricycles and pedal cars. You'll find Sesame Street as well as other brands of imported toys and a good selection of Japanese toys, puzzles, and games.

Special sales are held three or four times a year, and customers are notified by mail. To put your name on the mailing list, call the store or ask at the information counter. Special children's fairs are held on holidays such as Children's Day, Mothers' Day, Christmas, etc.

Play Areas

If the kids get restless in the afternoon, take them down to the ground floor for another organ concert which is held daily at 3:00 P.M. Sometimes, special concerts are held at noon as well. You will find seats for about 100 people at the foot of the giant cloisonne statue in the center of the store. The organist performs from his perch several floors above.

What's To Eat?

Coffee shops are located on almost every floor.

Seibu Department Store

21-1 Udagawacho, Shibuya-ku, Tokyo　東京都渋谷区宇田川町 21-1
☎ (03) 3462-3848 (Foreign Customer Liaison Office)
🚃 Shibuya Station, JR Yamanote, Ginza, Hanzomon, Inokashira, Shin Tamagawa, Toyoko lines
Hours: 10:00 A.M. to 7:00 P.M. Closed on Wednesdays.

There are three Seibu department stores in Tokyo, located in Ikebukuro, Yurakucho, and Shibuya. Serving the greater Tokyo area are the stores in Fujisawa and Kawasaki. In Osaka there is a branch in Takatsuki, and there are approximately twenty-four branches throughout the rest of Japan. All

Seibu branches have a bright, informal atmosphere particularly suited to the modern mother and her offspring. A good idea is to check out the members' clubs in the children's sections of Seibu stores. For example, Kids Farm Club in Seibu Ikebukuro will take care of your heavy bags, look after your baby, keep your children entertained while you shop, and also keep you informed of forthcoming events, parties, and sales—all for ¥5,000 per year.

Seibu in Shibuya is a great place to spend the day with the kids. The layout of the store, selection of merchandise, various services for parents and children, and rooftop playland all make Seibu a fun and unique shopping experience. If you intend to do some serious shopping, you can leave your children with a babysitter at Seibu. This service is known as Poppins Service and reservations are required.

Car parking is available in three locations near the store, but these lots are often crowded. We sometimes find parking on the street nearby, or take the train or bus to Shibuya Station and walk five minutes to the store.

Maternity/Newborn

On the fourth floor of their B Building (B *kan*) in Shibuya, Seibu offers many special services for pregnant women through the Mama and Babe Club. This club, also known as the Shibuya Seibu Baby Circle, is open to expectant mothers and children under three years of age. For ¥1,000, members can take advantage of such programs as: gifts for newborn babies; baby and child care counseling; maternity exercise and swimming classes; rental of baby goods; babysitting service in the store; registration for baby gifts; special discounts; and invitations to sales and other events.

Facilities for Baby

Near the maternity clothes is the Baby Room with changing tables, a padded sofa, and a private breast-feeding booth. There is also hot water, a washstand, scales, and vending machines with juice, diapers, and so on. A uniformed clerk is usually on duty if you need help.

Kids' Fashion and Toys

The children's clothing department on the fourth floor is clean, sleek, and well designed. Infant wear and baby gifts are displayed in clearly designated areas. Clothing for children is spread out over a vast area, with separate boutiques for each designer. A wide variety of styles is represented, from trendy to frilly.

On the same floor next to children's clothes is the toy section. The usual sample toys are here, as well as children's videos to keep the kids entertained. Each month a "Toy Fair" is held, and during Golden Week and

36

summer vacation special events are planned for children. There is also a toy hospital in this department (see chap. 4).

Special sales are held in spring, summer, and autumn which offer big discounts on baby and children's wear, in addition to toys. To be included on the invitation list, inquire at the children's department.

The Kids Wonder Club was recently established at Seibu to meet the needs of older children. The facilities of the club include a consulting room and a restroom for babies. The club also offers a program of activities for children, including Garakuta Land (an arts and crafts class for children aged three to twelve); Poppins and the Mythical Artist (art classes for children aged three to twelve); and English conversation classes for children aged three to five.

Play Areas
The rooftop play area has a number of ¥100 rides, a large carousel, and video games under cover in case of rain. There is also a pet shop on the roof level.

Sogo Department Store
2-18-1 Takashima, Nishi-ku, Yokohama   神奈川県横浜市西区高島 2-18-1
☎ (045) 465-2111
🚇 Yokohama Station (east exit), JR Yokosuka, Toyoko, Keihin Tohoku, Keihin Kyuko, JR Tokaido lines
Hours: 10:00 A.M. to 7:00 P.M. Closed on Tuesdays.

The Sogo Department Store in Yokohama is the largest department store in all of Japan. It is a great place for kids and parents at any time, but the rooftop playground and snack bar make it especially nice on sunny days.

There are twenty-seven Sogo stores around Japan, including locations in Kobe, Osaka, and Nara. Sogo in Yokohama is only a few minutes' walk from the east exit of Yokohama Station. There is parking for 1,500 cars.

Maternity/Newborn
Pregnant women and mothers with babies up to three years of age can join the Sogo Baby Circle. If you join, you will receive invitations to various events, opportunities for medical consultations, a present when your baby is born, discounts on baby snacks, and much more. For more information, contact the Baby Salon on the fifth floor, or call (045) 465-2111. A variety of maternity wear is available at Sogo. Some of the more popular brands are Baby It's You, Canlemon, Petimadore, and Wacoal. You can also purchase or rent breast pumps.

Facilities for Babies
In the Baby Salon on the fifth floor there are fifteen changing tables, hot

water for mixing formula, juice machines, and a nursing room with comfortable chairs for mothers. Changing facilities are also provided in the restrooms on other floors. Babysitting is available for two- and three-year-olds for up to two hours. The parent is given a beeper to wear while shopping in case he or she is needed.

Kids' Fashion and Toys

Clothes and toys for children of all ages are on the fifth floor. Every popular brand of clothing is here in all sizes from newborns to teens. As in most department stores in Japan, the toy displays allow you and your children to experiment with new products. This is the easiest way we know to keep the kids happy while you shop! There is a Sanrio shop on this floor as well.

Play Areas

Besides the toy department on the fifth floor, there is a rooftop play area with wooden climbing structures and a snack bar. These facilities close at 5:00 P.M., although the department store is open until 7:00 P.M.

What's to Eat?

When you get hungry, you can choose from any of the twenty-four coffee shops located throughout the store. The largest selection of restaurants is on the tenth floor, and on the B2 level you will find the food hall.

Takashimaya Department Store

2-4-1 Nihombashi, Chuo-ku, Tokyo　東京都中央区日本橋 2-4-1
☎ (03) 3211-4111
🚇 Nihombashi Station, Ginza and Tozai lines
Hours: 10:00 A.M. to 7:00 P.M. Closed on Wednesdays.

Takashimaya in Nihombashi has recently revamped its children's areas on the fifth floor, and the result is increased convenience and fun for parents and kids. We have always liked this department store, whose image is a little more elegant and cosmopolitan than some of the others.

Takashimaya has large branch stores in Nihombashi, Setagaya (see Tamagawa Takashimaya Shopping Center in this chapter), and Tachikawa. They also have stores in Osaka, Kyoto, Sakai, and Wakayama.

The Nihombashi store is easy to get to by subway. At Nihombashi Station simply follow the arrows to the exit into Takashimaya's basement. There is plenty of parking available if you drive.

Maternity/Newborn

The Hello Baby Salon is full of wonderful goodies for new babies. There is a wide variety of baby gifts and infant wear, including our favorite collection of Western-style christening gowns. The area has obviously been designed with pregnant women in mind. Comfortable chairs and small tables are scattered around the spacious room, which is separated from the rest of the children's floor. Clerks in pale blue uniforms are helpful and knowledgeable.

The maternity-wear section is adjacent to the Hello Baby Salon. Here you will find all manner of undergarments in addition to two kinds of breast pumps. The selection of maternity clothes by such designers as Mitsuko Tachibana and Pierre Cardin is fashionable, though like most Japanese maternity clothes the styles tend to be a bit on the cutesy side.

Facilities for Babies

The Baby Room has plenty of cots for naps or diaper changes. There is a feeding room with comfortable chairs and space for about five nursing mothers. One unique feature of this store is Baby Snack, a snack bar in the middle of the fifth floor. Even though there are only a few tables, it is a well-designed area, with highchairs and Mom-sized chairs as well. Uniformed waitresses are on hand to heat jars of baby food, which are sold there. You may also purchase yogurt, milk, and juice, all in baby-sized containers. A small basin is conveniently located for quick cleanups. This little restaurant can be crowded on weekends, but we have never had to wait very long for a place.

There is a "tutor room" on the fifth floor where two babysitters will watch your children while you shop. This service operates on a membership system, and appointments are necessary. Each Saturday, a counseling session on child care is available free of charge. An appointment is necessary for this service.

Kids' Fashion and Toys

Takashimaya carries many lines of European, American, and Japanese children's clothes. You won't find many bargains here unless you stumble upon a sale, but the selection is one of the best. At the Disney KKO clothes corner, look for the Winnie the Pooh video for the kids to watch while you shop.

Star Circle is a children's membership club at Takashimaya. There is no charge to join, but registration is necessary. Birthday parties for children who are members are held once a month. Special discount sales for children's clothing and toys are held three to four times a year for Star Circle members. Regular discount sales take place on the eighth floor in January, March, June, and October of each year. In September there is a toy fair featuring toys from around the world at reasonable prices.

Play Areas

Although Takashimaya cannot boast a rooftop playground, the entire children's department on the fifth floor has been designed with numerous play areas. In the central area, you will find rows of chairs where children—and adults—can watch Disney videos. In this same area, there are tables shaped like puzzle pieces where children can play with an assortment of display toys. There is also a long, white board on which to draw with eraseable pens. The different toy sections have been designed around a train theme. The "Yesterday Train" houses a very special collection of stuffed animals and dolls, while the "Tomorrow Train" features electronic toys of all shapes and sizes. Nearby is Lego Land, with enough Legos and Duplos to construct the Imperial Palace. Our kids enjoy watching the miniature electric train that runs beneath a clear plastic section of the floor and playing in the large wooden playhouse. Near the Sanrio shop there is a large wall with puzzles that children can create by turning the attached cranks. You will be amazed at the variety of activities available for all ages within this limited space.

What's to Eat?

If you are an infant, you will dine in style at the Baby Snack Bar on the fifth floor. Otherwise, you will have to visit Takashimaya's only restaurant, down in the B2 level. It is spacious, with highchairs and a decent menu for kids, but it is dreadfully crowded at mealtimes. We have always faced a long wait, which is a miserable experience with hungry kids. For a change of scenery, try taking the kids down to the food counters in the basement, where there is usually a selection of food samples from which to choose. Some of the delicacies are rather exotic, but you may be surprised at what your kids will try in these basement food halls. Our pickiest eater decided that he liked mushrooms after trying them sautéed in butter and soy sauce in a department store basement.

Tokyu Department Store

2-24-1 Dogenzaka, Shibuya-ku, Tokyo　東京都渋谷区道玄坂 2-24-1
☎ (03) 3477-3111
♨ Shibuya Station, JR Yamanote, Ginza, Hanzomon, Inokashira, Toyoko lines
Hours: 10:00 A.M. to 7:00 P.M. Main store closed on Tuesdays, Toyoko store closed on Thursdays.

Tokyu Department Store in Shibuya is known for its sales and bargains. The store has two buildings in Shibuya, one convenienently located in Shibuya Station (called the Toyoko store), and the main store, which is located next to the Bunkamura complex in Shibuya. Both stores offer a wide selection of goods, and a shuttle bus runs every fifteen minutes between the two. Information in English is available on the first floor of the main store. Tokyu has branches in Nihombashi, Kichijoji, Machida, and Tama Plaza.

Maternity/Newborn
Maternity wear and children's goods are available on the seventh floor of the main store and the sixth floor of the Toyoko store. Brand names for maternity wear include Wacoal (especially good for undergarments and nightwear) and Hiroko Koshino. Breast pumps are available by special order. The main store has a gift counter for help with the selection and delivery of gifts for newborns.

Facilities for Baby
Adjacent to the maternity wear departments in both stores is a Baby Room. Here there are cribs for changing diapers, hot water for mixing formula, and vending machines for juice.

Kids' Fashion and Toys
The main store in Shibuya has perhaps the largest variety of children's brand-name clothes in Tokyo. The Toyoko store has less variety, but is well known for its sales and bargain bins. You can join the Familiar Group of Friends club and Miki House club and receive a newsletter with advance notice of sales. Members receive birthday cards for their children and invitations to special sales. Both stores have display toys set up for children to play with and the usual brands of toys for sale. There is a toy repair service for certain types of toys; inquire at the toy counter in the main store.

Play Areas
There is a pet store on the rooftop level of the main store. Although within the stores there are no real play areas for children apart from the toy departments, the main store is adjacent to Bunkamura, a large cultural center that has theaters, a museum, gallery space, and two cinemas. There is also an art gallery on the eighth floor of the main store. For restless children, many of these spaces can provide a welcome diversion from continual shopping.

What's to Eat?
The eighth floor of the main store houses fresh food, delicatessens, and restaurants. There are casual coffee shops as well as fancier restaurants here. At the Toyoko store, a food fair is located in the basement.

Hankyu Department Store
8-7 Kakutacho, Kita-ku, Osaka-shi　大阪府大阪市北区角田町 8-7
☎ (06) 361-1381
🚆 JR Osaka Station, JR Tokaido Honsen, Hankyu Kobe, Osaka Loop lines
Hours: 10:00 A.M. to 7:00 P.M. Closed on Thursdays.

This department store aims to make customer service and satisfaction its number one goal. Most of the store's branches are conveniently located near railway stations, and they boast spacious floors conveniently arranged to make shopping a pleasant experience. As with most major department stores in Japan, Hankyu prides itself on keeping abreast of all of the latest in fashion and style.

Hankyu has three branch stores in Tokyo, at Yurakucho, Sukiyabashi, and Ooi. In Osaka, there is another store at Senri, and the Hyogo-ken stores are in Kawanishi and Kobe. There is also a branch in Kyoto at Shijo-kawaramachi.

The Osaka store is just a few minutes' walk from Osaka Station. There are no parking facilities, so you will need to find street or nearby lot parking.

Maternity/Newborn

On the fifth floor of the Osaka store is the Baby World Corner. Here you will find many international brands of baby and maternity products. Among the maternity wear brand names are Comme Ca Du Mode, Canlemon, and Wacoal. Special sales are featured in this department in the spring and fall in connection with its My Baby classes, which offer advice to new mothers.

Facilities for Baby

In the Baby World Corner, there is a nursing room with changing tables and other amenities for baby. The nursing room is closed on Thursdays and Sundays.

Kids' Fashion and Toys

Also on the fifth floor is an exciting array of children's toys and fashions for all ages. You will find a Sanrio shop on this floor as well.

What's to Eat?

Restaurants are located on the eighth floor.

SHOPPING DISTRICTS

At first glance, shopping in Tokyo may appear to be expensive and exhausting. There are certain shopping districts and specialty stores, however, that are well worth a visit because of their low prices and/or selection of merchandise. The following shopping areas have been chosen because they are easy to navigate and they have the most to offer families with children.

Azabu Juban

 Roppongi Station, Hibiya Line

The Azabu Juban shopping street is in one of the oldest neighborhoods in central Tokyo. Here you will find an interesting selection of stores selling everything from umbrellas to handmade Japanese rice crackers (*osembe*).

The main shopping street, about a 10-minute walk from Roppongi Station, runs parallel (one block from Roppongi) to the busy street coming from Shiba Park to Roppongi Tunnel via Ichinohashi. You can start with the Wendy's hamburger restaurant at the east end or the Sweden Center at the west end and take a leisurely stroll through several blocks. There are a number of good places to feed the kids along the way. The Chinese restaurant Toho Hanten is very accommodating to parents and young children. Our favorite restaurant is Sarashina, located on a corner near the Juban post office. This traditional Japanese *soba* (noodle) shop has been in business at the same spot for 200 years. If you have young children, ask for a table on the tatami. Our kids always enjoy a simple bowl of *tempura soba* (noodles with two pieces of fried shrimp) or *tori soba* (noodles with pieces of chicken). Just remember to clean up any mess before you leave. It is amazing how many strands of noodles can end up on the tatami when dining with kids!

Eating aside, there are many stores worth visiting in Azabu Juban. Our first stop is always the Kobayashi toy store on the corner, which carries a nice assortment of toys, including traditional Japanese ones that you do not often see in department stores. If you turn left here, walk one block, and turn right, you will be across the street from Blue and White, a special gift shop full of unusual things. Sometimes you will find children's clothes made out of traditional and not-so-traditional *yukata* (a cotton kimono) fabric, in addition to T-shirts and stuffed toys.

Next door to Blue and White is the Daimaru Peacock supermarket. The second floor has bargains in household products and Japanese dishes as well as inexpensive gifts and toys.

Back on the street to Kobayashi toys, walk in the opposite direction to the toy shop and Roppongi and you will see the Mary Poppins store. This corner shop has a lovely collection of imported children's clothes. Most of the merchandise is European, and the prices are reasonable. They also have Buster Brown shoes for boys and Mary Janes for girls.

If you go back to the covered main Azabu Juban shopping street, you will find several other stores that kids like to browse in. A Sanrio shop is located down the street from Kobayashi toys, and there is also a shop selling fish and aquariums. We like to stop for a snack at the outdoor *yakitori* (chicken kebab) stands and the *osembe* shops, where you can watch rice crackers being made the old-fashioned way—by hand.

In the summertime, the Windsor coffee shop on the corner sells refreshing *kakigori* (shaved ice flavored with fruit syrup), a real treat for the kids when the weather is hot. In August and early autumn, the annual Juban festivals are fun for the entire family (see chap. 8 under Japanese Holidays). If you live in the neighborhood, you might want to try the famous hot springs bath, which is located at the west end of the shopping street.

Harajuku–Omote Sando

🚇 Omote Sando Station, Hanzomon, Ginza, Chiyoda lines; or Meiji Jingumae Station, Chiyoda Line; or Harajuku Station, JR Yamanote Line

Although these two districts are not famous for their children's shops, no discussion on shopping in Tokyo would be complete without a description of sophisticated Omote Sando and funky Harajuku. For strolling and window-shopping, the wide Omote Sando boulevard cannot be beat. This is where the exclusive boutiques and streetside cafes are—the places to see and be seen.

Sunday is a great day for families on Omote Sando. The boulevard is closed to traffic, unless the weather is extremely bad, and you can stroll from Omote Sando Station all the way down the street across Meiji Dori to Yoyogi Park and Harajuku Station.

Don't forget to show the kids the revolving steel sculpture on top of the Hanae Mori Building. At the corner of this building, turn left to find Crayon House (see chap. 4 for details).

Continuing down the tree-lined boulevard, you will come upon a traditional piece of Japanese architecture painted bright orange. This is the Oriental Bazaar, our favorite place in town for gifts and trinkets. It basically caters to tourists, but the prices are cheaper than in other similar stores. It is convenient one-stop shopping for all your gift needs, from kimonos and cotton *yukata* to Japanese dolls and paper fans.

When you are ready for some food, Omote Sando has all the fast-food outlets you could possibly want: Shakey's Pizza (a few stores down from the Oriental Bazaar) and, across the street, Wendy's, Hagen Daaz, and McDonald's. There is a Kentucky Fried Chicken on Meiji Dori, and on Omote Sando near the Meiji Shrine end is El Polo Loco. A great change from hamburgers, El Polo Loco serves barbecued chicken, fast-food style. The only problem we have had in this area is finding a convenient place to change a diaper.

After lunch, don't forget to hit the toy stores. Kiddyland, Tokyo's most exciting toy store, is near the junction with Meiji Dori, and just around the corner is a Bornelund shop (see chap. 4 for details on both stores). On either side of Kiddyland are trendy outdoor cafes. We like to take a break and people-watch here. The kids can join you for a soda, or they can play in the street-turned-playground next door. This blocked-off street has swings, slides, and sandboxes stretched out over five or six blocks, running alongside the building that houses Shakey's Pizza. Directly across Omote Sando, this playground continues for a few more blocks.

Parallel to Omote Sando, from Meiji Dori to Harajuku Station, is the Harajuku shopping district, where Japanese teenagers and young adults flock each weekend. Sunday is the day to cut loose in Harajuku, and they come from far and wide to parade around in punk regalia and far-out hairdos. To work your way down to the Harajuku shopping street, look first for the LaForet building, which you can see from the intersection of Meiji Dori and Omote Sando. This building houses boutiques full of trendy fashions for adults. LaForet also has a number of deli and sandwich-type restaurants where you and the kids can pick out your lunches from the plastic food samples in the window.

This section of Meiji Dori is rapidly becoming a mecca for kids' shopping with the addition of the Carillon store, which opened in October 1991, next to Kids LaForet. At first glance Carillon looks like a terrific toy store, reminiscent of the famous FAO Schwartz stores in the U.S. However, Carillon is more than just another toy store.

Through the sale of stimulating and educational toys this company hopes to promote an awareness in children about important issues in the world today, such as the environment and international friendship. Throughout the store you will find everything from a section on science and the earth to all the latest Sesame Street toys.

The five floors are well designed, with a seating area on the first floor for children to view videos on a large screen. On other floors you'll find a selection of fashionable clothes, children's eyeglasses, and even a hair-cutting salon. On the basement level are kid's toiletries, other goods, and a restaurant.

Carillon offers a variety of interesting classes for children as well, such as music, drama, sports, crafts, nature study, and English conversation. These classes are available for members of Carillon, who also receive a 5% discount on purchases and 10% discount at the rental clothing boutique. The membership fee is ¥2,000 which is good for two years; privileges also include invitations to special events and a bimonthly magazine.

Carillon is open from 11:00 A.M. to 8:00 P.M. daily and is closed on Tuesdays.

For more information, write to Carillon at 1-8-9 Jingumae, Shibuya-ku, Tokyo, or call (03) 3796-1188.

Just down Meiji Dori from LaForet is a LaForet building exclusively for children. Dear Kids LaForet opened in the spring of 1990 and contains four floors of children's designer clothes and toys. From Ralph Lauren to Sonya Rykiel Enfant to Shirley Temple, to the children's art showroom on the top floor, this building is a child's paradise. Most of the stores are clothing stores, but they all have clever displays and gimmicks to attract the children's attention while you shop. To describe how "upscale" this building is, take for example the Jenny doll (Japan's equivalent to Barbie) store. Selections of outfits for Jenny hang from miniature racks, and dolls dressed in complete ensembles are perched on a dais at one end of the room. As if that weren't enough, a fashion show of Jenny dolls and accessories is projected onto one wall from a hidden projector while a narrator tells you about the various outfits. Definitely a little-girl's paradise. The top floor houses a play room called "D" Kids Studio (see chap. 12, Private Day-Care Centers) where children can be entertained by bilingual staff while you shop or go out to dinner. Next to "D" Kids Studio is a children's restaurant that is also available for birthday parties.

Back on Meiji Dori, get ready to turn left onto the first street you come to, Takeshita Dori. From here to Harajuku Station are trendy little stores, too numerous to count, with imported, vintage, classic, punk, and fashionable clothes for hip people of all ages. Many of the clothes in these stores are sized for Japanese teens and look rather small to us. If you have a twelve- or thirteen-year-old who wants to add some spice to his or her wardrobe, this is the place to shop. The prices are very reasonable compared with the department stores; here you get the feeling you have made a major find.

Up Takeshita Dori on the left is a Miki House children's clothing store with four floors of pure Miki House. Farther down the street on the right is a Leyton Kids store. As you continue toward Harajuku Station, the shops full of trinkets, stuffed animals, goodies to eat, and more just spill out onto the street. The atmosphere in this part of Harajuku is always alive and jumping. You may want to calm the kids down by taking a stroll through Meiji Shrine afterward. You can see the entrance to the shrine just behind Harajuku Station.

One warning about shopping on Takeshita Dori with children: It is always crowded, but especially so on Sundays. Since this is a narrow street, be careful to get out of the way when cars try to make their way through the chaos. If you do go to Harajuku on Sunday, we suggest you go to the end of Omote Sando near the National Olympic Stadium. This area is closed to traffic so that teenagers can enjoy dancing in the street. There are also several bands playing loud music. The kids enjoy all the noise and action, but it is wise to have a stroller on hand for tired feet. It is difficult to get a taxi here because the streets are closed. If you drive, parking is available by meter on the street or in the parking lots on Omote Sando and Meiji Dori. On Sundays, check out the National Olympic Stadium, too; sports fairs or exhibitions are often held here on weekends.

Jiyugaoka
🚆 Jiyugaoka Station, Toyoko Line

Jiyugaoka is a pleasant, compact shopping district that has a different feel from many of the shopping areas we have visited in Japan. Instead of the usual Japanese coffee shops and shoe stores, there is Laura Ashley, "American country," and health food. There are many cafes and restaurants where you can sip cappucino while you listen to classical music. If you want to window-shop without the crowds, this is the place to go.

Take the train to Jiyugaoka Station and you are at a great place to start your trek. If you drive, follow Meiji Dori to Jiyu Dori and turn down it toward the station. There is parking on the streets or in paid lots in this ten-to fifteen-block area.

If you start at the station, turn to the right and head up the street with the Jiyugaoka Department Store on it. Here, there are a number of independently owned shops on the street level that have toys and clothes for children. Walk all the way up to the XAX sports club and you'll find the Laura Ashley store, plus a cluster of stationery and kitchenware stores.

Next to XAX is the Children's Museum, which is not a museum at all but three floors of fine children's shops. In this building are housed ab's d' absorba, Mini-Batsu, bebe, and Granpapa stores, to name a few. Often there is a candy and popcorn vendor in front of the building, and there is a large *gelato* shop across the street.

If you continue down the street past the Children's Museum, you will come to a large Anna Miller's restaurant. If the kids are hungry, Anna Miller's has a children's menu and some of the best pies in town.

On the same street as Anna Miller's is a boutique with exquisite baby and children's clothes, just before the large pachinko parlor. If you turn left here and head back toward the station, you will find more small shops full of interesting things. On this street is a fabric store called Pico that carries a good selection of children's and interior print fabric. There are two other Pico stores in the area, so ask for a store map if you want to look for more fabric.

As you near the station, keep your senses alert for the sight and aroma of Mont Blanc bakery. They have all kinds of delicious goodies, and should you need a cake made in a special shape or design, Mont Blanc can do it for you.

Kichijoji

 Kichijoji Station, JR Chuo Line

Just twenty minutes from Shinjuku Station on the JR Chuo Line is a haven of bargain shopping for the entire family. Often referred to as Sun Road and Diamond City, the streets just across from Kichijoji Station are stuffed full of shops, both large and small, that offer great selection and even better prices.

If you take the central exit from Kichijoji Station, you will see a Mitsubishi Bank and a sign over the street next to it that says Sun Road. Head down this road and don't look back. Narrow pedestrian streets branch off this main street and continue for a couple of blocks to the next wide road that has a large Tokyu Department Store. Some of the streets are covered, others are out in the open, but they are all full of shops and restaurants. There are also many major banks in this area in case you run out of cash.

Both Isetan and Tokyu department stores have branches here. The stores are large and spacious and have a wonderful feeling of calm that you don't always find in the downtown branches. Isetan has children's clothes and toys on the fifth floor. Also on this floor is a great place they call "Kids Dessert and Hair Bar," a place where children can go to get a haircut, or just to order an ice cream soda at the bar. Throughout the floor there are chairs and tables for kids to sit at to play with toys and watch TV. Check out the Video Bus Theater, a large bus for kids to climb into and watch a video of their choice. There is also a "Hello Baby Salon" here (see the Isetan listing in this chapter); video games can be found on the roof level. The B1 level has the usual food fair, and there is plenty of parking in the basement.

In the Tokyu Department Store the sixth floor is for children. Here are the Sesame Street Club and a large Sanrio shop, as well as clothes and toys. On the roof there is a spacious outdoor playground with the usual ¥100 rides, a pet shop, and video games in a covered area. There is also food in the basement and two levels of parking below that.

For shopping on the street level, check out Rogers and Marble. Both are down the side street that turns off Sun Road to the left before McDonald's. Rogers is a large discount shop with everything from pet supplies to overcoats to sporting goods. We have heard that everything in the store is marked down 50 percent or more from the usual retail price. Across the street is Marble, a children's shop with cute and affordable clothes in a wide variety of styles.

No matter what street you end up on, you will come across small fabric and hobby shops, stationery and toy stores, electronic goods outlets, and numerous shoe stores (this is a great place to buy kids' sandals). Time for lunch? The bakeries, ice cream shops, take-home Japanese, and other popular fast-food stores will guarantee that no one in the family goes hungry for very long.

Musashi Koyama Shopping Area

4-4-1 Ebara, Shinagawa-ku, Tokyo　東京都品川区荏原 4-4-1
🚉 Musashi Koyama Station, Mekama Line

By car, the shops are only about a 10-minute drive from Gotanda Station, and you can usually find a parking space on a street nearby. If you're going by train, take the Mekama Line out of Meguro Station to Musashi Koyama Station. Most of the stores in the area are open every day except Tuesday from 11:00 A.M. to 7:00 P.M.

We love Musashi Koyama. Actually, we lived in Tokyo for years without knowing about this shopping mecca, but now we go there as often as possible to make up for lost time. An enticing arcade offers over 500 stores with bargains galore. You will find everything from futons to fur coats as you stroll down the long thoroughfare. For children, check out the cheap diapers, cute dishes, and discounted designer duds.

If you take the train to Musashi Koyama Station, look for the clock as you exit. Then head for the lane of stores that begins with a jewelry shop on the right-hand side. Just down that lane, look for Pocket Town 321, a women's clothing shop, and you'll be in our favorite arcade. Your best bet is to start at this end and stroll all the way down just to see the plethora of shops. Tokiwa Drugstore (they have cheap Pampers) marks the end of this arcade.

The great thing about shopping at Musashi Koyama is how much fun it is for the kids. Each time they start to get restless, don't worry as you will soon come across another toy store or Sanrio shop to explore. We warn you, however, that you will spend more time than you ever imagined browsing through the mall. It is a good idea to make it a full day's outing, especially on your first trip. Also, although many stores take credit cards, most of the smaller ones do not, so bring along plenty of cash.

We always get so preoccupied with the children's clothing bargains in this area that we forget to shop for women's and men's clothes. If you do take the time to look for adult fashions, you will find a stylish selection at very reasonable prices. Another good buy is bedding. Check out Bena for futons, blankets, and other bedding in all price ranges. Two interior shops, Interior Station Hoshinoya and Matsumura Interior, have some of the cheapest prices in town for window treatments, carpets, and household and bathroom goods. Several of the furniture shops carry inexpensive bookshelves and desks—items sometimes difficult to find in Tokyo.

Shinryudo and Total Fashion Seikado have casual clothes for kids in popular styles at bargain prices. Across from these shops is a large Sanrio store, look for the giant Hello Kitty popcorn machine in the mall, and remember this Sanrio store for holiday goodies around Halloween, Christmas, and Valentine's Day.

Next to Sanrio is Azuki, a tiny shop that makes delicious cream-filled (or, if you prefer, red-bean-filled) pastries. The warm cakes are especially yummy on a cold day. Directly across from Azuki you will see Tenyodo, another good shop for bargains in sleepwear, *asobigi* (playsuits for the park), and maternity clothes. Nearby is Tamuraya Kimono, where we buy inexpensive festival costumes for the kids. They also have a good selection of *hanten*, those padded coats that Japanese children wear instead of bathrobes.

In this same area, you will find the DoBe toy store, which is full of fun stuff for all ages. Look for the big red trolley at the entrance. Across the way are a couple of shops that carry children's designer clothes, such as NAF NAF, Miki House, and Mou Jon Jon. These stores usually have sale bins out front.

A few steps more and you are at McDonald's. This is one of the McDonald's in Tokyo that has a birthday room. The space (for a maximum of ten kids) can be reserved by calling (03) 3781-3417. The only charge is for what the kids eat, plus the birthday cake. There are several other restaurants in the area, including a fast-food sushi shop where sushi is served on a revolving belt.

If you are looking for baby clothes, don't miss the store with a picture of Dumbo on the sign out front. They carry cute baby and children's clothes and shoes. Throughout the mall, shoes are a prominent item. From kids' rainboots to "squeaky shoes" (sandals and shoes with a squeak in the heel), you will find everything you need in the shoe line here.

While at the mall you may want to take advantage of the low prices of groceries at the Hankyu Koei store (especially if you go by car). Look for the store's red canopy near the Funland video games and the Chaplin key shop.

Osaki New City

1-6-4 Osaki, Shinagawa-ku, Tokyo　東京都品川区大崎 1–6–4
☎ (03) 3490-2283
🚆 Osaki Station, JR Yamanote Line

Opened only a few years ago in Shinagawa, this gleaming white structure is a great place to shop for the whole family. Osaki New City is open every day from 10:00 A.M. to 7:30 P.M. and is conveniently located at Osaki Station. The station exit leads directly to the third-floor level, and car parking is available underground. On the third floor are some fast-food eateries and also a lovely outdoor water fountain and square where the kids can run around on a nice day.

Then take the elevator to the second floor and step out into a consumer's paradise with a giant shopping center called My Place on one side and a large supermarket on the other. My Place carries everything a family needs, from toys to chinaware. Complimentary strollers are available for the little ones, and the store accepts all major credit cards. Their selection of children's bikes and bike accessories, such as carriers and helmets, is especially good. You'll also find a terrific toy department with plenty of display items to keep the kids busy while you shop. Also on this floor you'll find a Sanrio shop, McDonald's restaurant, a shoe store, and a bookstore.

In the children's clothing section, there are many inexpensive brands in addition to designer duds by Mou Jon Jon and Mickey Mouse. Be sure to check out the sales as there are bargains throughout the store. In particular the *obento* boxes and thermoses in the kitchen and houseware department are very reasonably priced.

Shimokitazawa

🚆 Shimokitazawa Station, Odakyu, Inokashira lines

Shimokitazawa is an area in Setagaya that is famous for its large variety of restaurants and side streets crammed with shops. For adults, the bars and restaurants that line each alleyway are fun to explore in the evening. For parents shopping for the kids, two budget department stores and a plethora of small neighborhood shops offer bargains galore. The shops are conveniently located near Shimokitazawa Station; using either the north or south exit will put you in the heart of the main shopping area. If you drive, you can try to park as close to the station as possible, but many of the streets are narrow alleyways, and parking is limited. Most of the small stores do not open until 11:00 A.M., but there is usually enough happening at 10:00 A.M. to keep you busy for the first hour.

Start at the south exit for the largest concentration of shops. Just outside the station are the inevitable fast-food restaurants, as well as some fine bakeries. Each street is lined with small shops and restaurants, just waiting to be explored. If you walk down the street with the Shopping Center sign over it, you will come to Big Ben, the building that has the Rock n' Roll Diner in it. This restaurant is a great place to take the entire family for a fun evening of music and American food. If you head back to the station and continue around the corner to the left (as you face the station), you will see the Chujitsuya supermarket/department store, which has three floors of food, clothes, and household goods. On the third floor there are sale bins and toys.

To get to the other side of the tracks, go back to the station and cross over to the north exit. Just outside is the four-story Daimaru Peacock store. This large branch has groceries, children's and adults' clothing, and household goods at reduced prices. Across the street from Peacock there is a nice fabric store and more small alleyways and side streets to wander down.

Tamagawa Takashimaya Shopping Center

3-17-1 Tamagawa, Setagaya-ku, Tokyo 158　東京都世田谷区玉川 3-17-1
☎ (03) 3709-2222 (shops) and (03) 3709-3111 (Takashimaya Department Store)
🚇 Futakotamagawaen Station, Denentoshi, Oimachi, Shin Tamagawa lines

When we start to long for our modern shopping malls back home, this is where we go. The Takashimaya mall, as we call it, is the most modern, spacious indoor shopping center we know of. It is easy to get to, just off route 246 and across the street from the Futakotamagawaen Station. There is plenty of covered parking at the mall, and most stores are open daily from 10:00 A.M. to 9:00 P.M. The Takashimaya Department Store is closed on Wednesday.

Anchored at one end by a large Takashimaya, the mall comprises four buildings, all connected by glassed-over walkways. This mall underwent complete renovation in 1989, and the result is an interior that is a gleaming, highly polished, art deco statement of shopping in style. Whether you are shopping for something in particular at one of the mall's many specialty shops or just need to get out of the house with the kids, the wide marble hallways and stunning displays are a nice change of pace to shopping downtown. And best of all, everything is indoors, making the mall a great place to escape in rainy weather.

There is an information desk on the first floor with leaflets and information in English. On the second floor in the main building is a corridor a little off the beaten track (just past Laura Ashley) with huge, padded wicker chairs that is the perfect resting place for new or expectant mothers and tired shoppers. Throughout the buildings, you will find chairs and tables, drinking fountains, and spacious bathrooms that nicely accommodate parents with children.

Some of our favorite downtown stores have branches here, but the great thing is that here they are all together in one easy location. For imported decorations and goodies for the holidays, try the large Sony Plaza store in the south building on the basement level. Up on the third floor in the same building is a branch of Ginza's Itoya stationery store that always has an abundant supply of greeting cards and small gifts. Also on the third floor is Hobbyra Hobbyre (look under Hobbies in the mall directory), a fabric and yarn store that is full of hard-to-find 100 percent cotton calico imported from the United States.

In the main building, check out Laura Ashley for women's clothes and interior fabrics, and the many designer boutiques from Ginza. There is a fancy fabric store here called Maruchu which stocks fabric from Yves St. Laurent and other major names. For the flavor of the Southwestern United States, go to Uhn Good. It is a large store with imported dried flowers, pottery, and throw rugs.

The basement level is dedicated to food, and it is almost impossible to leave here hungry. Besides the usual department store Food City, there are restaurants to suit every taste and budget. If you cannot find what you want here, go to the sixth floor of the south building, where there is another group of restaurants.

MYCAL Honmoku

19-1 Honmokuhara, Naka-ku, Yokohama-shi, Kanagawa-ken
☎ (045) 624-2121   神奈川県横浜市本牧原 19-1
🚃 Negishi Station, JR Negishi, JR Keihin Tohoku lines; or Sakuragicho Station, JR Keihin Tohoku, JR Negishi, Toyoko lines
Hours: 10:00 A.M. to 8:30 P.M. (stores); 11:00 A.M. to midnight (restaurants); 10:00 A.M. to 11:00 P.M. (sports facilities) daily.

The MYCAL shopping plaza in Yokohama consists of seven fun-filled buildings of shopping and eating enjoyment. This new concept in Japanese shopping malls takes its cue from the sunny southern California life-style. The design is fresh and colorful, and in these buildings you can do your banking, shop for groceries, mail a package, visit the beauty salon, and see a movie—all without moving the car once! If you want to get out of the rat race of Japan for an afternoon, this is the place to go.

The names of the buildings reflect the trendy, informal outlook of the designers with their wacky use of English to describe what can be found inside. For example, block number one, "The Section For Young Urbanites And Their Families," is a five-story building containing children's fashions and toys, men's and ladies' apparel, and food. The first floor of this building has food and household goods, but the highlight of the building has to be the Fisherman's Wharf on this floor where you'll find yourself surrounded by huge fish tanks full of seafood. Lobsters, octopus, and many kinds of fish are here for you to choose from; you can take them home to cook yourself, or eat them there at the restaurant. They even have refrigerated coin-lockers for you to leave your purchases in while you complete your shopping. On the third floor of this building is a food-fair section where you can choose from a variety of food and eat it at the tables provided. There is something for everyone here!

Another building entitled "A Section Suggesting A Pleasant Atmosphere" not only sells home accessories and furnishings, but also offers an exterior/interior design consulting service. "A Section Featuring A Range Of Services For The Community" has parking for over 400 cars and real estate, banking, and postal services. "The International Section, Filled With The Sights And Sounds Of Other Countries" houses sports clubs, cinemas, international fashions, and restaurants featuring international cuisine. Throughout the buildings, there are clean, pleasant restrooms, many with changing tables for infants, and chairs where you could breast-feed a baby.

From Negishi Station, take bus #1 to Wadayamaguchi. From Sakuragi-cho Station take bus #8 or #58. Parking is available in almost all the buildings, with more than 1,000 parking spaces in total.

SPECIALITY AND DISCOUNT STORES

Throughout Japan, there are a number of chain stores that parents should know about. Some of these are discount stores that offer quality merchandise at discount prices. Others are specialty shops that market hard-to-find items. Here are brief descriptions of a few of these stores.

Daiei

4-1-1 Himonya, Meguro-ku, Tokyo　東京都目黒区碑文谷 4-1-1
☎ (03) 3710-1111
📍 Toritsu Daigaku Station, Toyoko Line
Hours: 10:00 A.M. to 7:00 P.M.

Daiei Co. has 189 discount-style department stores in Japan, forty-eight of which are in the Kanto area. There are five stores in Kobe and forty-four in the Osaka area. The company's head office can give you information about stores in your area if you cannot locate one. Their phone number is (03) 3495-7311.

The Himonya Daiei store on Meguro Dori is a great one-stop shopping center and is representative of what you will find in the larger Daiei stores. To get there by car, drive down Meguro Dori toward Jiyugaoka. After you pass Denny's restaurant on your left, look for the red-orange half-moon logo on the white, ten-story Daiei building, also on the left. Parking is available in two large lots behind the store or on the side streets. On foot, the store is fifteen minutes from Toritsu Daigaku Station.

The supermarket on the first floor has great prices on a wide selection of food, and throughout the store you will find bargains on everything from fabric to stereos.

In the children's clothing department, you can purchase good-quality styles at reasonable prices. Rain gear, backpacks, and lunch box supplies are all excellent buys here. They also have a section of Mou Jon Jon clothing, which are similar to Miki House in style but not, fortunately, in price. At the Mou Jon Jon counter, ask to register for their club to receive mailings on sales and a postcard on your child's birthday. For the best deals on the children's floor, check out the bargain bin of clothes in a corner of the store. If you are a seamstress, the fabric here is cheap, cheap, cheap.

Two of the nicest things about Daiei are the many restaurants throughout the store and the ¥100 rides on the landings between floors. The grocery store on the first floor has a wide selection of takeout food, perfect for a picnic in nearby Himonya Park (see chap. 5).

Daiei sells their own brand of certain products, such as diapers. For newborns, who don't need extremely thick diapers, a case of Daiei diapers is the best deal in town. The price is a fraction of what you would pay elsewhere, and the plastic on the outside of the pants is nice and soft. In fact, parents-to-be would do well to go on a prenatal shopping spree at Daiei. On the children's floors in Daiei you will find everything from Nuk pacifiers to strollers and car seats.

If you live near a Daiei store, you will save a bundle by shopping regularly for their low-priced groceries and household goods. For those a bit farther away, it is still worth your time to make the trip to Daiei once a month or so. In the Himonya store, there is only one elevator, plus a central escalator, so this is not a great place for a stroller. We use the stairs for speed and to reach the rides.

Tokyu Hands

12-18 Udagawacho, Shibuya-ku, Tokyo　東京都渋谷区宇田川町 12-18
☎ (03) 5489-5111
🚃 Shibuya Station, JR Yamanote, Hanzomon, Inokashira, Toyoko, Ginza lines
Hours: 10:00 A.M. to 8:00 P.M. Closed on second and third Wednesdays each month.

Tokyu Hands branches are located in Shibuya, Ikebukuro, Machida, Fujisawa, and Futakotamagawa. There are also stores in Osaka (Esaka branch) and Kobe (Sannomiya branch). The main store in Shibuya is located behind Seibu Department Store. Look for the large sign across from Hachiko Square in the heart of Shibuya.

Tokyu Hands is a one-stop hobby, fix-it, and do-it-yourself shop—a rarity in Japan. The large stores contain supplies for every craft and home-improvement project you can think of. Fabric, paper supplies, lumber, paint, silk flowers, gardening tools and plants, they are all here. The large Shibuya store also has a coffee shop where you can get ice cream and sandwiches.

The larger branches have customer service counters where you may be able to get help in English. Tokyu Hands can also arrange for an independent painter, builder, etc., to do work for you. They can make custom windows or kitchen counters, paint your house, or wallpaper your bedroom.

Even though there is nothing specifically for children at Tokyu Hands, parents with children will find the store invaluable both because there are so many items in one place and because the store can order or custom-make anything you need. We have gone to Tokyu Hands for shelving for the kids, rooms, fabric for Halloween costumes, plastic trash cans for storing toys, wallpaper paste for putting up a border in a child's room, custom blinds, and even artificial turf for the garage when we held a child's party there.

USEFUL SHOPPING DISTRICTS IN TOKYO

The three shopping districts described below have long been shopping havens for residents and tourists alike. They are not usually advertised as places for children's items, but we have found a surprising amount of gadgets, party supplies, and household goods that parents of young children could use. When visiting any of these three districts, you can either drive and park on the streets, or take the train or bus to the station of the same name. The shops and bargains you have heard so much about are in the stores in the backstreets just out of the station. If you want to explore, you can strike out on your own and check out the entire area, but we have always found more than enough things to buy within a few steps of the station exit.

Akihabara

🚇 Akihabara Station, JR Yamanote, JR Keihin Tohoku, JR Sobu, Hibiya lines

This shopping district, well known for its huge selection of electronic goods, has a surprising amount of things that parents and children can use. For low prices on humidifiers, electric heaters and fans, heated carpets, and hand-held vacuums, go to Akihabara. Should you want to buy something with adjustable voltage to take to another country when you leave Japan, go to one of the tax-free or export shops—usually identified by the international flags outside the shop.

Besides electronic goods, there are many small shops with interesting items on the busy streets here. On the way to our car from a large export shop one day, we passed a book and record store, a shop full of Sesame Street character goods, and a vendor selling miniature sponge lobsters that grow to life-size when you place them in water. You never know what you will find on the side streets of Akihabara, so take plenty of cash.

Asakusabashi

🚇 Asakusabashi Station, JR Sobu, Toei Asakusa lines

Asakusabashi is best known for its paper products, and rightly so. You will never have seen so many varieties of paper, nor so many shops devoted to selling it. *Washi* paper is available here all year round. If you are looking for holiday goods, you can usually shop a month or two in advance. For Christmas you can shop from October. Artificial trees and garlands, ribbons, bells, lights, and all other Christmas decorations imaginable can be found here.

Asakusabashi is also known for its craft stores, particularly those which sell kits and materials for making Japanese dolls. In this area there are also stores that sell kimono and *obi* fabric off the bolt—great for covering tea boxes and making other Japanese crafts.

We have found Asakusabashi to be a gold mine of trinkets and small gifts for children, as well as a good place to find costume and party supplies. Some stores in the Asakusabashi area are wholesale outlets, but we have never had any problem buying from them.

Kappabashi

 Tawaramachi Station, Ginza Line

Kappabashi is a wholesale district for restaurant and kitchen supplies west of Tawaramachi Station between Asakusa and Ueno. Paper products such as plates and cups are also a good deal here. Often stores will sell you only a large quantity of a certain item, whether it be china cups or paper napkins. This area is also the place to buy the infamous plastic food that is used as samples in so many restaurants in Japan. This artificial food is more expensive than most people think, but for the right person it makes a great gift.

CLOTHING SPECIALTY STORES

Familiar

6-10-16 Ginza, Chuo-ku, Tokyo　東京都中央区銀座 6–10–16
☎ (03) 3574-7111
Ginza Station (Matsuzakaya Department Store exit), Ginza, Hibiya, Marunouchi lines
Hours: 10:00 A.M. to 7:00 P.M. Closed on Wednesdays.

Familiar produces a line of children's clothing in Japan. Familiar products are sold in most department stores, and there are many Familiar stores throughout Japan. Their flagship store is in Ginza, and here you will find fine-quality clothing for infants and children. There is also a small restaurant serving sandwiches and cake overlooking Ginza, and a playroom and Baby Room for changing diapers or feeding a baby.

In addition to their own line, Familiar carries a fine selection of classic clothes with other brand names. They also stock a wide variety of imported shoes. Familiar's clothes are on the expensive side, but the quality is excellent. For beautiful infant knitwear, they are one of our favorite stores. Familiar's seasonal sales let you enjoy substantial discounts on Japanese designer clothes. At the store you will receive a member's card that is stamped after each purchase, entitling you to a discount when the card is full.

Besides their numerous smaller stores and boutiques in department stores, there is a large Familiar store in the Kobe Motomachi area.

Laura Ashley

6-10-12 Ginza, Chuo-ku, Tokyo　東京都中央区銀座 6-10-12
☎ (03) 3571-5011
🚇 Ginza Station (Matsuzakaya Department Store exit), Ginza, Hibiya, Marunouchi lines
Hours: 10:00 A.M. to 8:00 P.M. Closed on the third Wednesday each month.

Laura Ashley is known for her classic British clothes for women and children. The stores also have design books, interior accessories, and upholstery fabric. However, the Laura Ashley line of children's wear is only available at the branches in Jiyugaoka and Nagoya.

There are ten Laura Ashley shops in greater Tokyo, including those in Ginza, Aoyama, and Jiyugaoka. Nagoya and Hiroshima have large stores, and there are Laura Ashley boutiques in the Kintetsu Abeno and Kawanishi Hankyu department stores, both in Osaka, and in the Sogo Department Store in Kobe.

CLOTHES AS A HOME BUSINESS

Some Tokyo residents sell imported clothes from the United States and Great Britain as a home business. Ownership changes every few years owing to the mobility of foreign residents, but if you ask around at the international schools or at functions with foreign mothers, you will be able to find out who is selling what this year. These clothes are sold at private sales and at the international bazaars in Tokyo.

RENTAL CLOTHES

The Japanese often go to rental shops for a special party dress or for formal attire. Now that concept has expanded to include children's clothes. Throughout Japan, rental children's ceremonial kimono and Western-style formal wear are available through the stores and catalogs for baby equipment mentioned in chapter 3. In Tokyo, we recommend the following stores.

Allegretto

4-15-6 Minami Azabu, Minato-ku, Tokyo　東京都港区南麻布 4-15-6
☎ (03) 3280-3789
🚇 Hiroo Station, Hibiya Line
Hours: 11:00 A.M. to 6:00 P.M. Closed Tuesdays.

Here, you will find a selection of lovely dresses for girls and a few suits for boys available for rent. Most of the clothes are from the United States or

Italy, but there is an especially pretty line of dresses designed by the owner. Suits are available from age two to preteen. Patent leather shoes or traditional loafers can also be rented.

Wedding Service Watabe

1-30-1 Kabuki-cho, Shinjuku-ku, Tokyo　東京都新宿区歌舞伎町 1−30−1
☎ (03) 3208-7770
📮 Seibu Shinjuku Station, Seibu Shinjuku Line; or Shinjuku Station, JR Yamanote, Marunouchi, JR Sobu, JR Chuo, Keio, Odakyu lines
Hours: 10:00 A.M. to 8:30 P.M. daily.

Despite its name, this shop also rents out children's clothes. A girl's party dress can be rented for about ¥8,000. Or how about a kimono for the *shichi-go-san* festival (see chap. 8) starting from ¥20,000? The shop is on the sixth floor of Seibu Shinjuku Station Building and there is also a branch offering a similar service in the Bick Building, two doors down from Takashimaya Department Store in Nihombashi ((03) 3281-6761).

Piccolonova

2-1-5 Sanno, Ota-ku, Tokyo　東京都大田区山王 2−1−5
☎ (03) 3776-0808
📮 Omori Station, JR Keihin Tohoku Line
Hours: 10:00 A.M. to 8:00 P.M. Closed the third Wednesday each month.

This children's clothing shop also offers a rental service aimed at children from six months to fifteen years. The shop is on the second floor of the Omori Station Building.

RESALE OUTLETS

We have unearthed only a few shops that sell used children's clothes. Most Japanese do not like the idea of wearing a stranger's discarded clothes, and used clothing shops for children have not yet become popular. Foreigners, however, often do not mind buying used clothes for their children, especially when they are used Japanese designer clothes that are sometimes so well made that they don't show any wear and tear for years. If you want to sell or buy some children's clothes and you find a recycle shop in your area, go in and see what they have. Even if they do not have any children's clothes in stock, they may be willing to sell yours on commission.

Fukushi Center

1-12-20 Oogi, Adachi-ku, Tokyo　東京都足立区扇 1−12−20
☎ (03) 3896-1536
📮 Nippori Station, JR Yamanote Line

The Fukushi Center has large sales four or five times a year. You can obtain a schedule by calling the center. To get there, take a bus from JR Nippori Station for Adachi Ryutsu Center and get off at the Oogi Ohashi Kitazume stop.

Jelly Beans

6-18-8 Shimouma, Setagaya-ku, Tokyo　東京都世田谷区下馬 6–18–8
☎ (03) 3422-9997
📞 Gakugei Daigaku Station, Toyoko Line
Hours: 11:00 A.M. to 6:00 P.M. Closed on Mondays. English spoken.

As well as secondhand clothes, this recycle shop also carries a selection of imported children's clothing suitable for children from six months to twelve years of age. The shop is a 5-minute walk from Gakugei Daigaku Station.

Kaiten Mokuba

2-27-21 Nakaochiai, Shinjuku-ku, Tokyo　東京都新宿区中落合 2–27–21
☎ (03) 3954-0559
📞 Shimoochiai Station, Seibu Shinjuku Line
Hours: 10:00 A.M. to 6:00 P.M. Closed on Sundays.

This recycle shop's large selection of women's and children's clothes is sold at extremely competitive prices.

Ninjin

2-26-24 Kita, Asagaya, Suginami-ku, Tokyo　東京都杉並区阿佐谷北 2–26–24
☎ (03) 3339-3397
📞 Asagaya Station, JR Chuo Line
Hours: 11:00 A.M. to 4:00 P.M., Wednesday through Saturday. English spoken.

This recycle shop is completely devoted to children's goods and here you can find not only clothes but also secondhand books and toys at very reasonable prices. English is spoken so call for directions from Asagaya Station.

Salvation Army

2-21-2 Wada, Suginami-ku, Tokyo　東京都杉並区和田 2–21–2
☎ (03) 3531-3516
📞 Nakano Fujimicho Station, Marunouchi Line
Hours: 8:30 A.M. to 1:00 P.M.

The Tokyo Salvation Army store is famous for its great deals on like-new items. Get there early: Some people line up from 7:30, and the merchandise has pretty much been picked over by 10:00 A.M. The ticket-taker at Nakano Fujimicho Station has a map, and you can ask him or just about anyone else where the "*risaikuru shoppu*" (recycle shop) is.

SEW IT YOURSELF

Another alternative to outfitting the kids without busting the budget is to sew their clothes yourself. For those of you who enjoy sewing, either for your children or yourself, Japan has some terrific fabric shops. "Do-it-yourself" may not appear to be as popular here as in some other countries, but there are large numbers of people who sew for home decorating, for their children, or simply for their own enjoyment.

As a foreigner, you might consider purchasing some items in your home country to save time and money. We would suggest buying patterns, notions, and perhaps a basic supply of fabrics in colors that you use often. It is also helpful to subscribe to a sewing magazine that can supply you with the newest fashions in patterns from your home country. Most of the sewing supplies you will need can be found here, but some specialty items are difficult to locate. For example, we have yet to find a store that carries fine-quality cotton batiste for smocking little-girls' dresses. Also, the selection of swiss eyelet, in either trim or fabric, is limited and expensive.

Conversely, there are some things that you will find in abundance in Japan that may be hard to find elsewhere. You will see a wide selection of children's fabrics and prints for clothes or decorating in almost every store. Among our favorite fabrics in Japan is the 100 percent cotton stretch fabric that is available in a wide variety of colors and patterns.

The listing below contains a few select fabric stores in Tokyo. Most department stores have a small section of notions and fabric. Tokyu Hands has a whole floor full of sewing and knitting supplies in their store in Shibuya, and other locations also have sewing supplies. Throughout Japan, there are large craft stores that have floors and floors of buttons, lace, ribbon, and notions galore. You will also come across small neighborhood fabric stores that will have bolts of fabric but no notions. Whether you are an avid seamstress or just a fabric fanatic, you will enjoy browsing through the stores listed here.

Fabrications

Crossroad Bldg. 1F, 1-29-1 Shoto, Shibuya-ku, Tokyo　東京都渋谷区松涛 1-29-1
☎ (03) 3462-0233
🚇 Shibuya Station, JR Yamanote, Hanzomon, Inokashira, Toyoko, Ginza line
Hours: 10:00 A.M. to 8:00 P.M.

This store has a wide selection of interior and children's fabrics. They also offer classes and demonstrations on sewing for the home, and anything that they do not have in stock they will order. The store is conveniently located just past the main Tokyu Department Store and across from Bunkamura.

Horiuchi

2-25-6 Dogenzaka, Shibuya-ku, Tokyo　東京都渋谷区道玄坂 2–25–6
☎ (03) 3496-5411
Shibuya Station, JR Yamanote, Hanzomon, Inokashira, Toyoko, Ginza lines
Hours: 9:00 A.M. to 6:00 P.M. Closed on Sundays and the third Saturday each month.

This little shop is a great place to find notions, lining fabrics, interfacings, and knitting supplies. The store is across the street from the main Tokyu Department Store.

Laura Ashley

For locations throughout Japan, see the listing on page 59.

Most Laura Ashley outlets carry a small stock of upholstery and interior fabric. Should you want some design that they do not stock, they will try to find it in another of their stores in Japan for you. If they have to order it from England, there is a 5-meter minimum order. All branches can supply you with a catalog and fabric swatches for the entire Laura Ashley line. For top-quality British fabric and design, Laura Ashley is the place to go.

Shibuya Marunan

2-5-1 Dogenzaka, Shibuya-ku, Tokyo・東京都渋谷区道玄坂 2–5–1
☎ (03) 3461-2325
Shibuya Station, JR Yamanote, Hanzomon, Inokashira, Toyoko, Ginza lines
Hours: 9:30 A.M. to 8:30 P.M. daily

This store is easy to get to, is open late, and has a fabric stock representative of what you can expect to find in most stores in Japan. At first glance, the store seems tiny, but there are several floors to explore. Notions are also sold. Shibuya Marunan is across from the cylindrical 109 Building in the heart of Shibuya. Look for the bolts of sale fabric stacked outside the store as you walk from the station to the 109 Building.

Blue and White

2-9-2 Azabu Juban, Minato-ku, Tokyo　東京都港区麻布十番 2–9–2
☎ (03) 3451-0537
Roppongi Station, Hibiya Line
Hours: 10:00 A.M. to 6:00 P.M. Closed on Sundays and holidays.

A unique source for gift items, this store stocks an original selection of *yukata* fabric. All designs are made especially for Blue and White, and each motif is based on a traditional source. The *yukata* fabric is available in shades of blue and white, or red or pink and white.

Tamagawa Takashimaya Mall

At this mall, you will find many stores carrying imported and designer fabric. For a more detailed description, see the listing on pages 52–53.

Takatomi Elegance

1-10-13 Bakurocho, Nihombashi, Chuo-ku, Tokyo
☎ (03) 3663-3151　東京都中央区日本橋馬喰町 1-10-13
🚉 Bakurocho Station, JR Sobu Line
Hours: 10:00 A.M. to 6:00 P.M. weekdays, 10:00 A.M. to 5:00 P.M. Sundays and holidays. Closed the first and third Sunday each month.

This fabulous chain store specializes in fine fabrics. Branch stores are in Tokyo at Yurakucho, Kanda, Kitasenju, Omori, Ikebukuro, Meguro, and Shinjuku, and in Kanagawa-ken at Yokohama and Atsugi. They also have a chain of apparel stores by the same name. At the main branch you will find everything from imported British woolens to Chinese silks to sequined velvets; this store has the best quality and most expensive fabric available for sewing one-of-a-kind garments. Even if you settle for something out of the bargain bin—as we usually do—a trip to Takatomi is a must for fine-fabric lovers.

Okadaya

3-23-17 Shinjuku, Shinjuku-ku, Tokyo　東京都新宿区新宿 3-23-17
☎ (03) 3352-5411
🚉 Shinjuku Station (east exit), JR Yamanote, Marunouchi, JR Chuo, JR Sobu, Keio, Odakyu lines
Hours: 10:00 A.M. to 8:30 P.M. Closed the last day of February and August.

Paradise for any seamstress is to be found at Okadaya. A number of stores are grouped together near Shinjuku Station, and the easiest store to find is across the street from the east exit. Each floor of the four locations carries a different item—one floor for ribbon, one floor for buttons, one floor for lace, etc. This store is also a good place to find better fabrics as well as lace for evening wear and wedding dresses.

Yuzawaya

8-23-5 Nishi Kamata, Ota-ku, Tokyo　東京都大田区西蒲田 8-23-5
☎ (03) 3734-4141
🚉 Kamata Station, JR Keihin Tohoku Mekama, Ikegami lines
Hours: 10:00 A.M. to 7:00 P.M.

Yuzawaya is more than a store, it is a way of life. Actually it is a complex of ten stores conveniently located near the south exit of Kamata Station. Taking the correct exit will save time. Do not walk down the long corridors of the station to the main exit. Instead, take one of the exits close to the ticket booth (these have no name or number, so ask). From there it is a 5-minute walk straight down the street to the nearest store. At Yuzawaya you'll find not only clothing and interior fabrics at bargain prices, but also the materials for making any kind of craft imaginable. Stained glass, leather crafts, Japanese dolls, needlepoint, artificial flowers, kilns, more than 2,800 kinds of yarn . . . need we say more? Get there at 10:00 A.M. and stay all day.

CHILDREN'S CLOTHES—MAIL ORDER FROM ABROAD

We have used the following catalogs and have found the quality of their products and the reliability of their service to be excellent. Not only are the prices reasonable, but often the styles are a refreshing change from what you will find here. Even though the companies listed are all in the United States, you will find a wide selection of clothing from around the world. Cotton clothes from Sweden, *très* chic designs from France, and matching brother-and-sister outfits are just a few of the items these catalogs feature.

Biobottoms

P.O. Box 6009, Petaluma, California 94953, USA
☎ (707) 778-7945 fax (707) 778-0619

Children's sizes from newborn to 14. Good-quality cotton clothes and infant wear. Fashionable designs that are practical and durable.

Children's Wear Digest

P.O. Box 22728, 2515 East 43rd St., Chattanooga, Tennessee 37422, USA
☎ (615) 867-2342 fax (615) 867-5318

Children's sizes from newborn to 14. Sturdy, U.S. brand-name apparel for children. Great selection of Oshkosh overalls, jeans, and swimsuits.

Hanna Andersson

1010 N.W. Flanders, Portland, Oregon 97209, USA
☎ (503) 242-0920 fax (503) 222-0544 Japanese catalog also available

Children's sizes from newborn to teens, also adult sizes. Top-quality 100 percent cotton clothing made in Sweden for the entire family. Practical designs, beautiful colors, and lasting quality.

Heir Affair

625 Russell Drive, Meridian, Mississippi 39301, USA
☎ (601) 484-4323 fax (601) 484-4278

Advertised as carrying "today's treasures, tomorrow's heirlooms," this catalog offers some very special gifts for babies and children, such as christening gowns, hand-painted furniture, and unique toys.

Les Petits

6510 Eastwick Ave., Box 33901, Philadelphia, Pennsylvania 19142-0961, USA

Children's sizes from newborn to 16. French designs made in the United States. Best known for their polo shirts, corduroys, and other classic items.

Maggie Moore, Inc.

P.O. Box 1564, New York, New York 10023, USA
☎ (212) 543-3434

Children's sizes from newborn to 14. Great costumes, modern and classic styles of children's clothing. Some special wooden toys are included in the catalog as well.

Richman Cotton Co.

529 Fifth Street, Santa Rosa, California 95401, USA
☎ (707) 575-8924

Children's sizes from newborn to 14, also adults. A great selection of cotton clothing. They also have specialty items, such as diaper covers, baby carriers, and wooden toys.

Talbots Kids

175 Beal Street, Hingham, Massachusetts 02043-1586, USA
☎ (617) 749-7830 fax (617) 740-1772

Children's sizes from 4 to 14. The classic Talbots style and quality for children. Ask for their original women's wear catalog, too.

The Children's Shop

P.O. Box 625, Chatham, Massachusetts 02633, USA
☎ (508) 945-4811

Children's sizes from newborn to 14. Traditional clothing for children. Eton suits for little boys and classic dresses for the girls. Good selection of play clothes as well.

The Wooden Soldier

North Conway, New Hampshire 03860, USA
☎ (603) 356-7041

Children's sizes from 12 months to 14. Exquisite selection of dressy clothing for infants up to about age six. Brother-and-sister outfits and other matching sets for the family (some for Mom, too). Frilly and unique clothes.

3
Equipping
the
kids

THERE ARE ALSO CHILD-SIZED "FUTONS".

Baby Needs

Japan is full of wonderful things to buy for babies, from high-tech strollers to traditional futon. Many affordable and high-quality products are sold here. Even though many well-known products from other countries are not available now, with the internationalization of Japan baby products and accessories from the United States and Europe are showing up in the stores more frequently. If you decide to buy or rent these items here, you will find that outfitting baby in Japan can be as easy and as fun as it would be back home.

If you will be living in Japan for only a short time, you should consider renting baby equipment from any of the numerous companies that provide baby goods. Most publish catalogs full of a wide range of products from maternity clothes to cribs. The bulk of their stock is for rent, but some of the merchandise is for sale. See the section on baby equipment catalogs in Japan in this chapter for further information.

Tiny babies do not need a large crib for the first few months, and in Japan "Moses baskets" are popular for newborns instead of a traditional bassinet. There are also child-sized futons that the baby can sleep on next to your bed, which are especially convenient if you use a futon yourself. Both are portable and inexpensive options for baby's first months.

When you are ready to buy a full-sized crib, you will find many styles available. We would suggest shipping one if you have the option, as Western full-sized cribs are rather expensive in Japan. For a good selection of cribs, try the Nursery Collection by Grandoir. This company imports some very special baby furniture from France, Italy, and the United States, in addition to carrying lovely cribs, baby baskets, and chests of drawers.

Another company that sells a coordinated line of furniture and even baby dishes to match is Tan Tan Tan by Munehiro Minowa. See the listings below for store outlets for these companies.

Baby baths or bath seats are useful to have, and you can find some original models here. One that we like by Combi has a tilted bouncy seat that you strap the child into, and then place in the bathtub. Large plastic tubs, good for bathing babies on the counter or floor, are also available. For toilet training, there are plenty of cute potties for sale; one company's combination stepstool and toilet seat is a popular choice.

Baby walkers are also easy to find here, but we think the playpens are too expensive. The battery-operated swings that our children loved as infants are also pricey. Similar swings are available, but they are not as sturdy as the newest models from the United States.

Highchairs in Japan come in all shapes and sizes. Models that become a regular child's chair when baby has outgrown it and chairs so low that you have to sit on the floor in order to feed baby are both available.

The Japanese use front and back packs to carry babies, but they are usually soft-straps models. Metal-frame backpacks and baby slings, which are harder to find, can be mail ordered from the overseas catalogs listed in this chapter.

Some of the best strollers in the world can be found in Japan. Combi and Aprica are two of the most famous brands, and both are available in a variety of styles. Depending on your needs, you may want a large model that converts from a pram style to a regular stroller, or just a lightweight umbrella stroller. Some families buy one of each, but you will be surprised at the cost of the top-of-the-line designs. As one new dad complained, "My kid's new stroller cost as much as my first car!" A popular option is to buy a medium-sized stroller that is lightweight and folds down easily for travel but which also has storage under the seat and hooks on the handles for bags.

Car seats are an essential item if you plan on driving with baby. If you are using a regular-sized child's car seat for a newborn, try to get one of those newborn headrests to fit inside the car seat, or make your own by rolling a soft towel or blanket and placing it around the top of baby's head as a cushion.

When buying a regular-sized car seat, be sure to get one that your child will not outgrow too soon. Combi and Aprica both make good car seats, but we found Guardian's seat the roomiest for our kids to use up to about age four. Unfortunately, most Japanese parents do not view car seats as a necessity, and the prices are rather high. You can always watch the notice boards at grocery stores and look around the rummage sales at local churches. Make sure the model is recent (made within the last three to four years) to be assured of maximum safety. You also may want to buy a car seat that has been approved by the airlines if you plan on flying with baby.

PARENTING MAGAZINES

To find out what kinds of products are currently available in Japan, you may want to look at some Japanese parenting magazines. Of course, many foreigners can read Japanese, but even illiterates like ourselves enjoy seeing the pictures of new products and the latest kids' fashions. Check any bookstore or magazine stand for the following magazines.

Balloon
This publication focuses on pregnant women and new mothers, offering information on childbirth, maternity fashions, and parenting advice.

Kodomo Pia
Based on the adult magazine, Pia, which gives complete listings for virtually everything happening around Tokyo, Kodomo Pia will keep you uptodate with all events and information concerning children. From March 1992, the magazine will appear every other month.

Muffin
Muffin is geared toward mothers of young children, and features interiors, travel, and menus, in addition to tips on child-rearing and fashion.

P. AND
The unusual name of this magazine evidently stands for "Parenting and . . ." P. AND is very informative, with articles on pregnancy, childbirth, and breast-feeding. You will also see exercises for pregnant women, as well as fashion and menu ideas.

Sesame Magazine
This glossy magazine is mostly full of the latest fashions for young children. The photography is first rate, almost like a Vogue for kids.

Sweet Baby
Here you will find information for mothers and babies with articles on parenting, maternity fashions, and menus.

Watashi No Akachan (My Baby)
This magazine focuses on the needs and problems of new parents. You will find tips on cooking kids' meals and information on new products.

BABY EQUIPMENT STORES

Department stores in Japan (see chap. 2) carry a vast assortment of baby products and the shopping districts mentioned in chapter 2 are a good source of bargains in baby goods. The following stores have a particularly good selection of goods to meet your baby's every possible need.

Akachan Honpo

Head office: 3-3-21 Minami Honmachi, Chuo-ku, Osaka-shi, Osaka-fu
☎ (06) 251-0625　大阪府大阪市中央区南本町 3-3-21
Nihombashi branch: 1-6-8 Bakurocho, Nihombashi, Chuo-ku, Tokyo
☎ (03) 3662-7651　東京都中央区日本橋喰町 1-6-8
🚉 Bakurocho Station, JR Sobu Line
Hours: 9:00 A.M. to 5:30 P.M. daily

If you are outfitting baby on a budget, you will want to head straight for Akachan Honpo. Besides baby equipment, Akachan Honpo's more than thirty stores sell children's clothing and toys, maternity clothes and accessories, and gift items. To shop at the stores and take advantage of the wholesale prices, you must become a member by paying ¥2,000. The first time you go, ask at the checkout counter for a membership form. Members receive a card that must be shown each time you shop. You will also receive advance information on sales and special events at the stores. Other stores in the Kanto area are: Gotanda and Nakanobu (Shinagawa-ku), Funado (Itabashi-ku), Higashi-Hokima (Adachi-ku), Tanashi and Omiya (Saitama-ken), Yokohama and Ebina (Kanagawa-ken), Kashiwa and Yachiyo (Chiba-ken). Other branches are located in Sapporo, Izumi and Shinosaka (Osaka), Sendai, Aomori, Nagoya, Kyoto, Takamatsu, Kofu, Iizuka and Hakata (Fukuoka-ken).

Grandoir Nursery Furniture

Head office ☎ (052) 911-6451　東京都渋谷区富ヶ谷 1-16-4
Shibuya Branch: 1-16-4 Tomigaya, Shibuya-ku, Tokyo ☎ (03) 3469-5159
Aoyama Branch: Aoyama Bldg. 2F, Kita Aoyama, Minato-ku, Tokyo
☎ (03) 3408-7515　東京都港区北青山 1-2-3 青山ビル 2F

The Grandoir line of nursery furniture is sold at select locations in Japan. Call the head office to request a catalog from which you can order by phone. There are Grandoir showrooms in Shibuya and Aoyama, and you can buy Grandoir furniture at the following department stores: Tokyu in Machida and Shibuya, Takashimaya in Nihombashi, Seibu in Shibuya and Osaka, Tobu in Ikebukuro, Mitsukoshi in Nihombashi, Isetan in Shinjuku and Kichijoji, Sogo in Tama and Kobe, and Hankyu in Osaka.

Tan Tan Tan Nursery Furniture

1-8-10 Jingumae, Shibuya-ku, Tokyo　東京都渋谷区神宮前 1–8–10
☎ (03) 3322-5721
🚉 Harajuku Station, JR Yamanote Line; Meiji Jingumae Station, Chiyoda Line

Tan Tan Tan furniture and accessories are sold at their Harajuku shop in
Dear Kids, LaForet Building 3F, and in Osaka. Call the number above for
more information.

BABY EQUIPMENT CATALOGS (IN JAPAN)

Happy Bell Co., Ltd.

☎ (03) 3723-2039 or (06) 354-0322 for catalog.　東京都目黒区自由が丘 1–26–20
Jiyugaoka branch: 1-26-20 Jiyugaoka, Meguro-ku, Tokyo ☎ (03) 3724-3018
Kichijoji branch: 2-18-8 Kichijoji Honmachi, Musashino-shi, Tokyo
☎ (0422) 20-1281　東京都武蔵野市吉祥寺本町 2–18–8
Osaka branch: 2-2-27 Tenjin Bashi, Kita-ku, Osaka-shi, Osaka-fu ☎ (06) 354-0322

This is a baby and maternity goods store that also has a catalog from which
you can order.

King Baby Co.

Head office: 2-2-7 Senbanishi, Mino-shi, Osaka-fu　大阪府箕面市船場西 2–2–7
☎ (0727) 29-6666 fax (0727) 29-9204
Tokyo branch: Aoyama Kyodo Bldg. 4F, 3-6-18 Kita Aoyama, Minato-ku, Tokyo
☎ (03) 3407-3321 fax (03) 3407-9003　東京都港区北青山 3–6–18 共同ビル 4F

The King Baby Co. has a catalog with a large selection of baby products
and they will accept both mail and phone orders. Of special interest are
their good-quality cloth diapers and diaper covers, as well as maternity underwear and cotton baby clothes. Call or write for a catalog.

Marie Foret

Maternity Division: 7-22-17 Nishi Gotanda, Shinagawa-ku, Tokyo
☎ (03) 3494-3377 or (06) 251-3377 fax (03) 3494-2578
For a catalog, call toll-free 0120-003377　東京都品川区西五反田 7–22–17

This is a catalog of maternity and baby wear and accessories. You can
order by phone, postcard, or fax. Items are delivered within two to three
days, and payment is due within two weeks after receipt of the merchandise.

Paren Co.

Ichikura Bldg., 2-2-4 Yariyacho, Chuo-ku, Osaka-shi, Osaka-fu
☎ (06) 942-7858 from 10:00 A.M. to 5:00 P.M.　大阪府大阪市中央区鎗屋町 2–2–4

This company's catalog carries a big selection of all the goods necessary for
equipping baby in style. Call or write to request a catalog.

Senshu Kai

Cherie Maison Division, Evergreen Bldg., 4-3-24 Jingumae, Shibuya-ku, Tokyo
☎ (03) 3478-8177　東京都渋谷区神宮前 4-3-24 エバーグリーンビル

A large selection of baby and maternity products are available through this company's catalog.

The Safety Zone

3-1-27 Yuigahama, Kamakura, Kanagawa-ken　神奈川県鎌倉市由井ヶ浜 3-1-27
☎ (0467) 24-1006 fax (0467) 24-2304

This store stocks many imported safety-related baby products, such as cupboard latches, baby gates, and electric plugs. They also have a good selection of European and U.S. baby equipment and toys for older children. They will deliver anywhere in Japan and you can order from the catalog by phone or fax. English is spoken.

BABY EQUIPMENT CATALOGS (FROM ABROAD)

Anzan Industries

10062 Riverhead Dr., San Diego, California 92129, USA
☎ (619) 484-9639

Check out the lambswool blankets and car seat covers for babies.

Best Selection

2626 Live Oak Highway, Yuba City, California 95991, USA
☎ (916) 673-9798

This company offers a large selection of baby products, including many items not usually found in stores.

Hand in Hand

9180 LeSaint Drive, Fairfield, Ohio 45014, USA
☎ (513) 543-4343 fax (513) 860-5072

A good selection of baby products, bath toys, books, videos, toys, and clothing in sizes 2 to 6 is available from this catalog.

One Step Ahead

P.O. Box 46, Deerfield, Illinois 60015, USA
☎ (708) 272-8507 fax (708) 272-8509

This is the most comprehensive catalog for new parents and babies that we have ever seen. Convenient products, educational toys, bedding, and travel and safety items are all included. If you only order one catalog, make it this one!

Parenting Concepts

P.O. Box 1437, Lake Arrowhead, California 92352, USA
☎ (714) 337-1499 fax (714) 336-1347

This company has a small but special collection of accessories for babies and children. In addition to the Dr. Sears baby sling, an over-the-shoulder method for carrying children from newborn to about four years, several other unique items are offered.

Sweet Dreams

130 E. Wilson Bridge Road, Suite 205, Worthington, Ohio 43085, USA
☎ (614) 431-0496

This firm sells an amazing invention that attaches to a baby's crib and produces a vibration and sound similar to that of riding in a car. This easy-to-install clip helps babies sleep; in a recent study, it even reduced colicky behavior in infants.

The Perfectly Safe Catalog

7245 Whipple Ave. N.W., Canton, Ohio 44720, USA
☎ (216) 494-4366 fax (216) 494-0265

Every safety product and convenience item imaginable for your child is available from this catalog. A wide variety of travel products is also on offer.

Tot Tenders

30441 S. Highway 34, Suite 7-A, Albany, Oregon 97321, USA
☎ (503) 967-9133

The See and Snooze baby carrier is available from Tot Tenders. It allows a baby to be carried in six different positions, including facing outward. It also secures a baby in a grocery cart or adult chair.

BABY EQUIPMENT RENTAL OUTLETS

These rental outlets have baby equipment and supplies for rent and/or sale. Many of them also carry a selection of children's party clothes, ceremonial kimono, and maternity clothes. Call them and they will send you a catalog from which you can order.

GREATER TOKYO AREA

Baby Lease
☎ Toll-free 0120-158181 Tokyo: (03) 3281-0535

Hoxon Baby

☎ Toll-free 0120-240800 Tokyo: (03) 3580-2970 Yokohama: (045) 784-7503 fax (0482) 24-5783

Sanai Baby Lease

1-7-7 Inukura, Miyamae-ku, Kawasaki-shi, Kanagawa-ken ☎ (044) 977-7933

This company has outlets in Tokyo: (03) 3366-4450, Yokohama: (045) 311-9895, Tama: (0423) 75-9333, Sagamihara: (0427) 47-5911.

United Rental

Duskin Ltd., Baby Section, United Rental Division, Hokoku Bldg. 4F, 1-6-28 Nakatsu, Kita-ku, Osaka-shi, Osaka-fu

This company has outlets all over Japan. For a catalog, send a postcard with your name, age, address, and telephone number to the above address.

KANSAI AREA

Baby Futabado

☎ (075) 623-1717 toll-free 0120-172810

This company will deliver in Kyoto-shi, Osaka-fu, and Shiga-ken.

Osaka Baby Center

☎ (06) 972-5891

They will deliver in the Osaka area.

Baby Two-One

See the listing under Diaper Services in this chapter.

Kobe Baby

See the listing under Diaper Services in this chapter.

DIAPERS AND ACCESSORIES

Diapers are of course a necessity when outfitting any baby, and a variety of diapers are available in Japan. Disposable diapers have become more popular in the past few years, with many good-quality brands now on the market. At the time of writing, the only U.S. brand sold is Pampers, which are more expensive than Japanese brands. So far, no company has come out with moderately priced, biodegradable disposable diapers, but fortunately many diaper services make using cloth diapers easy and affordable. In Japan, nonbreathable plastic pants to put on over cotton diapers have been consigned to history. Instead, you will find "waterproof" cotton diaper covers, and the most wonderful wool and Goretex diaper covers. All of these covers close with Velcro at the front, so no pins are necessary.

We prefer the U.S. brands of baby wipes to the Japanese, but the only way to get them is through the Foreign Buyers Club (see chap. 10). The Japanese brands are expensive and flimsy—you need four or five for each diaper change. One suggestion is to buy Japanese-brand wipes when they are on sale and to use washcloths at home to save money.

DIAPER SERVICES

Some diaper services deliver cloth diapers, while others deliver both cloth and disposable diapers. If you use cloth diapers, you will need a large diaper bucket to store them in between pickup dates. Cloth diapers may come in two varieties—Western or Japanese. You may or may not be given a choice. What they call a Western-style diaper is most likely made of all-cotton—like a cotton dish towel, that can be folded into many sizes and styles. The Japanese-style diaper is usually made out of a cotton gauze-type fabric.

The following diaper services provide cloth diapers for rent only.

| GREATER TOKYO AREA |

Hemmy Diaper Service
3-38-3 Ebisu, Shibuya-ku, Tokyo　東京都渋谷区恵比寿 3-38-3
☎ (03) 3444-4491 English spoken

This company delivers both cloth and disposable diapers to hospitals and homes in central Tokyo once a week.

Seigyokusha
神奈川県川崎市中原区市ノ坪 264
264 Ichinotsubo, Nakahara-ku, Kawasaki-shi, Kanagawa-ken
☎ (03) 3700-5157, (03) 3467-7404, (03) 3682-1901 Only Japanese spoken

Delivery of both cloth and disposable diapers throughout Tokyo is available from this company. They will deliver twice a week.

Setagaya Baby Shokai
4-5-21 Kamiyoga, Setagaya-ku, Tokyo　東京都世田谷区上用賀 4-5-21
☎ (03) 3429-9071 Only Japanese spoken

This service only delivers disposable diapers. Service is available in Setagaya-ku, Meguro-ku, Ota-ku, and Suginami-ku, twice a week.

Tokyo Diapers

3-22-11 Shinjuku, Katsushika-ku, Tokyo　東京都葛飾区新宿 3-22-11
☎ (03) 3607-5231 Only Japanese spoken

Tokyo Diapers delivers within Tokyo once a week. They will provide both cloth and disposable diapers.

KANSAI AREA

Baby Two-One

Sunpia Bldg. 1F, Asahi-dori, Chuo-ku, Kobe-shi, Hyogo-ken
☎ (078) 242-1111 Some English spoken　兵庫県神戸市中央区旭通りサンピアビル 1F

This company delivers Japanese-style cloth diapers to Hyogo-ken and Osaka-fu once a week. They also rent baby necessities such as beds, strollers, walkers, and scales.

Kobe Baby

7-1-5 Mikage Honmachi, Higashinada-ku, Kobe-shi, Hyogo-ken
☎ (078) 452-1551 English pamphlet available　兵庫県神戸市東灘区御影本町 7-1-5

Kobe Baby delivers Western- and Japanese-style cloth diapers, and disposable diapers once a week. They also rent baby clothes. Call the head office in Kobe for information on delivery in prefectures from Hiroshima to Shizuoka and Nagano.

Sun Baby

☎ (078) 927-5821 Only Japanese spoken

This company delivers Japanese-style cloth diapers once a week in Hyogo-ken east of Kakogawa, and Osaka-fu west of Yodogawa-ku.

DECORATING THE KID'S ROOM

Decorating and organizing your child's room can be a challenge whether you live in a spacious house or a tiny apartment. No matter where you live, you will want your child's room to be fun yet functional. Many convenient accessories and products for decorating can be bought in Japan. For hard-to-find products from overseas, read through the mail-order section below.

The biggest problem facing most of us in Japan is lack of space, and we have a few suggestions on how to make the best of what you have. The world's greatest collection of storage containers is available here in a variety of colors, sizes, and shapes. Bright-colored plastic baskets and bins are just the thing for keeping kids' clutter organized, and we use them to store everything from Legos to bath toys. Look for them in local houseware and hardware shops.

Closet space can be doubled with the use of extenders made just for this purpose. The wire rods hook onto the clothes bar and hang down below, so another bar can then be extended between them on the lower level. Not only do you have twice the space with this system, but even the youngest child can reach his clothes. Extenders are sometimes available from overseas catalogs, but the same effect can be achieved with a home-made version. Take a bamboo pole and two pieces of wire or strong string. Tie the bar to the wire, trapeze-style, and suspend it from the original clothes bar at the right height for your child.

You should utilize every inch of storage space in your child's room. We found that a vinyl hanging shoe rack hung low on the back of the door was just the place to store mittens and other small items that are easily lost in drawers. Of course, it is always a good idea to have hooks that the kids can reach in the bedroom and bathroom, for hanging up towels, clothes, backpacks, and whatnot. If you like personalized coat racks, you can either make them yourself with a board, some paint, and markers, or order them from one of the catalogs listed in this chapter. Other hand-painted personalized items that kids love, such as wooden stools, rocking chairs, and nameplates, are not readily available in Japan but may be ordered from abroad.

Even if your child's room is the size of your closet back home, a color-coordinated look can enliven the space considerably. Most landlords in Japan will not allow you to put up wallpaper, but there are some alternatives. Try to coordinate the fabric on windows and beds, using a theme or character that appeals to your child. A variety of styles, from Sesame Street to ballerinas, can be ordered from catalogs such as J.C. Penny or Sears and Roebuck. You can purchase some adorable children's fabrics in Japan (see chap. 2), but unless you can sew, the cost of having anything custom made is quite expensive.

Another way to liven up the walls is to tape or tack up a matching wallpaper border. You can put it just below the ceiling level or at chair-back height. Posters and prints are also easy ways to decorate without spending too much time or money. Since children grow quickly and their tastes change, there is no need to have the posters framed. Just tack them securely to the wall with two-sided tape or thumb tacks. For a wide selection of wallpaper borders and posters, it is best to order from overseas. The selection in Japan is limited (mostly Disney characters), and prices are high.

Maps are a must for any family with children, and world and other maps are available—in Japanese, of course. Maps in English can be found at the major English-language bookstores (see chap. 4).

We suggest that you bring all the bedding that you will need when you move to Japan. From crib sheets to king-size beds, the size and selection in Japan is quite limited. Bassinet sheets are almost impossible to find. For options on sleeping arrangements for baby, see the introduction to this chapter. For toddlers and older children, duvets are a good choice. Kids can easily make their own beds using the duvet instead of a top sheet and blanket. The mail-order section of this chapter lists discount outlets for down comforters and bedding.

For a new baby, there are several essentials that make a lovely nursery. If you choose a crib, do not forget bumper pads, crib skirt, or canopy to complete the look. If you order items from overseas, make sure you allow enough time for delivery by sea mail to save money. In addition to crib fabric, a companion fabric that can be used for window treatments or a chair cushion and pillows is a good choice. If you are lucky enough to have a large shipment coming to Japan, make sure to include a comfortable rocking chair, as your only chance to find one here may be from a friend, through the want ads, or at international bazaars and flea markets. Also important to have is a changing table, a playpen, and a state-of-the-art highchair. An area rug in the same colors as the nursery is a nice addition that you can take with you when you move.

Most months of the year the morning sunlight will stream in through your windows bright and early. If you want your child to sleep past sunrise, you will need some form of window treatment to block out the sunlight. Blackout fabric, sold at custom drapery shops and some fabric stores, can be made into curtains or shades to fit behind your decorative window treatment. Another alternative is to use inexpensive miniblinds and top them off with a whimsical valance. You can make simple swags and bows and staple them up around the window. If you do not sew, just drape the fabric and staple at will. Full custom-made curtains for a child's room are not worth the price you have to pay here.

When buying overseas, remember that standard-size curtains often will not fit Japanese-size windows. If you want to order curtains that match your bedding but are not sure of the fit, either order two sets and sew them together or buy an extra set of sheets to make your own window treatments. Extra sheets also come in handy for pillows, cushions, and even covering a headboard.

Other suggested items to order from overseas or to bring with you include baby monitors, night lights and baby lamps, and mobiles for hanging above a crib.

If your only option is to use Japanese products for your child's nursery or playroom, be sure to go to a discount shop first to see what they have. If you are looking for Western-sized cribs and foreign baby equipment, place a want ad on a public bulletin board or in the English-language newspapers and magazines.

Perhaps you would like a Japanese theme for your child's room. Try some of the delightful patterns of *yukata* fabric for throw pillows and window treatments. One friend incorporated her collection of small, pastel-colored fans into a window treatment in her daughter's room by attaching them to a bamboo screen. For a boy's room, try hanging the brightly-colored Boys' Day carp streamers or paper kites from the ceiling or walls. These same carp streamers can be stuffed for an unusual bed pillow. A collection of traditional Japanese wooden toys makes an attractive bookshelf arrangement. Many products made from *washi* paper are suitable for decorating a child's room: mobiles, storage boxes, wastebaskets, picture frames, and more can all be used in decorative ways. Brightly-colored Noh masks are also fun for kids to collect and display on a bedroom wall. Japanese tea boxes, which come in many sizes, can be covered in colorful fabric and used as toy or clothes storage boxes.

DECORATING A CHILD'S ROOM (MAIL-ORDER FROM ABROAD)

The following companies have everything for decorating your child's room from posters and wall hangings to rocking chairs that you can order by mail. For more room accessories, look at the mail-order catalogs listed in chapter 4.

American Library Association

ALA Graphics, 50 E. Huron St., Chicago, Illinois 60611, USA
☎ (312) 944-6780

Posters from your favorite books, such as *Curious George* and *The Cat in the Hat*. These inexpensive posters are aimed at promoting reading and library use. American Express, VISA, and MasterCard are accepted.

Child Graphics Press

P.O. Box 7771, Hilton Head Island, South Carolina 29938, USA
☎ (803) 689-3030

Creative art posters from many favorite fairy tales.

Decorate It!

6320 Canoga Avenue, Suite 1600, Woodhills, California, USA
☎ (818) 595-1013

This company offers the newest trend in decorating kids' rooms. The products sold through this catalog use the Post-it Notes adhesive backing to allow you to apply and remove decorative decals time after time. The wall appliqués and borders are designed by some of the top children's illustrators. Easy to apply and suitable for almost any wall surface, these one-of-a-kind designs are ideal for decorating children's rooms in Japan.

Fun Furniture

8451 Beverly Blvd., Los Angeles, California 90048, USA
☎ (213) 655-2711

This is the most innovative idea in children's furniture that we have ever seen. Fun Furniture creates unique, architect-designed chairs, headboards, shelves, lamps, etc., in a variety of tantalizing colors. The furniture is either plastic-laminated or hand-painted, and the designs consist of castles, animals, and other whimsical motifs. The company will pack and crate the furniture and also help you arrange for overseas shipping. VISA, Master-Card, and American Express are accepted.

Hansen Planetarium Publications

1098 S. 200 W., Salt Lake City, Utah 84101, USA
☎ (801) 538-2242

A catalog full of spectacular posters. You can choose from scenes of planets, astronauts, the Space Shuttle, and more, all illustrated in beautiful color.

Teddy Bed

Premarq Inc., P.O. Box 840, Astoria, Oregon 97103, USA

Three versions of the famous net storage units are available. These nets hold soft toys and can be hung from the wall, in the shower, or on a stroller.

The Baby's Gallerie

P.O. Box 458, Whitesboro, New York 13492, USA
☎ (315) 736-5224 fax (315) 736-7559

A variety of baby furniture and accessories. Many new and unusual products as well as personalized items are available.

The Company Store

500 Company Store Road, La Crosse, Wisconsin 54601, USA

A fine collection of goose- and duck-down bedding, including cotton crib sheets, dust ruffles, and bumper pads. Also available from the catalog are 100 percent merino wool stroller throws, car seat covers, and playpen and crib mattress pads. VISA, MasterCard, DISCOVER, and American Express are accepted.

The Peaceable Kingdom

2980 College Ave., Suite 2, Berkeley, California 94705, USA
☎ (415) 644-9801

Posters of Peter Rabbit, Babar, Curious George, and many other characters from children's classics are to be found in this catalog. Maurice Sendak's *Where the Wild Things Are* is available, along with a special poster he created for the International Year of the Child.

Priss Prints

3960 Broadway Blvd., Suite 105, Garland, Texas 75043, USA

This company's stock of giant self-adhesive wall decorations includes characters from Disney, Sesame Street, My Little Pony, etc. The decorations are ideal for livening up your child's room and they are reusable on surfaces like furniture and painted or vinyl-papered walls.

Poster Originals

330 Hudson Street, New York, New York 10013, USA
☎ (212) 620-0522

This company offers a 100-page catalog filled with posters from museums around the world. Many are suitable for a child's room, and some are created just for children.

Rand McNally and Co.

P.O. Box 1697, Skokie, Illinois 60076-9871, USA
☎ (708) 673-9100

This is the place for globes, maps, and atlases for the home and office. American Express, VISA, and MasterCard are accepted.

4
Books, & toys, and Libraries

THANK YOU, DAD.

Just when you think your children have more than enough books, toys, and games, you find that the little rascals have grown out of them. Children advance in reading, toys break or become otherwise obsolete, and games are no longer a challenge. Children move on to new interests and activities. We have accepted the fact that our house is nothing more than a revolving door through which an unlimited number of books, toys, and games will pass as the children grow up.

Living in Japan is a mixed blessing in the endless cycle of book, toy, and game acquisitions. There is no question that some of the most intriguing toys are made here, and those that are not manufactured here are imported. Books and games in English are another story. Compared to other items for children, only a handful of these are available in Japan. We have found mail-order sources from abroad to fill the gap, however, and so our children's libraries continue to grow. Public libraries serve the same purpose in Japan as anywhere else, allowing children to borrow a book, enjoy it, and return it. Depending on where you live, public libraries can be a practical asset or a once-in-a-while outing.

BOOKS AND MAGAZINES

We know of a few special children's books available about Japan and its people that are good for entertaining and educating children about the Japanese way of life. *Sayonara, Mrs. Kackleman*, by Maria Kalman (Viking Penguin, 1989), is the most adorable, hysterically funny book we have ever seen about Japan. It is written from a child's point of view about a visit to Japan, and the whimsical pictures make the book a delight. The book can usually be found in the children's book section of Maruzen bookstore. Another book you may want to look for is *How My Parents Learned to Eat*, by Ina Friedman (Houghton Mifflin Co., 1984). This lighthearted tale takes place in Japan and is interesting for children age four and up.

There is also a series of coloring books about Japan called *American-Japanese Coloring and Talking Books* , illustrated by N. Sugimura (Charles E. Tuttle Co., 1952). Each book in the ten-volume series focuses on a subject of interest to children, such as fairy tale characters, animals, or holidays. It then compares the Japanese version of the subject with the American version using easy story lines and fun-to-color pictures. They make great gifts! A hardcover book called *Japanese Children's Favorite Stories*, edited by Florence Sakade (Charles E. Tuttle Co., 1953) is also available which contains twenty of Japan's best-loved children's tales. All these books make a great addition to anyone's collection.

BOOKSTORES

Crayon House

3-8-15 Kita Aoyama, Minato-ku, Tokyo　東京都港区北青山 3–8–15
☎ (03) 3406-6492
🚇 Omotesando Station (A1 exit), Ginza, Chiyoda, Hanzomon lines

This bookstore makes for a great outing with the kids. Not only do they have a fabulous selection of hardback and paperback children's books in English, French, German, and Japanese, but they have a nice family restaurant in the basement. From the menu to the kiddie seats to the staff that "ooh and ah" over your children, a visit to this restaurant is a treat for everyone. Go to the second floor for stationery goods and calendars with all of the popular storybook themes (Babar, Winnie the Pooh, etc.) and a great selection of imported wooden toys.

Crayon House also has a babysitting service; call ahead in Japanese to make a reservation. To get there, take the subway to Omotesando Station and go out the Hanae Mori exit (A1). Crayon House is located one block behind the Hanae Mori Building. The store is open daily from 11:00 A.M. to 8:00 P.M., and the restaurant is open from 11:00 A.M. to 10:00 P.M.

Jena Co.

5-6-1, Ginza, Chuo-ku, Tokyo　東京都中央区銀座 5–6–1
☎ (03) 3571-2980
🚇 Ginza Station (B5 exit), Ginza, Hibiya, Marunouchi lines

This three-story bookstore has a small selection of foreign books and magazines on the third floor. The children's selection consists mostly of hardbacks in English, ranging from board books for infants to the classics for three- to twelve-year-olds.

Jena is just outside the B5 exit. If you are walking from the center of Ginza, take the road with the Wako Building and the round Sanae Building for two short blocks. Jena is on the same side as the Sanae Building. The store is open Monday through Saturday from 10:30 A.M. to 7:50 P.M., and Sunday from noon to 6:30 P.M.

Kinokuniya Bookstore

3-17-7, Shinjuku, Shinjuku-ku, Tokyo　東京都新宿区新宿 3-17-7
☎ (03) 3354-0131
🚇 Shinjuku Station (east exit), JR Yamanote, JR Chuo, Toei Shinjuku, Marunouchi, Keio, Odakyu lines

The main store in a chain of bookstores, Kinokuniya in Shinjuku (easy to find near Isetan) has foreign books on the sixth floor. The children's selection is diverse, although small. Most of the books are top-quality hardbacks from the United States, Canada, and Great Britain. There are a few books in German and French. We were pleased to find a selection of children's Bible story books (not easy to find in Japan), as well as books about traditions and holidays from many countries around the world.

To get there, take the east exit of Shinjuku Station, turn right, and walk toward Isetan. Kinokuniya is a couple of blocks before Isetan on the same side of the street. The store is open daily from 10:00 A.M. to 7:00 P.M.

Another central Tokyo branch with foreign books is in Tokyu Plaza in Shibuya. Branches outside Tokyo include Osaka (Umeda store), Kobe, Hiroshima, Fukuoka, and Kumamoto. These stores carry only a small selection of books in English, but they will order specific titles from the main store in Shinjuku for you.

Maruzen

2-3-10 Nihombashi, Chuo-ku, Tokyo　東京都中央区日本橋 2-3-10
☎ (03) 3272-7211
🚇 Nihombashi Station, Tozai, Ginza lines

This is by far the best general bookstore in Tokyo for children's books in English. Located on the fourth floor is the children's section where you will find an exquisite collection of books in English and other languages. They have Caldecott medal winners, classics, and our favorite Elsa Beskow books. You can browse for hours among the selection, but don't forget to check out the maps, language tapes, and videos. For parenting or health books go to the second floor where most of the English books for adults are stocked.

The bookstore is directly across from Takashimaya Department Store, and one subway exit leads right into the basement level of Maruzen. Hours are Monday through Saturday, 10:00 A.M. to 6:30 P.M. The Ochanomizu branch in Tokyo also carries a large selection of books in English. The Osaka branches are at Shinsaibashi and Temma; the Kobe branch is at Motomachi.

Tuttle Bookshop

1-3 Jimbocho, Kanda, Chiyoda-ku, Tokyo　東京都千代田区神田神保町 1-3
☎ (03) 3291-7071
🚇 Jimbocho Station, Hanzomon, Toei Mita, Toei Shinjuku lines

Here you will find an excellent selection of books from a variety of publishers. Among their selection for children you will find pop-up books, coloring books, audio cassette and book sets, paint-with-water books, and almost anything else a child could want in a book. Our favorite coloring books, *American-Japanese Coloring and Talking Books*, are usually available at this store, although sometimes they have to be ordered.

The store is a 10-minute walk from Jimbocho Station. They are open Monday through Friday from 10:30 A.M. to 6:30 P.M. and on Saturday from 11:00 A.M. to 6:00 P.M. The Osaka branch is in the Wako Bldg., 2-7 Showa-cho, Suita-shi, Osaka-fu; phone (06) 382-5020.

Little America Bookstore

3-9-22 Heiwa, Chuo-ku, Fukuoka-shi, Fukuoka-ken 815
☎ (092) 521-8826 fax (092) 521-2288　福岡県福岡市中央区平和 3-9-22

This bookstore has everything you need to learn to speak, read, or write English; indeed, the store was originally opened to provide supplies for teachers of English as a second language. The result is a store with fun and educational games, tapes, and workbooks. The store has many hard-to-find items in English, such as maps, learning posters, card and board games, and flash cards. For the price of a stamp, they will send you a catalog from which you can order by mail.

National Azabu Bookstore

4-5-2 Minami-Azabu, Minato-ku, Tokyo　東京都港区南麻布 4-5-2
☎ (03) 3442-3181
🚇 Hiroo Station, Hibiya Line

Although called a bookstore, this is more like a stationery store. There is a good selection of greeting and holiday cards, wrapping paper, paper products for parties, small gift items, and foreign and local magazines for all ages. Their books consist mostly of best-selling paperbacks and books about Japan but they also stock a few children's storybooks and some activity-type books for preschoolers.

Located above the National Azabu Supermarket, across from Arisu- gawa Park, the bookstore is open daily from 9:30 A.M., Monday through Friday to 6:30 P.M. and Saturday and Sunday until 7:00 P.M.

The Bookworm

550-8 Kaitori, Tama-shi, Tokyo 206　東京都多摩市貝取 550-8
☎ (0423) 71-2141

 Keio Nagayama Station, Keio Sagamihara Line; Odakyu Nagayama Station, Tama Line (from Shinyurigaoka Station, Odakyu Line)

With over 20,000 volumes in stock, this is the largest bookstore in Tokyo for used English-language books. You can exchange your old books for other used books for a few hundred yen. Children's books are a hot com- modity here, with picture books being the most popular. If you are lucky, you can find a variety of children's books for all ages, but most of their stock consists of adult books. Ask for the mail-order book lists. They are open Tuesday through Saturday from 11:00 A.M. to 6:00 P.M.

OTHER SOURCES

Throughout the year, there are many opportunities to purchase books at the fairs and bazaars held by the international schools, churches, and private clubs around Tokyo. The books at these sales are usually provided by in- dividuals who sell books as a home business. Sometimes these sources provide mail-order catalogs.

La Leche League International

La Leche League (LLL) of Japan stocks copies of several English-language books that are unavailable in bookstores in Japan. The LLL manual, *The Womanly Art of Breastfeeding*, is always available in English and Japanese, and their cookbook, *Whole Foods for the Whole Family*, is very popular. They also sell books by Dr. William Sears, such as *Nighttime Parenting*, in addition to books on pregnancy, childbirth, and breastfeeding by other au- thors. Contact an LLL leader in your area if you are interested in purchasing books or borrowing from their library.

For more information, see the LLL listing in chapter 9.

My Favorite Books

Deidre Merrell-Ikeda, 2-6-18 Moto Azabu, Minato-ku, Tokyo 106
☎ (03) 3423-2067　東京都港区元麻布 2-6-18

A small company that published its first catalog in 1989, My Favorite Books, as the name implies, markets the favorite books of the owner and her child. The catalog lists an interesting assortment of reading material, from self-help books and New Age parenting to some very special books and tapes for children. Some of our own favorite books were recommended by Deidre herself: the parenting and relationship books by Joyce and Barry Vissell and all of Shakti Gawain's books. Having a My Favorite Books catalog is like having a friendly bookshop right next door, and is especially helpful for people who otherwise don't have access to books in English. Call Deidre for a catalog or write to her at the above address.

Telling Tales

Contact Julia Bonsall: A301 Komazawa Garden House, 1-2-33 Komazawa, Setagaya-ku, Tokyo; ☎ (03) 5481-8544 fax (03) 5481-6793. Or Pamela Edmonds: B406 Komazawa Garden House, 1-2-33 Komazawa, Setagaya-ku, Tokyo; ☎ (03) 3418-3386 fax (03) 3419-0071　東京都世田谷区駒沢 1-2-33 駒沢ガーデンハウス

Telling Tales is a company that imports high-quality British books for children up to about age twelve. The company is run by expatriate women, and they choose books from Great Britain that are not readily available in Japan, both old favorites and new releases. They sell at international bazaars in Tokyo and also in the relaxed atmosphere of their own homes. At these sales, you are encouraged to take your time in making selections and asking questions. Refreshments are usually offered and children are welcome. Call or write and ask to be put on their mailing list.

Usborne Books at Home

ABS Bldg., 2-4-16 Kudan Minami, Chiyoda-ku, Tokyo
☎ (03) 3221-9794 fax (03) 3239-2817　東京都千代田区九段南 2-4-16 ABS ビル

Usborne is a British publishing house known for its high-quality, educational books for parents and children of all ages. Their books are available in Japan through this sole distributor and are sold through their "Books at Home" scheme. You can invite a number of friends to your home and the Usborne distributor will provide the books for you to browse through and purchase at your leisure. The "Books at Home" method also lends itself to school or community group fund-raising campaigns. Call the number above for more information.

BOOK-OF-THE-MONTH CLUBS

Book-of-the-month clubs in the United States, Canada, and Great Britain sell books to members at reduced prices. Books range from the classics to early readers to special-interest books, depending on the club. Unfortunately, because of prohibitive shipping costs these clubs generally will not mail to individuals in Japan. There is one book club in Great Britain, however, that will mail to groups, such as schools and play groups, and reading circles. It seems that shipping large quantities is profitable for them, and as the books are priced 25 percent to 40 percent lower than in Tokyo bookstores, it is also worth it for you.

Again, we stress that this club is not intended for individual families, but for playgroups, school groups, and reading circles, etc. This means that if you can get six to ten families together for a reading circle, you can make use of this club! For more information, write: Baker Books Puffin Book Club, Manfield Park, Cranleigh GU6 8NU, Surrey, England, or phone 483-267888 or fax 483-267409

MAGAZINES FOR KIDS ONLY

Imagine the joy your child would experience at receiving his own magazine in the mail each month. Just as we hunger for new and up-to-date resources to feed our interests, so do our children. This list of magazines from the United States and Canada contains periodicals for children from two to fifteen years. The magazines are full of informative, educational, and insightful articles, stories, and projects and most are advertisement-free. Payment must be made in U.S. dollars or by VISA or MasterCard unless otherwise noted.

Chickadee Magazine

The Young Naturalist Foundation, 56 The Esplanade, Suite 306, Toronto, Ontario M5E 1A7, Canada
☎ (416) 868-6001 fax (416) 868-6009
For four- to nine-year-olds. This magazine contains articles, arts activities, and stories that aim to interest young children in the world around them in an entertaining and lively way.

Faces

30 Grove St., Peterborough, New Hampshire 03458, USA
☎ (603) 924-7209
For eight- to fourteen-year-olds. A fun and informative magazine on world cultures and history. Each issue focuses on a single subject or culture.

Highlights For Children

2300 West Fifth Avenue, P.O. Box 269, Columbus, Ohio 43216-0269, USA
☎ (614) 486-0695

For two- to twelve-year-olds. Full of entertaining stories, games, and puzzles, this magazine is one of the longest running and most popular magazines for children in the United States. The majority of the material is geared for eight- to twelve-year-olds to read to themselves and two- to seven-year-olds to listen to. There are special pages of interest for each age group so you can save the back issues and read them again as your child grows older.

National Geographic World

National Geographic Society, 17th and M Streets N.W., Washington, DC 20036, USA
☎ (202) 857-7000 fax (301) 921-1347

For eight- to thirteen-year-olds. This is a highly visual magazine with factual stories about animals, geography, sports, and outdoor adventure.

Sesame Street Magazine

P.O. Box 52000, Boulder, Colorado 80321-2000, USA
☎ (212) 595-3456

For two- to six-year-olds. All of the favorite Sesame Street characters are here! This publication, put out ten times a year by the people who bring us TV's "Sesame Street," is informative, educational, and—most of all—fun. Each issue contains games, projects, and stories to entertain your child for hours. An extra bonus is the accompanying Parent's Guide. The magazine is worth subscribing to just to get this guide full of parenting tips and stories. Published by the Children's Television Workshop. No credit cards accepted.

Kids City

P.O. Box 51277, Boulder, Colorado 80321-1277, USA
☎ (122) 595-3456

For six- to ten-year-olds. Published by the same publisher as *Sesame Street Magazine*, this magazine is full of humor, stories, and activities. No credit cards accepted.

3-2-1-Contact

same address as above

For eight- to fourteen-year-olds. A third magazine published by the Children's Television Workshop, this one is in the same exciting yet educational style as their TV show of the same name.

Stone Soup

Children's Art Foundation, Box 83, Santa Cruz, California 95063, USA
☎ (408) 426-5557

For four- to thirteen-year-olds. *Stone Soup* is a bimonthly literary magazine of writing and art, including fiction, poetry, book reviews, and artwork by kids through age thirteen.

Stork, Turtle, Humpty Dumpty, Children's Playmate, Jack and Jill, Child Life, and *Children's Digest*

Children's Better Health Institute, 1100 Waterway Blvd., Box 567, Indianapolis, Indiana 46206, USA

☎ (317) 636-8881 fax (317) 637-0126

For two- to fifteen-year-olds. These magazines are all published by the Children's Better Health Institute in the United States. Each magazine is geared for a slightly different age group, but all combine fun with learning in eight issues per year. Illustrated stories, poems, puzzles, games, and songs help children learn about health, nutrition, hygiene, exercise, and safety.

The Dolphin Log

The Cousteau Society, 8440 Santa Monica Blvd., Los Angeles, California 90069, USA

☎ (804) 627-1144

For seven- to fifteen-year-olds. This is an educational publication for children which covers marine biology, ecology, natural history, and other water-related topics. No credit cards accepted.

Your Big Backyard

National Wildlife Foundation, 1400 16th Street N.W., Washington DC 20036, USA

☎ (703) 790-4274 fax (703) 442-7332

For three- to five-year-olds. This is a wildlife magazine emphasizing ecology and conservation in an entertaining way for children. It offers nature lore and activities in addition to stories.

Ranger Rick

National Wildlife Foundation, 1400 16th Street N.W., Washington DC 20036, USA

☎ (703) 790-4274 fax (703) 442-7332

For six- to twelve-year-olds. From the same publishers as *Your Big Backyard*, this magazine is geared toward an older audience.

Zoobooks

P.O. Box 85271, San Diego, California 92138, USA

☎ (619) 745-2809

For all ages. A real treat for the whole family, these magazine-type books come every six weeks or so—there are ten per year. Each issue focuses on a different animal, exploring its prehistoric ancestors describing its anatomy, and illustrating where the different varieties of the species can now be found. Young children will enjoy the full-page illustrations and pictures. Older children can use them as reference books for school projects or for learning more about a favorite animal.

TOYS AND GIFTS

Although you may miss the bargain toy stores back home, you can find a wide variety of affordable children's toys here in Japan. In order to give you an idea of what is available, we have highlighted some of our favorite purchases over the years. Some of these items are so unique that you will want your kids to have one as a memento of their stay in Japan. Others are the perfect gift to send back home without spending a fortune.

For those of you with very young children, the selection of riding and push toys here is unbeatable. The cars, trucks, and animals come in all colors and designs, with a plastic bar across the back for your child to hang onto as he learns to walk. Pick one with all the extras, such as a telephone, beeping horn, and hidden compartments. Your children will spend hours scooting around on these and the price is only about ¥5,000 (less if you go to a discount store—see chap. 3).

Many toys made in Japan are designed with the parent in mind. This is especially true of the tricycles that come with a steering stick in the back for parents to guide their child along the road. No more stiff backs from pushing little ones whose feet do not touch the pedals. These trikes even have foot-rests and a safety bar around the seat that can be removed as the child grows.

The spiffiest pedal cars in the world are right here in Japan. From age two to three, one of our children practically lived in his miniature red Mercedes pedal car. He would insist on "driving" it wherever we went in the neighborhood, and if it was raining outside, he would bring it inside and sit in it while eating or watching TV! The cars are quite small, so a large three-year-old might not fit, but they are safe for even a one-year-old. Pedal cars come in every model imaginable, from Mercedes to Volkswagens, police cars to fire engines. They can be found at department stores and toy stores for around ¥15,000.

Sesame Street toys and accessories are now sold in Japan, but many of the products are different from those sold overseas. We have found some inexpensive gifts that are very "Japanese," such as *obento* boxes and *oshibori* containers with the Sesame Street characters on them.

Sanrio Co. makes a Hello Kitty series of Velcro-and-plastic food sets that children of all ages enjoy. Children love to "slice" the food with the plastic knife and then put it all back together again. There are vegetable sets, fruit sets, sandwich sets, and more. When we send these overseas, we always buy the sushi set as a unique gift from Japan. Sanrio shops also carry a mind-boggling assortment of Japanese character items that make great gifts. In addition to *obento* boxes, you may choose from travel toothbrush sets, Band-aids, towels, or thermoses, all designed with character or color-coordinated themes. The best thermos design is the kind with the straw that pops up when the lid is snapped open. It is leak-proof and easy to use when traveling. Our friends back home always ask for more of these when we go back on vacation.

Everyone knows Hello Kitty, but don't forget the other Sanrio characters, such as The Runabouts and Little Twin Stars. Rice bowls, fork and spoon sets, and chopsticks are all available with these characters on them. We have started a collection of different pieces for several of our friend's children; additions over the years are easy and affordable.

We have had our best luck finding unusual toys in small neighborhood toy or stationery stores. Japanese paper balls, miniature pen sets, and sticker packs are all very lightweight to mail as gifts. Japanese bath toys can be found just about anywhere, and the animals that change color in different water temperatures are our favorites. Many of the toys in the smaller shops are seasonal, so keep your eyes open year-round for the best bargains.

Every summer we buy "squeaky shoes" for our kids to wear to the pool. These sandals are brightly colored and emit a loud squeak with every step. They are available only in sizes up to about age three, but they are a big hit with that crowd. We give them as gifts along with Japanese summer pajamas or T-shirts.

Gifts that educate a child about Japan are always appreciated. We often give the plastic money sets that include yen coins, bills, and a small abacus. These are cheap (¥500) and can be found in any small toy store or festival booth during the summer and fall.

Japan has many traditional toys to offer. Spinning tops, kites, dolls, and other toys made of bamboo and wood are a special part of Japan that your child should experience. At New Year, buy a *hagoita* for the whole family to enjoy. This is a wooden paddle, often elaborately decorated, that is used to bat a tiny shuttlecock in a game similar to badminton. Other traditional toys are made from *washi* paper and can be used as decorations in a child's room. In Tokyo, these can be found at very low prices in Asakusabashi (see chap. 2); they can also be purchased at a shop in Roppongi called Washikobo (see Traditional Japanese Toys section). Origami is fun for all ages, and sets of fancy paper with instruction books in English are available in toy and book stores. There are many beautiful dolls available in Japan but they are rather expensive. For little girls, it is perhaps safer to buy the soft dolls in kimono with the pretty plastic faces that look like porcelain. They are less destructible than the fancier dolls, and cheaper. Another option is the *kokeshi* doll. These hand-painted wooden figures are often inexpensive, and the different types are fun to collect.

Of course, the electronic gadgets and robot toys available in Japan are ideal for older children. Akihabara (see chap. 2) is famous for the wide variety and the latest designs in home video games and portable Game Boys. An inflatable robot that we mailed home one Christmas was a big hit, and our own children are fascinated by the robot toys that can be taken apart and transformed into several vehicles. Just make sure that your kids are old enough to figure out how to put it all back together again because the instructions are usually in Japanese.

TOYS IN DEPARTMENT STORES

As you can imagine, the toy selection at major department stores is extensive. There is always a new gadget or gizmo on display, and you can find a large selection of Japanese toys in addition to imported ones from Fisher Price and Playskool. All major department stores display sample toys to keep the kids busy while you shop—a real advantage for parents. Department stores are forever changing their floor layout and their merchandise in an effort to stay ahead of the competition. Generally, however, all department stores carry the same products. See chapter 2 for detailed descriptions of each department store.

TOY STORES

Bornelund

Hara Bldg. 1F, 6-10-10 Jingumae, Shibuya-ku, Tokyo
☎ (03) 5485-3430　東京都渋谷区神宮前 6-10-10 原ビル 1F
Hours: 11:00 A.M. to 8:00 P.M.
🚃 Meiji Jingumae Station, Chiyoda Line; Harajuku Station, JR Yamanote Line
Osaka: Crest Shinsaibashi 1F, 4-12-9 Chuo-ku, Osaka-shi, Osaka-fu
☎ (06) 244-9231
Hours: 11:00 A.M. to 7:00 P.M.

Bornelund is a toy manufacturer from Denmark, and the store carries educational toys and games, as well as baby rattles, beautiful German dolls, and a very expensive line of clothing from the Netherlands. From either station, walk four blocks from the Meiji and Omote Sando intersection toward Shibuya Station.

Froebel-Kan

3-1 Kanda Ogawamachi, Chiyoda-ku, Tokyo 東京都千代田区神田小川町 3-1
☎ (03) 3292-7781
Hours: 10:00 A.M. to 6:00 P.M.
🚇 Ogawamachi Station, Toei Shinjuku Line; or Jimbocho Station, Toei Mita, Toei Shinjuku Lines; or Awajicho Station, Marunouchi Line

Although this showroom is primarily for selling to preschools and kindergartens, individuals may also purchase their sturdy and imaginative toys. There is a large selection of wood toys in addition to outdoor play equipment.

Gran Papa

New Aoyama Bldg., 2nd floor, 1-1-1 Minami Aoyama, Minato-ku, Tokyo
☎ (03) 3475-1388 東京都港区南青山 1-1-1 新青山ビル西館 2F
Hours: 11:00 A.M. to 7:00 P.M.
🚇 Aoyama Itchome Station, Hanzomon, Ginza lines

This chain carries fine-quality imported toys from Europe. Some of the outstanding items are dolls from Germany that come with matching outfits for the dolls and their owners (little girls of all ages) and exquisite stuffed animals that make special gifts for newborns. Gran Papa's main store in Aoyama Twin Towers also carries Japanese dolls. Other stores are in Ginza, Shinjuku, Ogikubo, Asakusa, Jiyugaoka (see Shopping Districts in chap. 2), and Yokohama. To get to Aoyama Twin Towers, take the train to Aoyama Itchome Station and exit into the basement, or drive and park on a side street off Aoyama Dori.

Hakuhinkan Toy Park

8-8-1 Ginza, Chuo-ku, Tokyo 東京都中央区銀座 8-8-1
☎ (03) 3571-8008
Hours: Toy store, 11:00 A.M. to 8:00 P.M. daily. Restaurant floors, 11:30 A.M. to 10:00 P.M.
🚇 Ginza Station, Ginza, Hibiya, Marunouchi lines

This spacious store has a different atmosphere from many other toy stores—it is almost luxurious. A wide, carpeted, spiral stairway leads from each of the four floors to the next (there is also an elevator), and soothing music plays over loudspeakers. The toys are not crammed together but neatly displayed on large shelves. The mood is very relaxed—except on weekends when the store gets crowded. Adult toys and games—fancy remote-control cars, golf putting kits, stationery goods, and video games—are on the first two floors. The third and fourth floors have a wide selection of Japanese and imported toys. Character toys, electronic games, beautiful

Japanese dolls, and a toy hospital are all to be found here.

To get a bite to eat, try the coffee shop in the basement or the sandwich shop on the second floor. For more serious eating, the fifth and sixth floors house French, pasta, steak, and Japanese restaurants. Concerts and other shows are held at the éighth-floor theater. For information, ask at the ticket counter on the first floor.

To get to there, go out the A5 exit. This will put you in the heart of Ginza. Walking away from the main intersection, you will find Haku-hinkan at the end of the street—past Matsuzakaya Department Store, Familiar, Wendy's, and McDonald's—just before the Shuto Expressway.

Kiddyland

6-1-9 Jingumae, Shibuya-ku, Tokyo　東京都渋谷区神宮前 6-1-9
☎ (03) 3409-3431
Hours: 10:00 A.M. to 8:00 P.M. Closed every third Wednesday.
🚇 Meiji Jingumae Station, Chiyoda Line; Harajuku Station, JR Yamanote Line

This is probably the best single toy store in Tokyo, but do not try to navigate it with the little ones on a weekend. The crowds are horrendous and the layout, even though there are five floors, is cramped and confusing. We also try to avoid Kiddyland on weekday afternoons, when hordes of giggly adolescents clog every aisle. When we do make the trip, however, we always find an abundance of toys for all ages and plenty of new displays. Our favorite floors are the preschool collection on the third floor and the Sesame Street Club in the basement. Throughout the store, there are enough displays to keep the kids busy while you look around. There is only one small elevator, so you may end up taking the stairs. This is difficult with a stroller, so plan your strategy before leaving home. Despite the inconvenience, Kiddyland is the ideal toy store according to just about every kid we know. The store is near the intersection of Meiji Dori and Omote Sando.

Kids Crimson

Prestige Nishi-Azabu Bldg., B2F, 4-22-10 Nishi-Azabu, Minato-ku, Tokyo
☎ (03) 5485-1533　東京都港区西麻布 4-22-10 プレステージ西麻布 B2F
Hours: 10:00 A.M. to 7:00 P.M. Sundays noon to 6:00 P.M.
🚇 Hiroo Station, Hibiya Line

This is basically an import store. Among the goods they carry are two popular brands from the United States, Little Tykes toys and Oshkosh clothing for kids (newborn to size 6 or 7). Little Tykes makes sturdy, good-quality plastic toys that range from train sets and blocks for babies to large

97

doll houses, slides, and easels for older children. The store will order any items that you want from the Little Tykes catalog. The store is located at the end of Nisseki Dori shopping street, across from the Red Cross Hospital.

Niki Tiki Toy Shop

Daikanyama: Park Side Village BO2, 9-8 Sarugaku-cho, Shibuya-ku, Tokyo
☎ (03) 3770-4686　東京都渋谷区猿楽町 9-8 代官山パークサイドビレッジ B02
Hours: 10:00 A.M. to 6:00 P.M.
🚃 Daikanyama Station, Toyoko Line
Kichijoji: 2-28-3, Kichijoji Hon-cho, Musashino-shi, Tokyo
☎ (0422) 21-3137　東京都武蔵野市吉祥寺本町 2-28-3
Hours: 10:00 A.M. to 7:00 P.M.
🚃 Kichijoji Station, JR Chuo Line

Niki Tiki Toy Shop has one of the most extensive collections in town of wooden toys, games, and ornaments from Sweden and Germany. They also have collector-quality dolls and a good selection of Ravensburger puzzles and games. Most of their hand-painted Christmas ornaments and decorations are on display year-round. The Shibuya store is located one block from the main Daikanyama shopping street, just past the NTT B Building. The Kichijoji store is down the side street to the right of the main entrance to Tokyu Department Store.

Sanrio Gallery

2-7-17 Ginza, Chuo-ku, Tokyo　東京都中央区銀座 2-7-17
☎ (03) 3563-2731
Hours: 11:00 A.M. to 8:00 P.M. Closed three Tuesdays a month.
🚃 Ginza Station (A13 exit), Hibiya, Marunouchi, Ginza lines

Something about the Sanrio Gallery in the Ginza reminds our kids of Disneyland. Perhaps it's the talking trees or the fantasylike appearance of it all. This two-story shop is the flagship store for Sanrio, maker of Hello Kitty products and many other popular character toys. The Ginza store is a larger version of their small shops in department stores and stationery stores around town. Usually, there is a candy section where the kids can fill up their baskets with individually wrapped goodies. In the Ginza store this section has been replaced with a prepackaged candy counter, so you will have to go to one of the department stores to find this special Sanrio feature. Most of the items in the store are small and inexpensive, making it a great place to let the kids spend their pocket money or buy gifts.

To get there, go out the A13 exit and you will find the store next to Ito-ya. There are also large Sanrio stores in Kobe and Sannomiya.

Toys R' Us

953-95 Aza Uzurano, Ami-cho, Inashiki-gun, Ibaraki-ken   茨城県稲敷郡阿見町字
🚇 One kilometer north-east of JR Arakawaoki Station   うずら野 953-95

After the Japanese government revised the Large-scale Retail Store Law, the world's largest retail toy chain, Toys R' Us, opened a store in Ibaraki-ken in December 1991. The chain sells 15,000 children's items including toys, clothing, and nursery goods, of which about fifty percent is imported. The company plans to open ten more stores in Japan, seven of which are due to open by the end of 1992.

For more information, write the head office at Recruit Higashi Kawasaki Bldg. 10F, 3-1 Ekimae Honcho, Kawasaki-ku, Kanagawa-ken, or call (044) 246-1851.

TRADITIONAL JAPANESE TOYS

Bingoya

10-6 Wakamatsu-cho, Shinjuku-ku, Tokyo   東京都新宿区若松町 10-6
☎ (03) 3202-8778
Hours: 10:00 A.M. to 7:00 P.M. Closed Mondays.
🚇 Waseda Station, Tozai Line; Akebonobashi Station, Toei Shinjuku Line

Bingoya is a Japanese folk-craft shop in the finest tradition. Pottery, hand-woven fabric, paper products, carved wood, and, best of all, traditional kids' toys from all over Japan fill this five-story store. The basement is stuffed full of *kokeshi* dolls from almost every prefecture in Japan, each in the area's own traditional style. There are also huge paper kites, in the shape of warriors, fish, and other traditional Japanese symbols. The papier-mâché figurines come in animal shapes representing the years of the zodiac in addition to sumo wrestlers and kimono-clad women. Any of these crafts is suitable for collecting or for decorating a child's room. We were also delighted to find many hand-painted wooden pull-toys at Bingoya. These are similar in style to the wooden toys of West Germany, but they have a Japanese look to them and are reasonably priced. Don't forget to explore the other floors for gifts for the whole family. The hand-blown glass, hand-made pottery, and baskets are of the finest quality and are one-of-a-kind, something you don't often find in department stores these days.

Bingoya is a 15-minute walk from Akebonobashi Station or Waseda Station. To get there by car, drive down Meiji Dori through Shinjuku, turn right at the second major intersection past Isetan Department Store and follow the street for about five minutes. Bingoya is on the left-hand side of the street; you will pass a Benten grocery store on the way. By bus, catch bus #76 (for Akihabara or Iidabashi) or #74 (for Tokyo Joshi Idai) at Shinjuku Station's west exit. Get off at the eighth stop, Kawada-cho, which is just past the store.

Washikobo

1-8-10 Nishi Azabu, Minato-ku, Tokyo　東京都港区西麻布 1-8-10
☎ (03) 3405-1841
Hours: 10:00 A.M. to 6:00 P.M. Closed on Sundays and the second Saturday each month.
🚇 Roppongi Station, Hibiya Line

In addition to all the toys and accessories made out of *washi* (Japanese paper) that you could ever wish for, Washikobo has a large selection of other Japanese traditional toys. Washikobo is conveniently located a few minutes walk from Roppongi Crossing,

OTHER SOURCES

Omocha Bijutsukan (Toy Museum)

2-12-10 Arai, Nakano-ku, Tokyo　東京都中野区新井 2-12-10
☎ (03) 3387-5461
Hours: 10:30 A.M. to 5:00 P.M. Closed Fridays.
🚇 Nakano Station (north exit), JR Chuo Line; Arai Yakushimae Station, Seibu Shinjuku Line

More than just a museum, this three-story building with showroom and play space aims to introduce children to toys from all over the world. Children and parents are welcome to join groups to learn how to make toys from recycled goods. Toys may also be borrowed every Saturday free of charge for two weeks. Admission is ¥500.

Educational Toy Library

9-2 Hachiyama-cho, Shibuya-ku, Tokyo　東京都渋谷区鉢山町 9-2
🚇 Shibuya Station, JR Yamanote, Ginza, Hanzomon, Inokashira lines

This is not really a toy store, nor a library in the traditional sense, but rather a toy-borrowing center. Located at the Tokyo Baptist Church on Kyu Yamate Dori in Shibuya, the toy library is run by the Tokyo International Learning Community (TILC) (see chap. 11). The library has a wide variety of educational toys for all ages, and of special interest is the selection of therapeutic toys for handicapped children.

For more information, call TILC at (03) 3780-0030 or (03) 3224-6946 (afternoons only).

TOY HOSPITALS

Seibu Department Store Toy Hospital
Shibuya Branch-B kan (building) 4F, 21-1 Utagawa-cho, Shibuya-ku, Tokyo
☎ (03) 3462-3249　東京都渋谷区宇田川町 21-1 渋谷西武 B 館 4F
📵 Shibuya Station, JR Yamanote, Inokashira, Ginza, Hanzomon lines

From dolls to computer games, this hospital will take in any broken toy. To save further tears, call for advice and information between 11:00 A.M. and 5:00 P.M. The hospital charges about a third of the original price of the toy.

Meguro-ku Shohisha Center Toy Hospital
2-4-36 Meguro, Meguro-ku, Tokyo　東京都目黒区目黒 2-4-36 区民センター内
☎ (03) 3711-1121
Hours: 1:00 P.M. to 3:00 P.M. Sundays only. Closed every third Sunday
📵 Meguro Station, JR Yamanote, Mekama lines

This consumer center run by the metropolitan government on the fourth floor of the Meguro Kumin Center will repair dolls, electrical toys, picture books, even antique wind-up toys—and all for free.

MAIL-ORDER BOOKS AND TOYS FROM ABROAD

The book, cassette, video, and toy catalogs listed below offer a variety of products from around the world.

A Child's Collection
151 Avenue of the Americas, New York, New York 10013, USA
☎ (212) 691-7266 fax (212) 691-9154

This catalog has a lovely selection of books for children from newborns to twelve-year-olds and up, including award winners and new authors. American Express, VISA, and MasterCard are accepted.

Animal Town
P.O. Box 2002, Santa Barbara, California 93120, USA
☎ (805) 682-7343

Animal Town specializes in children's tapes, books, and puzzles with animal and environmental themes. They also have a good selection of noncompetitive and nature-oriented games for children and adults.

Anthroposophic Press
Box 94 A-1, R.R. 4, Hudson, New York 12534, USA
☎ (518) 851-2054 fax (518) 851-2047

This catalog contains many educational and spiritual books for adults, but their selection of children's books is interesting and unique. Many beautifully illustrated fantasy books are available, and they also carry a comprehensive list of printed lectures and books by Rudolf Steiner, founder of Waldorf education, in addition to other books about early childhood education and parenting.

Little America

3-9-22 Heiwa, Chuo-ku, Fukuoka-shi, Fukuoka-ken 810
☎ (092) 521-8826 fax (092) 521-2288

Call for a free catalog of imported games and toys.

Book of Wonder

132 Seventh Avenue, Dept. AD, New York, New York 10011, USA
☎ (212) 989-3270

This large New York City bookstore sends out fabulous catalogs containing virtually every children's book you have ever heard of. A monthly newsletter, Books of Wonder News, is available at no charge. They have several different catalogs, one of which is devoted only to signed editions of children's books. Searching for hard-to-find books is one of their specialties. VISA, MasterCard, American Express, and DISCOVER are accepted.

Chinaberry Book Service

2830 Via Orange Way, Suite B, Spring Valley, California 92078-1521, USA
☎ (619) 670-5200

One of the most comprehensive book catalogs we know, Chinaberry offers a wide range from picture books for toddlers to safety books for preschoolers, to adventure and fiction for the advanced reader. Many of the classic storybooks for children are available here in updated, beautifully illustrated editions. There are also many parenting books available, as well as craft and family project books, videos and cassette tapes.

A Gentle Wind

P.O. Box 3103, Albany, New York 12203, USA
☎ (518) 436-0391

This catalog has cassettes of traditional songs as well as new music and recorded stories for all ages. The independent children's recording label, A Gentle Wind, has won numerous awards for its special music.

Kiddie Cat

P.O. Box 429, Waterbury, Vermont 05676, USA

This is a comprehensive catalog of children's music on cassette tapes.

From lullabies to the newest contemporary tunes, this company has it. They also offer a selection of children's stories on tape and some children's books and videos.

Music for Little People

Box 1460 Redway, California 95560, USA
☎ (707) 923-3991

A beautiful catalog filled with music cassettes, music videos, and musical instruments for you and your children. You will find more than just the ordinary selections of children's tapes here. There is every kind of music imaginable—from Afro-Cuban to Indian to jazz. American Express, DISCOVER, VISA, and MasterCard are accepted.

Spoken Arts

310 North Avenue, New Rochelle, New York 10802, USA
☎ (914) 636-5482

This company offers recordings of stories, poems, and speeches. Children's classics, such as *Peter Rabbit,* are available as well as fairy tales. For older children, try Aesop's fables or Mark Twain yarns. Recordings are available in several different languages, and there are also tapes for adults.

Parent Care

25 Independence Court, P.O. Box 417, Folcroft, Pennsylvania 19032-0417, USA

This company produces an all-video catalog that contains the top 75 children's videos from the United States. Included are Disney classics, *Ninja Turtles, Sesame Street,* and storybook classics such as *Anne of Green Gables.* The only catalog you need for videos.

Hearth Song

P.O. Box B, Sebastapol, California 95473-0601, USA
☎ (707) 829-1550

A truly exquisite catalog containing unusual and creative toys, books, and games. Many are made exclusively for Hearth Song from natural fibers and wood. This catalog also includes many old-fashioned and country craft projects for older children and adults. VISA, MasterCard, American Express, and DISCOVER are accepted.

Metropolitan Museum of Art Children's Catalog

Special Service Office, Middle Village, New York 11381, USA
☎ (718) 326-7050

This well-known museum publishes a separate catalog just for children, which is full of beautifully illustrated books and fine toys and games. Some of these items are designed exclusively for the Metropolitan Museum of Art, such as a song book illustrated with artwork from the museum.

Pied Piper

2922 N. 35th Ave., Drawer 11408, Phoenix, Arizona 85061-1408, USA
☎ (602) 272-1853

The *Gifted Children's Catalog* available from Pied Piper contains a fine selection of children's toys, games, books, and project kits from around the world. All of the products emphasize the educational aspects of fun. VISA, MasterCard, American Express, and DISCOVER are all accepted.

Aristoplay

P.O. Box 7529, Ann Arbor, Michigan 48107, USA
Fax (313) 995-4611

This catalog contains a choice selection of educational and cooperative games for adults and children over the age of four. The games are based on such themes as pollution, great composers, and geography, our favorite being Friends Around the World, a game of world peace. This catalog is a must for international families.

Toys to Grow On

P.O. Box 17, Long Beach, California 90801, USA
☎ (213) 603-8890

This catalog for educational and imaginative play offers a vast selection of toys and school materials for all ages. American Express, VISA, and MasterCard are accepted.

Rose's Doll House Store

5826 West Bluemound Road, Milwaukee, Wisconsin 53213, USA
☎ (414) 259-9965

This is a catalog full of unique doll houses, doll house furniture, dolls, toys, and miniatures. VISA, MasterCard, and American Express are accepted.

Shoppe Full of Dolls

39 N. Main Street, Dept. C, New Hope, Pennsylvania 18938, USA
☎ (215) 862-5524

This catalog carries a spectacular collection of dolls. Every style imaginable is represented, from baby dolls to Barbies to porcelain collector's items. Our personal favorite was the series of dolls from *Gone With the Wind*. This enormous selection of dolls has to be seen to be believed.

Public Libraries

Public libraries abound in Japan—there are over 260 libraries owned and operated by the Tokyo Metropolitan Government alone. You have access to all of them just by working, studying, or living in Japan. Each ward or city has a number of libraries under its care, and your local ward or city office is the first place to look for information regarding the one nearest you. Some areas that have more foreign residents (e.g., Minato-ku) will have better selections of books in English. Remember that you are able to register at and use *any* of the public libraries, not just the ones in your particular ward or city.

Children's books in English are popular, and most libraries will have a fairly large selection of them. Adult books are another matter; the number of good books in English will vary from library to library. Ward- and city-operated libraries are great places to go on a rainy day, as most of them offer story time, children's movies (often from the United States), and other activities for kids. To register at the library, you will need your Alien Registration Card or some other proof that you live, work, or study in Japan. If you do not speak Japanese, you might consider taking along someone who does so that the numerous rules and regulations of the library can be explained to you.

Private Libraries

As a foreigner living in Japan, you may also have access to private libraries that serve the foreign community. Contact your local embassy or consulate for more information. Also, many private clubs have libraries which are available to members.

Below is a short list of libraries containing reference books and information in English that adults may find helpful while living in Japan.

The American Center Library

2-6-3 Shiba Koen, Minato-ku, Tokyo　東京都港区芝公園 2-6-3 ABC 会館 11F
☎ (03) 3436-0901
Hours: 10:00 A.M. to 7:00 P.M.
🚊 Shiba Koen Station, Toei Mita Line

This library has an 8,000-volume collection on many subjects relating to America, but mostly for adults. Unfortunately, these books can only be read on the premises. It also subscribes to 200 magazines and journals from overseas. The library is located in the ABC Kaikan, a 3-minute walk from the station.

The British Council Library

1-2 Kagurazaka, Shinjuku-ku, Tokyo　東京都新宿区神楽坂 1–2
☎ (03) 3235-8031
Hours: 10:00 A.M. to 8:00 P.M.
🚇 Iidabashi Station, JR Chuo, Tozai, and Yurakucho lines

Open to any resident of Japan, this library lends books and videos for a ¥3,500 annual fee. They have a good selection of children's books and books on Japan, as well as English literature.

The Japan Foundation Library

3-6 Kioi-cho, Chiyoda-ku, Tokyo　東京都千代田区紀尾井町 3–6
☎ (03) 3263-4504
Hours: 10:00 A.M. to 5:00 P.M., Tuesday through Friday; noon to 5:00 P.M. Saturdays.
🚇 Kojimachi Station (Hotel New Otani exit), Yurakucho Line

This library is a fabulous source of information on Japan and things Japanese. All you need to do is apply for a free member's card. The library is a 3-minute walk from the Hotel New Otani.

Tokyo Metropolitan Library

5-7-13 Minami Azabu, Minato-ku, Tokyo　東京都港区南麻布 5–7–13
☎ (03) 3442-8451
Hours: 9:30 A.M. to 8:00 P.M. Tuesday through Friday; 1:00 P.M. to 8:00 P.M. Monday. Open until 5:00 P.M. on weekends and national holidays.
🚇 Hiroo Station, Hibiya Line

Located in Arisugawa Park, this is the central library of the metropolitan government library system—over one million books are here! They also have many periodicals, videotapes, films, newspapers, and music tapes and records which unfortunately cannot be taken out. You must be over sixteen years of age to use this library.

World Magazine House

3-13-10 Ginza, Chuo-ku, Tokyo　東京都中央区銀座 3–13–10
☎ (03) 3545-7227
Hours: 10:00 A.M. to 7:00 P.M. Monday through Saturday.
🚇 Higashi Ginza Station (exit 3), Hibiya and Toei Asakusa lines

Well, it's not really a library, but we can't subscribe to all the magazines we love, so we read them here. You will find approximately 1,300 periodicals in over fifty languages here. It is fun to see articles on fashions, food, and sports from around the world but leave the kids at home unless you are a fast reader. Magazines cannot be bought or checked out.

5

Parks, Playgrounds, and Gardens

There is no question that much of Japan is crowded, especially the cities. While living here, you may miss your suburban backyard, but there is probably a nice neighborhood park within walking distance of your residence. Many of these neighborhood parks are now being designed with small children in mind, and we have listed some from the twenty-three wards in Tokyo. In addition to small parks, you will also find many large ones with vast areas of open space. Some parks are more enjoyable than others for young children. This selection of parks, playgrounds, and gardens should provide the most fun for children under six with a minimum of hassle for everyone involved.

NEIGHBORHOOD PARKS

In each ward, there are many parks or playgrounds with facilities ranging from simple swings to giant slides and sandboxes. An excellent way for your child to make friends in the neighborhood—and for you to meet some of the parents—is to visit the park. During the week, many mothers bring their children to the park at the same time every day. If your schedule is flexible, you might try going at different times to meet a variety of children. Perhaps you will find a particular group whose company you enjoy enough to meet regularly. In any case, there are a few basic rules you should learn to make you feel more comfortable and to fit in at the playground in Japan.

You will notice that other mothers readily offer your child a snack—often candy—so you might want to bring along something to share with other children who may be at the park. Besides bringing healthy snacks, it is a good idea to bring your *oshibori* with you, as playgrounds are usually dirty. Almost all neighborhood parks have water fountains, restrooms (don't forget to bring tissues), and even clocks, but, unfortunately, no grass. If you bring sandbox toys, label them so you know which are yours and prepare your child to be ready to share with other children because they (or their parents) will almost always offer to share toys with him.

There are a few important words that should be part of your playground vocabulary. You will often hear mothers saying "*abunai yo!*" and "*ki o tsukete!*" *Abunai yo* means "Look out—that's dangerous," and *ki o tsukete* means "Be careful." You might also find that your child picks up the word "*dame*" rather quickly. This is what other children will say to him if he knocks down their sandcastle. *Dame* means "Stop it!" in a very firm manner. It's a good idea to learn early on how to say thank you (*arigato*) and excuse me (*sumimasen* or *gomen nasai*), since they are frequently used playground words as well.

If you have ever lamented the difficulties involved in chasing a crawling baby around a dirty playground, or worse, not taken your infant to the playground for fear of him getting dirty, then you'll be delighted to hear about the Japanese *asobigi*. This baggy coverall is made with elastic at the wrists and ankles and pulls over whatever baby is wearing. Your inquisitive baby or toddler can then be free to explore without ruining a full set of clothes with the infamous "Tokyo dirt." When it's time to leave the park, just give the hands a good wash, pull off the *asobigi*, and you've got a clean baby once again. These suits come in all colors and sizes, with lightweight cotton fabric for summer and sturdier denims and corduroys for cold weather. Look for them in any department store or neighborhood clothing store.

A new concept in neighborhood playgrounds is a "*shinsui* park." *Shinsui* means literally "to be friendly with water." A *shinsui* park is one with plenty of water attractions that provide children with a chance to get used to water by playing in it. These parks are often found within a larger park or playground, and most of them have a shallow wading pool and educational water toys and games in a small playground area. These spaces attract parents and kids year-round and are especially refreshing during the oppressive summer heat.

The neighborhood parks that we have listed are popular with families and have something special just for children. These parks are listed according to wards, and cover greater Tokyo from north to south.

ADACHI-KU

Higashi Ayase Koen

3-4 Higashi Ayase, Adachi-ku, Tokyo　東京都足立区東綾瀬 3-4
☎ (03) 3605-0005
Area: 15.6 ha
📵 Ayase Station, JR Joban, Chiyoda lines

This is a relatively new park in a nice residential area, made mostly to house sports facilities and for strolling or jogging.

Minumadai Shinsui Koen

4-5 Toneri, Adachi-ku, Tokyo　東京都足立区舎人 4-5
☎ (03) 3980-5261
Area: 1,720 meters long
📵 Takenozuka Station, Tobu Line

This popular "friendly with water" park has lots of free play space for kids.

KATSUSHIKA-KU

Mizumoto Koen

3-2 Mizumoto Koen, Katsushika-ku, Tokyo　東京都葛飾区水元公園 3-2
☎ (03) 3607-8321
Area: 61.4 ha
📵 Kanamachi Station, JR Keisei Line

Opened in June 1989, this man-made beach is fabulous for children. The large, open areas of sandy beach are ideal for playing, fishing, and water sports. From the south exit of Kanamachi Station take a Keisei bus leaving from #2 bus stop and get off at the Mizumoto Koen Mae stop.

Shinkoiwa Koen

1-1-3 Shin-Koiwa, Katsushika-ku, Tokyo　東京都葛飾区新小岩 1-1-3
Area: 4.7 ha
☎ (03) 3696-9512
📵 Shinkoiwa Station, JR Sobu Line

This general-purpose park, with sections for water, family, and sports play, is a 5-minute walk from Shin-Koiwa Station.

ITABASHI-KU

Akatsuka Koen

3-1 Takashimadaira, Itabashi-ku, Tokyo　東京都板橋区高島平 3-1
☎ (03) 3938-5715
Area: 22.9 ha
📵 Takashimadaira Station, Toei Mita Line

This park has many sports facilities and is good for walking. Walk from Takashimadaira Station.

Nishidai Koen

1-23-1 Nishidai, Itabashi-ku, Tokyo　東京都板橋区西台 1–23–1
☎ (03) 3964-1111
Area: 0.6 ha
🚉 Nishidai Station, Toei Mita Line
Popular with children, this park has an athletic park, forest, and a small stream.

Ukima Koen

2-15-1 Funado, Itabashi-ku, Tokyo　東京都板橋区舟渡 2–15–1
☎ (03) 3969-9168
Area: 11.6 ha
🚉 Ukima Funado Station, JR Saikyo Line
There are good picnic areas and some scenic lakes in this park.

KITA-KU

Asukayama Koen

1-1-3 Kita Oji, Kita-ku, Tokyo　東京都北区王子 1–1–3
☎ (03) 3910-8882
Area: 6.1 ha
🚉 Oji Station, JR Keihin Tohoku Line
Asukayama Koen is famous for its cherry blossom trees which were planted in the Edo period. There is also a large water fountain, a steam locomotive, and a rotating observatory.

NERIMA-KU

Hikarigaoka Koen

4-1-1 Hikarigaoka, Nerima-ku, Tokyo　東京都練馬区光が丘 4–1–1
☎ (03) 3977-7638
Area: 60.5 ha
🚉 Narimasu Station, Tobu Tojo Line
Located in two cities, this is a huge park with vast green open spaces.

Johoku Chuo Koen

1-3-1 Hikawadai, Nerima-ku, Tokyo　東京都練馬区氷川台 1–3–1
☎ (03) 3931-3650
Area: 20.2 ha
🚉 Uesakabashi Station, Tobu Tojo Line; Hikawadai Station, Yurakucho Line
This sports park is good for family picnics.

Shakujii Koen

1-26-1 Shakujiidai, Nerima-ku, Tokyo　東京都練馬区石神井台 1-26-1
☎ (03) 3996-3950
Area: 16.8 ha
🚃 Shakujii Koen Station, Seibu Ikebukuro Line
This fairly large park with a picturesque lake in the center of the grounds
has an impressive array of cherry trees in spring. A visit to Shakujii Koen
can easily become a full-day's outing because of the many attractions
available, including swimming and boating.

ARAKAWA-KU

Arakawa Yuen

6-35-11 Nishiogu, Arakawa-ku, Tokyo　東京都荒川区西尾久 6-35-11
☎ (03) 3893-6003
Area: 0.4 ha
🚃 Arakawa Yuen Station, Arakawa Line

This park has a children's playground and a small petting zoo. Presently
undergoing major renovation, a new "friendly with water" park is scheduled for completion in 1991.

Nippori Minami Koen

5-19-1 Higashi Nippori, Arakawa-ku, Tokyo　東京都荒川区東日暮里 5-19-1
☎ (03) 3802-3111
Area: 3,500 sq. meters
🚃 Nippori Station, JR Yamanote Line
This park features an attractive playground for children.

TOSHIMA-KU

Nishi Ikebukuro Koen

3-20-1 Nishi Ikebukuro, Toshima-ku, Tokyo　東京都豊島区西池袋 3-20-1
☎ (03) 3981-1111
Area: 8,759 sq. meters
🚃 Ikebukuro Station, JR Yamanote, Tobu Tojo, Marunouchi, Yurakucho, JR Saikyo,
Seibu Ikebukuro lines
There are athletic facilities in the grounds of this park and a "friendly with
water" park. The park is a 10-minute walk from the west exit (*nishi guchi*)
of Ikebukuro Station.

Minami Ikebukuro Koen

2-21-1 Minami Ikebukuro, Toshima-ku, Tokyo　東京都豊島区南池袋 2-21-1
☎ (03) 3981-1111

Area: 7,811 sq. meters

🚇 Ikebukuro Station, JR Yamanote, Tobu Tojo, Marunouchi, Yurakucho, Saikyo, Seibu Ikebukuro lines

Here there is a children's swimming pool and lots of open space for playing freely. The park is a 6-minute walk from the east exit (*higashi guchi*) of Ikebukuro Station.

Higashi Ikebukuro Chuo Koen

3-1-6 Higashi Ikebukuro, Toshima-ku, Tokyo　東京都豊島区東池袋 3-1-6
☎ (03) 3981-1111
Area: 6,189 sq. meters
🚇 Ikebukuro Station, JR Yamanote, Tobu Tojo, Marunouchi, Yurakucho, JR Saikyo, Seibu Ikebukuro lines

This neighborhood park offers a small pond and open space. Leave Ikebukuro Station by the east exit (*higashi guchi*) and you'll find the park next to the Sunshine Building about eight minutes from the station.

TAITO-KU

Sumida Koen

A large park in both Sumida-ku and Taito-ku. See Sumida-ku for details.

Ueno Koen

Connected to Ueno Zoo. See chapter 6 under zoos for information.

BUNKYO-KU

Kyoiku No Mori Koen

3-29 Otsuka, Bunkyo-ku, Tokyo　東京都文京区大塚 3-29
☎ (03) 3944-6342
Area: 2.1 ha
🚇 Myogadani Station, Marunouchi Line

This park has an open area for children and a nice playground with lots of trees.

Hongo Kyusuisho Koen

2-7 Hongo, Bunkyo-ku, Tokyo　東京都文京区本郷 2-7
☎ (03) 3816-1517
Area: 7,271 sq. meters
🚇 Hongo 3-chome Station, Marunouchi Line

Here you can enjoy a Japanese-style garden, a rose garden with forty-eight varieties, and a children's playground.

Heiwa no Mori Koen

3-37-6 Arai, Nakano-ku, Tokyo 東京都中野区新井 3-37-6
☎ (03) 3385-4150
Area: 2.5 ha
 Numabukuro Station, Seibu Shinjuku Line; Nakano Station, JR Chuo, Tozai lines
This park has a pond, a playground, and a children's corner. Also here are replicas of Yayoi period (ca. 200 B.C.–A.D. 250) houses and pottery. It is a 6-minute walk from Numabukuro Station or 17 minutes from Nakano Station.

Tetsugaku-do Koen

1-34-28 Matsugaoka, Nakano-ku, Tokyo 東京都中野区松が丘 1-34-28
☎ (03) 3951-2515
Area: 5.2 ha
Nakano Station, JR Chuo, Tozai lines
This neighborhood park with sandbox, swings, slides, baseball field, tennis courts has plenty of trees. From Nakano Station take a bus to Tetsugaku-do.

SUMIDA-KU

Sumida Koen

1-2-5 Mukojima, Sumida-ku, Tokyo 東京都墨田区向島 1-2-5
☎ (03) 3871-1528 or 3626-3151
Area: 16.4 ha (in both Sumida-ku and Taito-ku)
Honjo-Azumabashi Station, Toei Asakusa Line; Asakusa Station, Ginza, Toei Asakusa lines
This is a nice park with an old Japanese garden. There is also a "friendly with water park" to delight any youngster. Sumida Koen is conveniently located two blocks from Honjo-Azumabashi Station or just a short walk across the river from Asakusa Station.

Kinshi Koen

4-15-1 Kinshi, Sumida-ku, Tokyo 東京都墨田区錦糸 4-15-1
☎ (03) 3624-4483
Area: 5.6 ha
Kinshicho Station, JR Sobu Line
Here there are sports facilities and a square with a fountain and pool.

SHINJUKU-KU

Shinjuku Chuo Koen

2-11 Nishi Shinjuku, Shinjuku-ku, Tokyo 東京都新宿区西新宿 2-11
☎ (03) 3209-1111

Area: 8.2 ha

🚉 Shinjuku Station (west exit), JR Yamanote, JR Chuo, Marunouchi, Toei Shinjuku, Keio, Odakyu lines

This park with its lovely fountain in a central square is a breath of fresh air in Shinjuku. Also here are a variety of flowering plants and a playground. The park is located behind the Hotel Century Hyatt.

SUGINAMI-KU

Wada Bori

1 Omiya, Suginami-ku, Tokyo　東京都杉並区大宮 1
☎ (03) 3313-4247
Area: 11.5 ha
🚉 Nishi-Eifuku Station, Inokashira Line

A nice, spacious park which not only has many recreational facilities for children but also houses some old relics. It is ideal for family outings, cycling, and picnicking.

Zempukujigawa Ryokuchi

2 Narita Nishi, Suginami-ku, Tokyo　東京都杉並区成田西 2
☎ (03) 3313-4247
Area: 16.4 ha
🚉 Hamadayama Station, Inokashira Line

This is actually two parks along the Zempukuji River.

EDOGAWA-KU

Komatsugawa Sakaigawa Shinsui Park

1 Hon-Isshiki, Edogawa-ku, Tokyo　東京都江戸川区本一色 1
☎ (03) 3652-1151
Area: 3.2 kilometers long
🚉 Shin-Koiwa Station (south exit), JR Sobu Line

This is a large "friendly with water" park along a river with many flowering plants. To get there, take bus #21 or #22 from the south exit of Shin-Koiwa Station.

Kasai Rinkai Koen

6-2-1 Rinkai-cho, Edogawa-ku, Tokyo　東京都江戸川区臨海町 6-2-1
☎ (03) 5696-1331
🚉 Kasai or Nishi-Kasai stations, Tozai Line; or ferry from Hinode Pier near JR Hamamatsucho Station

Opened in 1989, this park includes two man-made beaches for sunbathing and picnicking. Don't miss the large aquarium (see page 145).

CHIYODA-KU

Shimizudani Koen

2-1 Kioi-cho, Chiyoda-ku, Tokyo　東京都千代田区紀尾井町 2–1
☎ (03) 3264-0151
Area: 1 ha
📶 Akasaka Mitsuke Station, Ginza, Marunouchi lines; Nagatacho Station, Hanzomon, Yurakucho lines

This is a small park with a few swings located across from the New Otani Hotel, eight minutes from Akasaka Mitsuke Station.

SHIBUYA-KU

Nabeshima Shoto Koen

2-10-7 Shoto, Shibuya-ku, Tokyo　東京都渋谷区松涛 2–10–7
☎ (03) 3409-3280
Area: 5,012 sq. meters
📶 Shinsen Station, Inokashira Line

Here, there's a playground with slides and swings, and a nice-size pond surrounded by trees.

KOTO-KU

Yumenoshima Koen

3-2 Yumenoshima, Koto-ku, Tokyo　東京都江東区夢の島 3–2
☎ (03) 3521-8273
Area: 40.8 ha
📶 Toyocho Station, Tozai Line; Shin-Kiba Station, Yurakucho Line

This park built on reclaimed land has a large playground, coliseum, and baseball stadium. Also here is the Yumenoshima Tropical Botanical Garden with over 4,300 trees of 127 species under one glass dome. The garden is open Tuesday through Sunday, 9:30 A.M. to 4:00 P.M. Admission is ¥200 for adults; no charge for children under twelve.

Sendaihorikawa Koen

6-6 Toyocho, Koto-ku, Tokyo　東京都江東区東陽 6–6
☎ (03) 3647-9111
Area: 10.4 ha
📶 Toyocho Station, Tozai Line; Oshima Station, Toei Shinjuku Line

At this park, there's not only a "friendly with water park" but also a cherry tree boulevard, cycling road, open square, and pond for fishing. The park is a 10-minute walk from either station.

Kameido Chuo Koen

9-37-28 Kameido, Koto-ku, Tokyo　東京都江東区亀戸 9-37-28
☎ (03) 3631-9732
Area: 10.2 ha
🚉 Kameido Station, JR Sobu Line

At this park, look out for the children's playground with a wooden swing bridge and other playground equipment. There is also a rest house in the center of the park.

CHUO-KU

Tsukishima Daichi Jido Koen

4-2-1 Tsukishima, Chuo-ku, Tokyo　東京都中央区月島 4-2-1
☎ (03) 3543-0211
Area: 3,700 sq. meters
🚉 Tsukishima Station, Yurakucho Line

A great place for the kids to burn off some energy on the swings, slides, balancing bar, and wooden climbing equipment. There is also a sandbox.

Tepozu Jido Koen

1-5-1 Minato, Chuo-ku, Tokyo　東京都中央区湊 1-5-1
☎ (03) 3543-0211
Area: 2,900 sq. meters
🚉 Hatchobori Station, Keio, Hibiya lines

Here there's a shallow wading pool, sandbox, swings, and slides.

MINATO-KU

Ichinohashi Koen (Pirate Ship Park)

3-9-1 Higashi Azabu, Minato-ku, Tokyo　東京都港区東麻布 3-9-1
Call Minato-ku office (03) 3578-2111 for more information.
🚉 Roppongi Station, Hibiya Line

Completed in April 1990, this is the first "friendly with water" park in Minato-ku. It is nicknamed the "Pirate Ship Park" by local residents because of the big pirate ship climbing structure in one part of the park.

Shizen Kyoiku-en

5-21-5 Shiroganedai, Minato-ku, Tokyo　東京都港区白金台 5-21-5
☎ (03) 3441-7176
Area: 20 ha
🚉 Meguro Station, JR Yamanote, Mekama lines

Opened to the public in 1949 as a nature education park, this is an ideal place to examine various plants and waterfowl. The Tokyo Metropolitan

Garden Museum is next door. Hours for the park vary with the seasons, so call before you go. Admission is ¥170 for adults, ¥50 for children. The park is a 10-minute walk from the station.

SETAGAYA-KU

Kuhonbutsu Jido Koen

7-41-50 Okusawa, Setagaya-ku, Tokyo　東京都世田谷区奥沢 7-41-50
Call Setagaya-ku office (03) 3412-1111 for more information.
Area: 718.21 sq. meters
🚉 Kuhonbutsu Station, Oimachi Line

There is a small playground here with swings, slides, and a sandbox.

Setagaya Koen

1-5-27 Ikejiri, Setagaya-ku, Tokyo　東京都世田谷区池尻 1-5-27
☎ (03) 3412-7841
🚉 Ikejiri Ohashi Station, Shin Tamagawa Line

The highlight of this park is the steam locomotive that actually runs. You can ride it on Saturdays, Sundays, and holidays from 10:00 A.M. to noon and 1:00 P.M. to 3:00 P.M. for a small fee. There is also a small playground, outdoor pool, and go-carts.

MEGURO-KU

Komaba Koen

4-3-55 Komaba, Meguro-ku, Tokyo　東京都目黒区駒場 4-3-55
☎ (03) 3715-1111
Area: 4.0 ha
🚉 Todaimae Station, Inokashira Line; Shibuya Station, Ginza, Hanzomon, JR Yamanote, Shin Tamagawa, Inokashira, Toyoko lines

Once a private garden, it is now a quiet place for a walk or picnic. There is a small play area for children, and lovely grounds. The park is a short cab ride from Shibuya Station.

SHINAGAWA-KU

Jusango-chi Koen

1 Higashi Yashio, Shinagawa-ku, Tokyo　東京都品川区東八潮 1
☎ (03) 3521-8273
Area: 5.4 ha
🚉 Monzen Nakacho Station, Tozai Line; Shinagawa Station, JR Yamanote, Keihin Tohoku, JR Tokaido, JR Yokosuka, Keihin Kyuko lines

This is an ocean-side beach park built on reclaimed land. Bring sand toys, and binoculars to view boats and ships. From the east exit of Shinagawa Station take a bus bound for Monzen Nakacho and get off at the Kaijo Koen bus stop.

Rinshi no Mori

2 Koyamadai, Shinagawa-ku, Tokyo　東京都品川区小山台 2
☎ (03) 3710-4022
Area: 4.3 ha
🚾 Fudomae or Musashi Koyama stations, Mekama Line
This park has large and small fields, an adventure forest, and seven play areas with various themes. There is a day camp for children in the forest section from May to September. The park is a 10-minute walk from Musashi Koyama Station.

Togoshi Koen

2-1-30 Yutakacho, Shinagawa-ku, Tokyo　東京都品川区豊町 2-1-30
☎ (03) 3782-8811
Area: 1.8 ha
🚾 Togoshi Koen Station, Oimachi Line
Mountain scenery and a path around the lake make this small park special. Also here is an outdoor stage and an old locomotive.

OTA-KU

Higashi Chofu Koen

5-13-11 Minami Yukigaya, Ota-ku, Tokyo　東京都大田区南雪谷 5-13-11
☎ (03) 3720-1692
Area: 25,000 sq. meters
🚾 Ontakesan Station, Ikegami Line
A typical playground area where your little ones can enjoy playing. There is also a miniature traffic park where they can learn about safety and traffic rules. In the summer, there are several swimming pools open, and two are just for children. The park is a 10-minute walk from the station.

Ikegami Honmonji Temple

1-1-1 Ikegami, Ota-ku, Tokyo　東京都大田区池上 1-1-1
☎ (03) 3752-2331
🚾 Ikegami Station, Ikegami Line
The grassy areas around this temple are nice for strolling with the children. There is a special festival day each year on October 12.

Garakuta Koen (Junk Park inside Haginaka Kotsu Koen)

3-24-26 Haginaka, Ota-ku, Tokyo　東京都大田区萩中 3–24–26
☎ (03) 3743-0991
🚃 Otorii Station, Kuko Line

This is a playground featuring old pieces of equipment for children to climb on and is popularly called the Junk Park. The old bus and trolley car are perhaps the safest and most fun for the under-six set. Kids can sit in the driver's seat and drive or pretend to ride the bus. Adjacent to the park is a grassy area with a large sandbox and climbing equipment. At the nearby Haginaka Traffic Park, children can ride bikes along a small course complete with traffic signs. To get there, go to Keikyu Kamata Station on the Keihin Kyuko Line and transfer to the Kuko Line for Otorii Station. If you are like us, you can follow the people with children to the park, or ask at the station for the way to Garakuta Koen, about an 8-minute walk. Another possibility is to get off at Kamata Station on the Keihin Tohoku Line and take a bus bound for Haneda Airport which stops by the park.

OUR FAVORITE PARKS, PLAYGROUNDS, AND GARDENS

The following list of parks, playgrounds, and gardens contains descriptions of their facilities and suggestions for enjoying them. All of these places have a diversity that makes you want to visit them again and again. Each time you visit, in different seasons and with different friends, it is a whole new experience!

If you are looking for the children's playground inside one of these vast spaces, just say, *kodomo no yuenchi wa doko desu ka?* which means "Where is the children's playground?" You may have to repeat this phrase along the way, but it should eventually get you there.

To let you know at a glance which of these special spots you might want to visit, we have devised a rating system. We took into account the location, ease of getting there, condition of the park, the cost involved, availability of food, toilets, quiet places, and things kids like. Then we rated the parks in this section using these criteria. Check our ice cream cone rating system: one cone for mediocre, three for average, five for great.

BUNKYO-KU

Chinzanso Garden and Restaurant 🍦🍦🍦

2-10-8 Sekiguchi, Bunkyo-ku, Tokyo　東京都文京区関口 2–10–8
☎ (03) 3943-1111

Area: 6 ha

🚉 Mejiro Station, JR Yamanote Line

If you are looking for a special spot to take the kids in Mejiro, you will be pleased to hear about Chinzanso. June is the best time of year to visit Chinzanso because of their famous firefly festival. The many flowers and plants on the premises make it a nice place to observe the change of seasons. We have often made reservations for lunch or dinner and included the children. Not only is the tatami a comfortable choice for infants and toddlers, but you don't have to worry about your noise level interrupting other diners because each party eats in a small house separated from the others. The food is Japanese barbecue, and although the cost is about ¥8,000 for an adult meal, it is well worth it.

Most of the garden winds up and down stone steps, so you will need a firm grip on your toddler if he is not too steady on his feet. It is not a large area, so you do not need a backpack or stroller; just park the car, or take a bus or taxi from Mejiro Station, and enter the rather modern-looking building called Chinzanso Restaurant. The garden area is located out the back door.

SHINJUKU-KU

Shinjuku Gyoen 🌷🌷🌷

11 Naito-cho, Shinjuku-ku, Tokyo　東京都新宿区内藤町 11

☎ (03) 3350-0151/35

Area: 9 ha

🚉 Sendagaya Station, JR Sobu Line; Shinjuku Gyoenmae Station, Marunouchi Line; Shinjuku Station (east exit), JR Yamanote, Marunouchi, Keio, Odakyu, Toei Shinjuku, JR Chuo, JR Sobu lines

This is a vast, open park with beautiful old trees and a lake. There is no car parking on the grounds, but we sometimes stop by with the kids after a shopping trip in Shinjuku. It is easy enough to park a few blocks away near the Wendy's hamburger restaurant on Yasukuni Dori and walk to the park for a picnic lunch.

There is one playground in a corner of the park, and a large greenhouse in the grounds that houses exotic plants from around the world. The greenhouse is open from 11:00 A.M. to 3:00 P.M., and admission is ¥100 for adults and ¥50 for children.

The park is a 3-minute walk from Sendagaya or Shinjuku Gyoenmae stations, or a 10-minute walk from Shinjuku Station.

CHIYODA-KU

Hibiya Koen 🌷🌷🌷

1-6 Hibiya Koen, Chiyoda-ku, Tokyo　東京都千代田区日比谷公園 1-6
☎ (03) 3501-6428
Area: 16 ha
🚇 Hibiya Station, Hibiya, Toei Mita, Chiyoda lines; Yurakucho Station, Yurakucho, JR Yamanote lines

This sprawling park has a large fountain in the center where our toddlers love to watch the changing water patterns and chase the pigeons. Near the fountain there is a small concession stand selling snacks and drinks. We use the entrance across from the Imperial Hotel that leads directly to the fountain. A minute's walk from there is an excellent playground that never seems to be very crowded, possibly because it is located downtown and away from most residences. After riding the coiled koala bears and playing the giant bead game, the kids can wander over to the pond and throw stones into the water. This park is a refreshing break in the Ginza-Hibiya district. If one parent works in this area or the nearby Otemachi-Marunouchi business district, you could arrange a midday picnic here for all the family. If you want to drive, parking is available underground.

Kitanomaru Koen 🌷🌷🌷🌷

1-1 Kitanomaru, Chiyoda-ku, Tokyo　東京都千代田区北の丸公園 1-1
☎ (03) 3211-7878
🚇 Takebashi Station, Tozai Line; Kudanshita Station, Tozai, Toei Shinjuku, Hanzomon lines

Near the Imperial Palace grounds you will find a park with grassy lawns and winding paths. Kitanomaru Park is easy to maneuver with strollers, and the outer moat is great for a longer walk. For the young ones, the Chidorigafuchi rowboat area is always lots of fun. Hours are from 9:30 A.M. to 4:30 P.M. from March 1 to December 15; they close a little later in July and August. The cost is ¥200 per hour. This is one of our favorite spots to watch the changing seasons, and it is rarely crowded. The nearby Fairmont Hotel is a good place to park the car, freshen up, and perhaps have an ice cream.

SHIBUYA-KU

Yoyogi Koen 🌷🌷🌷🌷🌷

2-1 Yoyogi-Kamizono-cho, Shibuya-ku, Tokyo　東京都渋谷区代々木神園町 2-1
☎ (03) 3469-6081
🚇 Harajuku Station, JR Yamanote Line; Meiji Jingumae Station, Chiyoda Line

A park for all seasons, Yoyogi Park is located at one end of Meiji Shrine in Harajuku. It is just right for kite flying and picnics, long walks and quiet times, or just about anything you would want to do in an outdoor setting. It is also one of the few parks with convenient parking nearby. If you park at the west end, a stroll up the sidewalks will lead you to the bicycle area where small tricycles and bikes are available for children free of charge from 9 A.M. to 4 P.M. daily. This is not your typical paved bike lot, but a nice open spot surrounded with trees and lots of grass for parents to sit on and watch the kids.

Heading back across the open spaces will lead you to the perfect picnic spot. You will find a concession stand near the south entrance that sells kites in addition to snacks and drinks. The iris garden of the shrine is famous for its beauty, and is an ideal spot to take some pictures. The shrine itself is one of the most popular in Tokyo for residents and tourists alike. The paths of the shrine are gravel, so don't try to take your stroller. This sprawling park becomes fairly crowded on weekends, but Yoyogi has something for everyone.

CHUO-KU

Hama Rikyu Teien (Hama Detached Palace Garden) ♟♟♟♟
1-1 Hama Rikyu Teien, Chuo-ku, Tokyo　東京都中央区浜離宮庭園 1−1
☎ (03) 3541-0200
Area: 25 ha
🚃 Daimon Station, Toei Asakusa Line; Shimbashi Station, Ginza, Toei Asakusa, JR Yamanote, JR Keihin Tohoku, JR Tokaido, JR Yokosuka lines

Located on the banks of the Sumida River, this spacious Japanese garden is a great place to turn the kids loose. There is a lake in the grounds with a charming Japanese bridge across the middle. At one end of the park is a pier where you can board a double-decker sightseeing boat. The cruise up the river and back is enjoyable for all ages and a great choice for entertaining out-of-town guests. You can purchase snacks on board or take your own picnic lunch.

The five tennis courts on the grounds are open from April to November and can be reserved by calling (03) 3541-0200.

To get there, we suggest taking a cab for the 5-minute ride from either Daimon or Shimbashi stations. If you are driving, you will see the park on the water side as you drive under Shuto Expressway No. 1 between these two stations. Park on the street nearby.

Arisugawa No Miya Kinen Koen ♟♟♟

5-7-19 Minami Azabu, Minato-ku, Tokyo　東京都港区南麻布 5-7-19
☎ (03) 3441-9642
Area: 3.6 ha
🚋 Hiroo Station, Hibiya Line

This is a quiet, rambling park in the heart of Azabu. There is a swing set located near the entrance across from National Azabu Supermarket. The best playground, however, is up the hill near the German Embassy. In addition to jungle gyms, swings, and slides, there is a large sandbox and an open space nearby for playing ball or riding bikes. A 2-minute walk deeper into the park from here will take you to a pond where children can go fishing. We've never had any luck, but we have seen other children catching fish. If you bring some bread crumbs, you can feed the ducks or the carp in the pond. This park is conveniently located, and we often use it as an incentive to get our toddlers to sit still in the grocery cart at National Azabu.

From the station, it is a 5-minute walk to the park. If you drive, look for parking on small neighborhood streets.

Nezu Art Museum and Park ♟♟♟

6-5-1 Minami Aoyama, Minato-ku, Tokyo　東京都港区南青山 6-5-1
☎ (03) 3400-2536
🚋 Omotesando Station, Ginza, Hanzomon, Chiyoda lines

Your children will enjoy the many features of this Aoyama retreat. We lived nearby when the children were barely walking, and there was always something to interest them. There is a small museum just as you enter the gates, but the exhibits of porcelain are more interesting for adults. The quiet, tree-lined garden is just the place for an adventure walk. Our favorite spot is the bridge over a small pond where giant carp swim. Look for the stone statues of animals as you wander along the paths. Renovation of the small museum and a new wing was completed in September 1990.

Happoen Gardens ♟♟♟

1-1-1 Shiroganedai, Minato-ku, Tokyo　東京都港区白金台 1-1-1
☎ (03) 3443-3111
Area: 5 ha
🚋 Meguro Station, JR Yamanote, Mekama lines

A visit to this 500-year-old garden in Shiroganedai is best on weekdays since it is a favorite spot for weddings on weekends. Parents will appreciate the quiet serenity of the surroundings, and children will be delighted by the large pond full of colorful mallards and carp. There is a gazebo at the water's edge from where it's fun to watch the fish literally jump into the air to eat the crumbs thrown by children. Since this is a private garden, picnics and excessive noise are discouraged. The restaurant is a good place to stop for an ice cream before heading home.

When you're ready to leave, there are always taxis waiting in front of the restaurant; or you can come by car and park free of charge. From Meguro Station it is a 10-minute bus or taxi ride down Meguro Dori. If you drive, look for the large sign for Happoen restaurant near the Miyako Hotel.

Aoyama Bochi (Aoyama Cemetery) ♪♪♪

2-32-2 Minami Aoyama, Minato-ku, Tokyo　東京都港区南青山 2-32-2
☎ (03) 3401-3652
Area: 26.3 ha
🚃 Gaienmae Station, Ginza Line

Aoyama Cemetery is one of the best spots to view the changing of the seasons in Tokyo. Whether it is autumn leaves or cherry blossoms that you see overhead, you and your family will enjoy a stroll along the paths of this centrally located cemetery (see more on cherry blossom season in chap. 15). Most cemeteries in Japan are not viewed as parks or picnic spots, but Aoyama Cemetery is the exception in Tokyo because of its location and outstanding beauty all year round. There are always joggers and people with children strolling through the grounds. There is a main road cutting through the middle of the area, but the side paths are grassy and safe.

One of the nicest things about Aoyama Cemetery is that it is rarely crowded. Of course, there are more people out in the spring for cherry-blossom viewing, but it is not overrun by hordes of sightseers as some popular spots are.

You can take a taxi to the middle of the cemetery, or walk ten minutes or so from Gaienmae Station. If you go by car, be aware that there is no parking in the cemetery, though it is easy enough to find parking nearby. We have had no problem parking on the bridge just before you enter the main intersection.

Shiba Koen ♪♪

4-10-17 Shiba Koen, Minato-ku, Tokyo　東京都港区芝公園 4-10-17
☎ (03) 3431-43591
Area: 1 ha
🚃 Hamamatsucho Station, JR Yamanote; JR Keihin Tohoku lines; Daimon Station, Toei Asakusa Line

This park is a collection of buildings and sports centers. Included in its grounds are Tokyo Tower, Zojoji Temple, the Tokyo Prince Hotel, some sports facilities, a bowling alley, a golf range, public tennis courts, and swimming pools. The one real playground with climbing bars and swings is on the other side of Zojoji Temple from Tokyo Tower, down Hibiya Dori to the right as you face away from the temple. There are a couple of other areas with pull-up bars and benches, but they cannot really be called playgrounds.

The sidewalks around the park make for nice strolling with children. The paths inside the park are mostly dirt (mud when it has been raining) or sand, and in some spots they are like hiking trails in the mountains. There is a small waterfall just below Tokyo Tower, and the kids can have some real adventures here if you don't mind the mud.

The best time to visit this area with kids is in conjunction with an outing to one of the attractions on the grounds or a visit to the doctors or pharmacy at the Tokyo Medical and Surgical Clinic. Zojoji Temple is a great background for a photograph, and if you have guests who want to go sightseeing, this is a good spot. You could combine a trip to the temple with a stop at McDonald's (on Kaigan Dori, the street that leads from the front of the temple, about five-minutes' walk toward the bay) then finish up at Kyu Shiba Rikyu Garden (see below). This park provides plenty of opportunities for a taste of Japanese history without traveling a great distance.

For adults, there are three tennis courts in the park, open from April to December; call (03) 3431-4359 one month in advance for a reservation. There is also an outdoor public swimming pool complex with three pools of varying depths. They are open from mid-July to the end of August, 9:30 A.M. to 11:30 A.M. and 12:30 P.M. to 4:30 P.M. Night swimming is also available from mid-July to September 1, 6:00 P.M. to 8:00 P.M. A ticket is good for two hours' worth of swimming.

If you drive, it is best to park in a paid lot at one of the attractions, or off one of the streets that intersect Hibiya Dori.

Kyu Shiba Rikyu Garden 🌷🌷🌷
(Garden of the Former Imperial Detached Palace)

1-4-1 Kaigan, Minato-ku, Tokyo　東京都港区海岸 1-4-1
☎ (03) 3434-4029
Area: 4.3 ha
🚉 Hamamatsucho Station, JR Yamanote, JR Keihin Tohoku lines

Located directly down the street from the entrance of Zojoji Temple is this beautifully landscaped garden. On the street side is a playground with swings, slides, and climbing equipment. There are benches here where you can eat a picnic, or you can stop at the McDonald's up the street halfway to Zojoji Temple. Just behind this playground is the entrance to the garden. There is no admission charge for children under twelve, and admission for adults is ¥300. The garden is open from 9:30 A.M. to 4:00 P.M. daily except Monday. This Edo period (1615–1868) garden, one of Tokyo's oldest, still maintains its miniature landscapes featuring famous mountains, and a pond, connected to the sea, that rises and falls with the tides. It is an excellent choice for photographs, and a good plan is to combine it with one of the attractions in Shiba Koen (see above).

For those who drive, we suggest parking along Kaigan Dori, the street that comes out from the front of Zojoji Temple (off Hibiya Dori).

Kokuritsu Shizen Kyoiku-en (National Park for Nature Study) ♀♀

5-21-5 Shiroganedai, Minato-ku, Tokyo　東京都港区白金台 5-21-5
☎ (03) 3441-7176
Area: 20 ha
Meguro Station, JR Yamanote, Mekama lines

This is a heavily wooded nature reserve full of gigantic old trees. As you walk along the paths, you may see rabbits and squirrels hopping among the trees. In the ponds and marshes are ducks, swans, and geese, and our kids have been enthralled by huge spider webs glistening in the sunlight. When you are looking for some peace and quiet in the hustle and bustle of Tokyo, this is the place to go.

Strollers are a bit difficult to navigate over the pebbled path so front or back carriers are helpful. For youngsters who are fascinated by insects, be sure to visit the Insect House, open from April to November from 10:00 A.M. to 11:00 A.M., Sundays only. Inside is a marvelous collection of colorful butterflies and other insects.

SETAGAYA-KU

Komazawa Olympic Koen ♀♀♀♀♀

1-1 Komazawa Koen, Setagaya-ku, Tokyo　東京都世田谷区駒沢公園 1-1
☎ (03) 3421-6121
Area: 41 ha
Komazawa Daigakumae Station, Shin Tamagawa Line

This large sports complex was built for the 1964 Olympic Games. The park is split in two by Komazawa Dori, and there are three playgrounds spread throughout the park. You will find kilometers of paved paths for bike riding and lots of fresh air and open spaces for exercising and playing all year round.

There is a family area in the park with a small bike course for children (open 9:30 A.M. to 4:00 P.M., except Mondays), which is free of charge, and another bike path where you can ride a two-person pedal cart. (If there are two adults on the bike, you cannot put your child in the kid's seat. Only two people *total* allowed.) Near the bike course is a play area with a few swings and some old climbing structures. There are two other playgrounds, referred to by the regulars as the "squirrel" playground and the "pig" playground, because of the animal-shaped climbing structures. The "pig" playground, preferred by our friends, is on the Tamagawa Dori side of the park by the track and field stadium. The "squirrel" playground is across Komazawa Dori, off Jiyu Dori.

The park's public swimming pools are open July 1 to September 15 from 10:00 A.M. to 5:00 P.M. daily except Monday. Tennis courts are available from 8:30 A.M. to 4:30 P.M. daily except Monday and must be reserved two months in advance. Inside the large stadium is a training center where adults can work out from 9:00 A.M. to 5:00 P.M. and from 6:00 P.M. to 8:45 P.M. daily for only ¥300 for two hours. The training center is closed on the third Monday of each month.

If possible, it is best to ride or take your bike to this park so you can make use of the long bicycle course and sidewalks. If you drive, there is parking available in paid lots adjacent to the park, or you can park on one of the side streets. To get to the park from Ebisu Station take the Sakura Shinmachi bus to the Tokyo Daini Byoin-mae (Tokyo National Hospital No. 2) stop, near the corner of Komazawa Dori and Jiyu Dori. The park is a 10-minute walk from Komazawa Daigakumae Station on the Shin Tamagawa Line.

Kinuta Ryokuchi Koen ♪♪♪

1-1 Kinuta Koen, Setagaya-ku, Tokyo　東京都世田谷区砧公園 1-1
☎ (03) 3700-7059
Area: 38.3 ha
🚇 Yoga Station, Shin Tamagawa line

For residents of Setagaya, this park is a refreshing oasis of green with excellent facilities for picnics and playing. There is a cycling course and bike rental for children under fifteen years of age. The area is actually divided into two parks, and children will have the most fun in the section where they can climb on an old locomotive and enjoy the playground equipment. The adjacent Setagaya-ku Sports Center has three outdoor swimming pools with shallow pools for the little ones. Even though Kinuta Park is a little difficult to get to, (thirty to forty minutes by car or bus from Shibuya), it is a great choice for birthday parties. Not only can you find an abundance of picnic tables just off the playground, but you can also rent a party room in case of rain. There is a water park next door that is fun for older kids as well as adventurous four- or five-year-olds, and it also has a miniature water slide for the little ones. Free parking is available in the park grounds.

Baji Koen 🎀🎀🎀🎀

2-1-1 Kami Yoga, Setagaya-ku, Tokyo　東京都世田谷区上用賀 2-1-1
☎ (03) 3429-51011
Area: 8.5 ha
🚃 Shibuya Station, JR Yamanote, Inokashira, Ginza, Toyoko, Shin Tamagawa lines

Baji Koen, or Horse Park, is a well-kept, spacious park that was used for equestrian events during the 1964 Olympic Games. Events are held at the park each month, such as free horse rides and carriage races. In addition to the well-designed playground, there is an area of natural woods where the children can go exploring. The park has many lovely details in its layout, such as hedges carved in horse shapes and water fountains with horse-head statues. It is an ideal place for picnics—drinks are available from vending machines—or lunch at the restaurant next to the information office. Baji Koen is open daily all year round. To get there, take a 30-minute bus (bus #24 bound for Seijo Gakuen) or taxi ride from Shibuya Station. Get off at Noda Mae bus stop and walk three minutes to the park. Parking is not available at the park.

MEGURO-KU

Himonya Koen 🎀🎀🎀

6-9-11 Himonya, Meguro-ku, Tokyo　東京都目黒区碑文谷 6-9-11
☎ (03) 3714-1548
🚃 Gakugei Daigaku Station, Toyoko Line

As parents of young children, this park in Meguro was one of our most exciting discoveries. Not only is there a real petting zoo, but there is also a boating pond, and pony rides for ¥100. The petting zoo is open every day except Monday from 10:00 to 11:30 A.M. and 1:30 to 4:30 P.M. Next to the petting zoo is a ticket machine for the pony rides. A park worker guides the ponies, so the rides are safe even for the youngest cowboy or cowgirl. There is also an arena for horseback riding lessons, which can be arranged by calling (03) 3714-1548. Riding lessons are from 3:00 P.M. to 5:00 P.M., but you must reserve far in advance.

In Himonya Park there is enough space for kicking a ball around and a nice playground with a sandbox. If you are brave enough to row a boat with young children, the price is ¥50 but each child must be accompanied by an adult. An enjoyable activity for all ages is feeding bread to the ducks.

The park is across the street from Gakugei Daigaku Station and several blocks away from the Daiei Department Store on Meguro Dori. If you drive, you can usually find a parking place on a side street.

OTA-KU

Nishi Rokugo Koen "Tire Park" 🌷🌷🌷

1-6-1 Nishi Rokugo, Ota-ku, Tokyo　東京都大田区西六郷 1-6-1
☎ (03) 3731-1811
🚉 Kamata Station, JR Keihin Tohoku, Mekama, Ikegami lines

A visit to Tire Park is an experience like no other in Tokyo. In the park, there are hundreds of tires in every shape and size imaginable, and they are used in the most creative ways. Some are sculpted into robots or dragons, and there are tunnels and mountains that are perfect for climbing. This park boasts the best swings for parents and babies to swing in together; big, comfortable tire swings that accommodate adults of every shape and size. Because of the tires, it can be a bit dusty on a hot day, so be sure to bring your *oshibori* and use the row of water faucets to clean up afterward. On one side of the park there is a snack bar with popsicles and ice cream and a few picnic tables.

We are usually fortunate enough to find car parking on the street that runs in front of the park. If you go by train, you can walk the fifteen minutes from Kamata Station or take a taxi to "Taiya Koen."

Senzoku Koen 🌷🌷🌷🌷

2-14-5 Minami Senzoku, Ota-ku, Tokyo　東京都大田区南洗束 2-14-5
☎ (03) 3726-2427
Area: 2.5 ha
🚉 Senzoku-ike Station, Ikegami Line

This very special pond with an adjacent playground is one of the most scenic places you will come across in Tokyo. Children will be delighted by the large swan and duck paddle boats available for hire. The swan boats are roomy and safe even for two adults and two children. For ¥400 you can paddle across the pond for thirty minutes while your little one mans the steering wheel. Less exotic duck paddle boats are available for ¥300. After a ride on the paddle boats, you can head through the Senzoku Temple grounds to the small playground. A quicker way to get there is to go along a back street to the right of the pond. We have visited this temple on the first weekend in September, during the annual autumn festival. It was especially festive at dusk, with red lanterns reflecting on the surface of the water. In addition to the usual booths of food and games, there was an artist demonstrating the art of candy sculpture. The kids were fascinated as he created various animal shapes from a ball of warm taffy.

If you are driving to Senzoku-ike, go along Nakahara Kaido in Ota-ku and you'll see the pond. There is no parking lot, so you will have to park on the narrow side streets near the playground. The train is quite convenient as Senzoku-ike Station is located just across the street from the paddle boat entrance. There is a nice terrace cafe for meals or snacks in the building that houses the boats.

WEST TOKYO

Tomin no Mori 🌷🌷🌷🌷🌷

7146 Kazuma, Hinohara-mura, Nishitama-gun, Tokyo　東京都西多摩郡檜原村7146
☎ (0425) 98-6006
Area: 197 ha
🚃 Musashi Itsukaichi Station, Itsukaichi Line

This "forest" park is a wonderful chance for Tokyo residents to experience the great outdoors. Built by the Tokyo Metropolitan Government in 1990 in the Chichibu Tama National Park, this park comprises five "zones" created to give children a chance to exercise their bodies and their imaginations.

For example, at the entrance is the "Forest of Encounter," where you can get information about the park. Refreshments are available at the forest villa, and here you will also find the wooden craft center, where you can watch craftsmen at work. You can also learn how to make various crafts on the second floor of this building.

Zone 2 is the "Forest of Daily Life." Here you can study how charcoal is made, find out which mountain vegetables are edible, and learn other nature-related skills. Other zones have names such as the "Forest of Adventure," with sports equipment and obstacle courses; the "Forest of Wild Birds," with wildlife exhibits; and the "Forest of Trees," with a breathtaking view of Mt. Fuji.

The park is open from 9:30 A.M. to 4:00 P.M., and admission is free. To get there, take the JR Chuo Line to Tachikawa Station, change to the

JR Ome Line and get off at Haijima Station. From there, take the Itsukaichi Line to Musashi Itsukaichi Station, where a shuttle bus leaves for Kazuma. From Shinjuku, the trip will probably take about 2½ hours. If you go by car, take the Shuto Expressway to the Tokaido Interchange and change to the Chuo Expressway. At Kamakawanori, change to the Shinohara Kaido, which will lead you to Kazuma.

The Tokyo Metropolitan Government is planning two other forest parks in the near future. "Taiken no Mori" or Experience Forest Park, is scheduled to be completed by 1993 in Okutama, and Model no Mori, or Model Forest, will be completed in Hachioji in 1996. The Ministry of Construction plans to build ten more nature parks for children throughout Japan during the 1991–92 fiscal year.

Musashi-Koganei Koen ♀♀♀♀♀

1-13-1 Sekino-machi, Koganei-shi, Tokyo 東京都小金井市関野町 1–13–1
☎ (0423) 85-5611
 Musashi-Koganei Station, JR Chuo Line

We are always looking for a new place for a school outing, company picnic, or to take visitors from abroad. This park is a great choice, as there is something for everybody here. Unless you live in west Tokyo, it takes a little effort to get there (about one hour on the train from central Tokyo), but it is well worth it.

The grounds of the park are large, with no fences or gates to make you feel hemmed in, and immediately upon arriving you feel as if you are in the country. The large trees are of many species, and the grounds have a wild look to them that is refreshing in this society where gardeners love to clip and trim. There are many picnic tables, paved and dirt paths, and open areas to choose from. You can stay away from the crowd for a private party, or join the fun with everyone else near the sports center and the playground.

The playground at Musashi-Koganei Park is one of the newest and nicest we have seen in Tokyo. There is also a small play area for babies (under two years old) with scaled-down slides, swings, and climbing toys, located well away from the older children and their activities.

For older children, there is a pyramid-type structure built into a hill that has stairs, dirt paths, rope ladders, and grassy knolls all around it leading up to the top. There are three levels to the top, all with a variety of slides, hidden sandboxes, and daredevil paths to explore. Just below this pyramid is an open area with an obstacle or workout course (*Trimm dich Pfad*) set up.

The equipment is new and made for adult use, but children of all ages play on the balance beam, monkey bars, and pulley swing.

Just next to this course is a hill covered with artificial turf in a fenced-in area, that at first glance looks like a putting green. There is a gate at the bottom, and a pile of red plastic sleds. It is actually a slide and is free of charge. Children do much better on a sled by themselves without an adult to weigh them down or tip them over. (Important note: The sleds are unstable with two people in them. We watched an adult holding a child in the sled and when the sled tipped over, the child was hurt.). Next door is a paved area for bouncing balls or gently hitting a tennis ball. There is also the usual bike area for children with bikes to use free of charge and a snack stand with drinks, chips, and ice cream for sale.

Also on the grounds is the Musashino Museum (Musashino Kyodo Hakubutsukan), which has a collection of local (Kanto Plain) archaeological objects inside, and some models of old houses and farm structures outside.

Next to the playground is a new members-only sports center. They don't offer anything for children under six years of age, but they have many activities for adults. The phone number for the sports center is (0423) 81-1336.

To get there, catch bus #3 from Musashi-Koganei Station and get off at Koganei Koenmae (it's about a 10-minute ride). If you are driving and want to use the parking lot, turn right off Koganei Kaido onto Itsukaichi Kaido. You will see the park to your left; turn at the third street and drive to the lot. The sports center and playground are to your right as you face the park.

Inokashira Koen ♪♪♪♪

1-18-31 Gotenyama, Musashino-shi, Tokyo　東京都武蔵野市御殿山 1-18-31
☎ (0422) 44-3796
Area: 28 ha
🚉 Kichijoji Station, JR Chuo Line; Inokashira Koen Station, Inokashira Line

Park, small zoo, and pond are all combined here to make for a terrific outing in west Tokyo. The playground facilities located near the pond are excellent, and it is a scenic spot for a picnic. To arrange boating on the pond, call (0422) 47-1538. The zoo, called Suiseibutsu-en, has fish and birds and is open from 9:30 A.M. to 4:30 P.M. daily except Monday. Children under twelve are admitted free, and adult tickets are ¥300. Our children delight in petting the guinea pigs and chasing the peacocks. The zoo is actually rather clean if a bit smelly.

Located adjacent to the park is the Inokashira Nature and Culture Park (Inokashira Shizen Bunka-en). Here there is an amusement-park atmosphere with ¥100 rides and small carnival rides. There is also a greenhouse and aviary, a small natural history and sculpture museum, and another zoo-type attraction called Hon-en. This zoo has deer and peacocks that are free to roam about. The ticket for Suiseibutsu-en is good for Hon-en too, so don't throw it away.

The park is a short walk from Kichijoji Station or Inokashira Koen Station. If you drive, there is parking at the park, although there is often a long line on weekends.

Showa Memorial Park 🌷🌷🌷🌷

3173 Midori-cho, Tachikawa-shi, Tokyo　東京都立川市緑町 3173
☎ (0425) 28-1751
Area: 89 ha
🚉 Nishi Tachikawa Station, JR Ome Line

This lovely park has slides, swings, and climbing equipment for all ages. A lake with rowboats (¥300 per half hour) and pedal boats for rent (¥600 per half hour) is the centerpiece of the park. Bike courses and jogging courses crisscross the park, and they have over 600 bicycles of all types for rent. In the winter months, there is ice-skating daily.

To get there, take the JR Chuo Line to Tachikawa Station. Change here for the JR Ome Line to Nishi Tachikawa Station. The park is a 5-minute walk from the station.

6

Amusement Parks, Aquariums, and Zoos

For a special outing with children, you cannot go wrong with an amusement park, aquarium, or zoo. Japan has plenty of all three, with new ones springing up every year. Because of the time involved in getting to many of these places, especially with young children, these outings are often full-day trips.

Most amusement parks, aquariums, and zoos have restrooms and snack areas. The snacks for sale are the usual chips, ice cream, and pop. Sometimes there are restaurants selling sandwiches and *obento* lunches. You will find souvenir booths full of goodies, and there is almost always a section with ¥100 rides, which are especially delightful for babies and toddlers.

Many of the attractions listed in this chapter could fall under more than one category. The aquariums are generally on the small side and are often combined with another attraction. Some amusement parks have small petting zoos (usually a few rabbits and goats), while most zoos have a ¥100 rides. Many of the amusement parks run an ice-skating rink in the winter and swimming pool in the summer. Amusement parks may have a theme, and include playground or athletic equipment as well as the usual rides—roller coasters, tilt-a-whirl, etc. For the most part, children under age eight or so will be thrilled with the hustle and bustle of these theme parks. Older children may be disappointed at the small scale of things, but if you prepare them, and yourself, in advance, you can all have a great time. If you consider the day trip a cultural experience and an opportunity for the family to spend some time together, these attractions should have something to keep everyone happy.

As with most popular holiday spots in Japan, these attractions will be much less crowded if you visit during the week. However, all the places in this chapter are spacious enough to enjoy on weekends, too, although the gaggles of young couples at the high-tech aquariums on Sundays can be a bit overwhelming. One of the places where lines can be a real problem is Tokyo Disneyland, but *there* the wait is worth it! In all cases, arriving as early as possible any day you go is your best bet.

There is usually a good deal of walking involved if you attempt to see all the exhibits in any of these outings, so be sure to bring a stroller for tired feet. Some places offer strollers for rent, but they go quickly on a busy day.

We suggest that you try at least a few of the outings listed below with your kids. Hours tend to change from season to season so it's a good idea to call for more information before you visit. You may find the zoos and aquariums in Japan a bit more cramped than some of the more spacious and modern habitats in other countries, but if your child is thrilled at the idea of seeing a real giraffe or live dolphin, the trip will be worth the effort.

AMUSEMENT PARKS

KANTO AREA

Arakawa Amusement Park

6-35-11 Nishiogu, Arakawa-ku, Tokyo   東京都荒川区西尾久 6-35-11
☎ (03) 3893-6003
🚃 Arakawa Yuenchimae Station, Toden Arakawa Line

Renovated in 1989, this amusement park also houses a small zoo. The park is closed Mondays and at New Year, and there is free admission for children under middle school age. To get there, take the JR Keihin Tohoku Line to Oji Station and then change to the Toden Arakawa Line to Arakawa Yuenchimae Station.

Asakusa Hanayashiki

2-28-1 Asakusa, Taito-ku, Tokyo   東京都台東区浅草 2-28-1
☎ (03) 3842-4646
🚃 Asakusa Station, Ginza, Toei Asakusa lines

One of the oldest amusement parks in Tokyo, this park has recently been renovated. The park is open from 10:00 A.M. to 5:30 P.M. (9:00 P.M. in summer), six days a week. It is closed Tuesdays, except during school holidays, when it is open daily. Admission is ¥400 for adults, ¥200 for children. The park is just behind Asakusa Kannon Temple.

Korakuen Amusement Park

1-3-61 Koraku, Bunkyo-ku, Tokyo　東京都文京区後楽 1-3-61
☎ (03) 3811-2111
🚃 Korakuen Station, Marunouchi Line; Suidobashi Station, JR Chuo Line

This is a typical amusement park, with rides to thrill the teens as well as the usual assortment of smaller rides. It is connected to Tokyo Dome stadium and is next to Koishikawa Botanical Garden. The park is open from 10:00 A.M. to 7:00 P.M. daily and until 9:00 P.M. in summer. Admission is ¥1,100 for adults, ¥650 for children.

Lake Sagami Picnic Land

1634 Wakayanagi, Sagamiko-machi, Tsukui-gun, Kanagawa-ken
☎ (0426) 85-1111　神奈川県津久井郡相模湖町若柳 1634
🚃 Sagamiko Station, JR Chuo Honsen Line

Picnic Land is made up of 150 hectares of camping sites with a playland, ranch, and a wading pond. It is open from 9:30 A.M. to 4:30 P.M. every day except Tuesdays. Summer hours are daily from 9:00 A.M. to 5:00 P.M. The entrance fee is ¥1,000 for adults, ¥600 for children. From Sagamiko Station, take a Kanagawa Chuo Kotsu bus bound for Mikage from bus stop #1 and get off at Picnic Land Mae. The trip takes about eight minutes.

Mukogaoka Amusement Park

2-8-1 Nagao, Tama-ku, Kawasaki-shi, Kanagawa-ken
☎ (044) 911-4281　神奈川県川崎市多摩区長尾 2-8-1
🚃 Mukogaoka Yuenchi Station, Odakyu Line

This park is situated in a 23-hectare garden, and much of the beauty of the garden is still here for your enjoyment. There is swimming in the summer, ice-skating in the winter, and the usual small-scale rides and amusements. The park is open from 9:00 A.M. to 5:00 P.M. daily, and admission is ¥1,300 for adults and ¥700 for children. From November through March the park is closed on Wednesdays. From Mukogaoka Yuenchi Station, change to the monorail which takes you directly to the amusement park in just three minutes.

Nippon Land HOW Amusement Park

2427 Aza Fujiwara, Suyama, Susono-shi, Shizuoka-ken
☎ (03) 3376-1127 (Tokyo office)　静岡県裾野市須山字藤原 2427
🚃 Gotemba Station, Odakyu Line

Situated at the foot of Mt. Fuji, this is a combination outdoor sports plaza, amusement park, and resort center. HOW stands for Humanity Opening World, and what it really means is there is something here for everyone, all year round. Golf, ice-skating, skiing, hiking, and a large amusement park are just a few of the attractions. Hotel accommodation is available for those wishing to stay overnight. For reservations, call the Japan Tourist Bureau at (03) 3257-8543. All the attractions are reasonably and individually priced. For information on fees, snow conditions, and hours, call the Tokyo office of Nippon Land. From Gotemba Station, Nippon Land is a 50-minute ride by Fuji Kanko Bus.

Pony Land

3-12-17 Shinozaki-cho, Edogawa-ku, Tokyo　東京都江戸川区篠崎町 3-12-17
☎ (03) 3678-7520
🚃 Koiwa Station, JR Sobu Line; Shinozakicho Station, Toei Asakusa Line

At Pony Land, the kids can ride ponies and stagecoaches for free. Park hours are 9:30 A.M. to 11:30 A.M. and 1:30 A.M. to 3:30 P.M. They are closed Mondays and New Year. From the south exit of Koiwa Station, take bus #72 bound for Mizue, Ichinoe, or Edogawa Sports Land. The trip takes about fifteen minutes; get off at the Pony Land Mae stop.

Seibu-en

2964 Yamaguchi, Tokorozawa-shi, Saitama-ken　埼玉県所沢市山口 2964
☎ (0429) 22-1371
🚃 Seibu Yuenchi Station, Seibu Shinjuku Line

At Seibu-en you will find about twenty rides in a big amusement park. They are open Monday through Friday from 10:00 A.M to 5:00 P.M and Saturday and Sunday from 10:00 A.M to 8:00 P.M. They are closed on Wednesday from November through March. Entrance fees range from ¥500 for one- to five-year-olds, to ¥1800 for adults. The park is connected by train with UNESCO Village (seven minutes from Seibu Kyujomae Station on the Yamaguchi Line). UNESCO features scaled-down versions of houses from each country represented in the United Nations. Hours for UNESCO are 10:00 A.M. to 5:00 P.M. and fees are ¥400 for children, ¥800 for adults.

Sesame Place

403 Ajiro, Itsukaichi-machi, Nishitama-gun, Tokyo
☎ (0425) 96-5811　東京都西多摩郡五日市町網代 403
🚃 Akikawa Station, JR Musashi Itsukaichi Line

Sesame Place is a theme park based on the popular TV show "Sesame Street." Built around the theme "play and learn together," the park is set up so that parents and their children can interact and learn with each other. The Tokyo park's special theme is "internationality," and they hire foreign guides—whom they call "play leaders"—to ensure that Japanese children

..e of international life. At the park you will find Big Bird, Cookie
Monster, and many of the other original Sesame Street characters. There is
also a model of 123 Sesame Street, just like the one used on the TV show.
Instead of roller-coasters and merry-go-rounds, Sesame Place uses outdoor
activities and educational games to give the children their thrills. The park
is aimed particularly at children from the age of three to twelve, and so
even the youngest child can join in the fun. Besides the restaurants for the
general public, there are also nice restroom facilities with baby changing
and feeding areas.

The park is located in Akikawa, near Summerland (see the entry in this
chapter). Hours vary with the seasons, so call for opening and closing
times. As the park has several attractions only for children, admission is
¥2,100 for adults and ¥2,600 (this price includes all attractions) for children from the age of three to twelve.

Nikko Edomura

470-2 Karakura, Fujiwara-cho, Shioya-gun, Tochigi-ken
☎ (0288) 77-1777　栃木県塩谷郡藤原町柄倉 470–2
🚆 Kinugawa Onsen Station, Tobu Kinugawa Line

This unusual park features daily shows by ninja warriors, and all attractions
around the 16-hectare park are based on the theme of Japan in the Edo period (1615–1868). Nikko Edomura is open from 9:00 A.M. to 5:00 P.M.
daily. The admission ticket, which includes all the attractions is ¥3,500 for
adults and ¥2,300 for children.

Tama-tech

5-22-1 Hodokubo, Hino-shi, Tokyo　東京都日野市程久保 5–22–1
☎ (0425) 91-0820/4
🚆 Tama Dobutsu Koen Station, Keio Line

This is an automobile amusement park run by Honda Motor Co., which is
reflected in the various vehicles (battery powered) that feature in some of
the rides. The rest are the usual roller coaster, ferris wheel, and so on. There
is ice-skating in the winter months. The park is open daily from 9:30 A.M. to
4:30 P.M. in winter and 9:00 A.M. to 5:30 P.M. in summer. Admission is
¥1,200 for adults, ¥600 for children. To get there from Tama Dobutsu
Koen Station, take a bus bound for Tama-Tech or walk for fifteen minutes.

Tokyo Disneyland

1-1 Maihama, Urayasu-shi, Chiba-ken　千葉県浦安市舞浜 1–1
☎ (0473) 54-0001
🚆 Maihama Station, JR Keiyo Line

This is the real thing. This park is just like the original California Disneyland, with the Disney characters played by American actors and park signs in English. A day here is like a day in the United States. Disney's impeccable landscaping and professional staff are consistent throughout the world. The park has special attractions all year round, with Christmas decorations and shows in December, and late hours and evening fireworks in the summer months. They are open Monday through Thursday from 10:00 A.M. to 7:00 P.M. and Friday, Saturday, and Sunday from 9:00 A.M. to 10:00 P.M. Hours may vary in the winter months so call before you go. The "passport" ticket, valid for all rides, is ¥4,400 for adults and ¥3,000 for four- to eleven-year-olds. There are many ways to get there, but the best option may be to go to the new Maihama Station that is right in front of the Disneyland main gate. To get there, take the Yurakucho Line to Shin Kiba Station and transfer to the JR Keiyo Line to Maihama Station. You can also take the Tozai Line to Urayasu Station, walk to the shuttle bus terminal and pay the small fee for the 15-minute ride to Disneyland on their special bus. Yet a third way is to take one of the direct Disneyland shuttle buses from Tokyo Station, Ueno Station, or Yokohama Station. These buses run every fifteen minutes or so, and the charge is ¥600 one way for adults and ¥300 for children.

Tokyo Summerland

600 Shiraiwa, Kamiyotsugi, Akikawa-shi, Tokyo   東京都秋川市上代継白岩 600
☎ (0425) 58-6511
🚉 Hachioji Station, JR Chuo Line; Keio Hachioji Station, Keio Line; Akikawa Station, JR Musashi Itsukaichi Line

This is a medium-sized amusement park with a few large rides. The real attraction, and reason for the name, is the unique wave pool. Here, man-made waves wash over swimmers, and intermittent tropical rains fall all year round—all within a domed structure. There are outdoor pools as well, which are open in the summer, and all pools have shallow areas for babies and toddlers. Believe it or not, in the winter months there is ice-skating. From the north exit of Hachioji Station take a cab or bus #12 for the 20-minute ride to Tokyo Summerland.

Toshimaen

3-25-1 Koyama, Nerima-ku, Tokyo   東京都練馬区向山 3–25–1
☎ (03) 3990-3131
🚉 Toshimaen Station, Seibu Ikebukuro Line

This is the oldest amusement park in Tokyo, with fifty attractions. Large adult rides, haunted houses, and a special children's section are all features of the park. Also on the grounds is an outdoor theater with shows nightly during the summer season and every Sunday during the winter. During the summer there is also a fireworks show here that is famous in Japan. The park is open from 9:00 A.M. to 5:00 P.M. daily and closed on Wednesdays from mid-November to mid-March. A one-day pass including entrance and all rides is ¥3,900 for adults and ¥3,300 for children.

Yomiuriland

3294 Yanokuchi, Inagi-shi, Tokyo   東京都稲城市矢野口 3294
☎ (044) 966-1111
🚉 Keio Yomiuri Land Station, Keio Sagamihara Line; Yomiuri Land Mae Station, Odakyu Line

This is a huge park with thrilling rides, including, as of 1989, the world's fastest roller coaster. There is also an aquarium with dolphin and seal shows and an entire section of children's rides. Roller skating is available year-round, and there are outdoor swimming pools in the summer and ice-skating in the winter. The park is open from 10:00 A.M. to 5:00 P.M. Monday through Friday, 9:00 A.M. to 5:00 P.M. Saturday and Sunday, and closed on Tuesdays except for school holidays. Admission is ¥1,200 for adults, ¥600 for children. To get there take the Keio Line from Shinjuku to Chofu Station; change to the Keio Sagamihara Line and get off at Keio Yomiuri Land Station, from where you can ride the "skyroad escalator" to the park. An alternative is to take the Odakyu Line from Shinjuku Station to Yomiuri Land Mae Station and then catch a special bus to the park.

KANSAI AREA

Space World

8-1 Edamitsuhoncho, Yahata Higashi-ku, Kitakyushu-shi, Fukuoka-ken
☎ (093) 672-3600   福岡県北九州市八幡東区枝光本町 8–1
🚉 Edamitsu Station, JR Kagoshima Line

Opened in the spring of 1990, this is the world's first space-oriented theme park. Covering more than 300,000 sq. m., the park includes large-scale rides, pavilions, restaurants, and a space camp. The space camp gives young people the opportunity to learn about space travel and experience what it is like to travel in space. Besides the youth camp programs, there is a two-day program for adults. Another main attraction at Space World is the Space Dome, the largest amusement pavilion in the world which includes several space-simulation attractions. Space World is open from

9:00 A.M. to 7:00 P.M. on weekdays, with extended hours on weekends, holidays, and school vacations. Admission to the park is ¥1,800 for adults, ¥1,200 for students, and ¥800 for children under twelve. Admission to the attractions is charged separately; either ¥500 or ¥300 each. Space World is thirty minutes by bus from Kokura Station on the JR Shinkansen Line, or just a 5-minute walk from Edamitsu Station on the JR Kagoshima Line.

Kobe Portopialand

8-7-1 Minatojimanakamachi, Chuo-ku, Kobe-shi, Hyogo-ken
☎ (078) 302-2820   兵庫県神戸市中央区港島中町 8-7-1
🚃 Minami Koen Station, Port Island Line

This recently-built amusement park on Port Island has plenty of large-scale rides for the older kids but not much here specifically for the under-six set. The park is open daily except Wednesday from 10:00 A.M. to 5:30 P.M., March through January, with extended summer hours. Admission to the park is ¥1,000 for adults, ¥500 for children, with rides extra.

Banpaku Koen Expoland

1-1 Banpaku Koen, Senri, Suita-shi, Osaka-fu   大阪府吹田市千里万博公園 1-1
☎ (06) 877-0560
🚃 Ibaraki Station, JR Tokaido Honsen Line

This amusement park was built as part of Expo '70, which was held in Osaka. There are a number of large rides and other standard amusements for children. Inside the park there is a playground for younger children, as well as the usual ¥100 rides. A library in the grounds has a large selection of children's books in the international section. The park is open year-round, and is closed on Wednesdays except in August. Hours are 9:30 A.M. to 5:30 P.M., and until 9:00 P.M. in summer. Admission is ¥1,100 for adults and ¥550 for children. To get there, take bus #4 from Ibaraki Station. If you are traveling by car, the park is next to Suita Junction just off the Meishin Expressway.

Sanrio Theme Parks

The Sanrio Company, makers of Hello Kitty, The Runabouts, and many more character toys and accessories, has opened two new theme parks since 1990. These parks have been years in the making, and no expense has been spared in their design and execution. Although quite different from one another, Puroland and Harmonyland are Japanese theme parks at their best.

Puroland

1-31 Ochiai, Tama-shi, Tokyo　東京都多摩市落合 1-31
☎ (0423) 72-6500
🚋 Tama Center Station, Keio or Odakyu lines

Sanrio's Puroland is a six-story indoor amusement park. All the attractions are made with the latest technology, and with active participation in mind. Sanrio says that each amusement is designed for 80 percent entertainment and 20 percent participation. Once inside the large, domed plaza, you can take your pick from six floors of theme-oriented amusements and restaurants. Much of the park is animated with robots, and all of the restaurants have either entertainment or service by robots. The amusements have themes like "Fantastic Puro Adventure," where you can ride a boat around Puro Village and learn the story of the birth of Puroland, and "Time Machine of Dreams," where you can experience a trip through time via special effects. Of course, the Sanrio characters are present in abundance, and all the attractions are built with both children and adults in mind. Puroland's controlled admissions policy means that you can enjoy the attractions to the full because the park is never overcrowded. You must reserve a ticket, and to do that, phone the reservation center at (03) 5705-1110, not more than one month before you want to visit; you pay for your ticket on the day you visit the park. Reserved tickets can also be ordered through the major travel agencies. Admission is ¥3,000 for adults, ¥2,700 for twelve- to seventeen-year-olds and ¥2,000 for three- to eleven-year-olds. The park is open from 10:00 A.M. to 10:00 P.M. on weekdays and 9:00 A.M. to 10:00 P.M. on weekends and it is closed on Tuesdays. The park is a 10-minute walk from Tama Center Station.

Harmonyland

5933 Oaza Fujiwara, Hiji-machi, Hayami-gun, Oita-ken ☎
(0977) 73-1110　大分県速見郡日出町大字藤原 5933
🚋 Hiji or Kitsuki stations, JR Nippo Honsen Line

Opened in the spring of 1991, this park exhibits a new concept in children's theme parks. Harmonyland is a vast area filled with miniature villages, parks, and whimsical shops. Focusing on fantasy, a Time Machine and a Dream World are just a couple of Harmonyland's many fairy-tale-like creations. The park is a 35-minute taxi ride from Oita Airport. If you're traveling from the direction of Kitakyushu or Oita airport, the nearest station is Kitsuki on the Nippo Line. From the direction of Beppu and Oita city, the nearest station is Hiji on the same line. From both stations the park is twenty minutes by bus—look for buses with the sign HL (Harmonyland).

AQUARIUMS

KANTO AREA

Itabashi Ward Aquarium

3-50-1 Itabashi, Itabashi-ku, Tokyo　東京都板橋区板橋 3-50-1
☎ (03) 3962-8419
Itabashi Kuyakushomae Station, Toei Mita Line

This is a small freshwater aquarium located in Higashi Itabashi Park. It is open from March through November from 10:00 A.M. to 4:30 P.M., and December through Feburary from 10:00 A.M. to 4:00 P.M. It is closed Mondays and holidays.

Kasai Rinkai Aquarium (Tokyo Sea Life Park)

6-2-3 Rinkai-cho, Edogawa-ku, Tokyo　東京都江戸川区臨海町 6-2-3
☎ (03) 3869-5151
Kasai Rinkai Koen Station, JR Keiyo Line; Nishi-Kasai Station, Tozai Line

Opened in October 1989, Tokyo Sea Life Park is one of the largest aquariums in Tokyo. Its modern design lets you observe exotic sea life up close; the "room full of tuna" being particularly spectacular. Future construction projects include an aviary, a cycling course, and a promenade and "Sea Breeze Square" for ocean viewing. Open from 9:30 A.M. to 5:00 P.M. daily except Monday, national holidays, and at New Year's. When Monday is a national holiday, it is closed the following day.

Shinagawa Aquarium

Shinagawa Kumin Koen, 3-2-1 Katsushima, Shinagawa-ku, Tokyo
☎ (03) 3762-3431　東京都品川区勝島 3-2-1 品川区民公園内
Omori Kaigan Station, Keihin Kyuko Line

Opened in October 1991, this aquarium is home to a large variety of fish and a school of dolphins that performs daily. The aquarium also features an underwater tunnel allowing visitors a fish's-eye view of life underwater without getting wet once. Open daily except Tuesdays, hours are from 10:00 A.M. to 4:30 P.M. Admission is ¥800 for adults, ¥500 for elementary and junior high school students, and ¥300 for children age four to seven. The aquarium is a 5-minute walk from Omori Kaigan Station.

Sunshine Kokusai Aquarium

Sunshine City, 3-1-3 Higashi Ikebukuro, Toshima-ku, Tokyo
☎ (03) 3989-3466　東京都豊島区東池袋 3-1-3
Higashi Ikebukuro Station, Yurakucho Line; Ikebukuro Station, Marunouchi, Yurakucho, JR Yamanote, JR Saikyo, Tobu Tojo, Seibu Ikebukuro lines

This is a large aquarium with 20,000 fish of over 400 species on display. It is open daily from 10:00 A.M. to 6:00 P.M. and to 6:30 P.M. on Sundays and national holidays. Admission is ¥1,440 for adults and ¥720 for children. The aquarium is located on the tenth and eleventh floors of the World Import Mart in Sunshine City.

Tokyo Tower Aquarium

4-2-8 Shiba Koen, Minato-ku, Tokyo　東京都港区芝公園 4-2-8
☎ (03) 3434-8833
🚃 Kamiyacho Station, Hibiya Line; Hamamatsucho Station, JR Yamanote, JR Keihin Tohoku lines

Centrally located in Shiba Koen, this small aquarium boasts over 800 species of fish. The aquarium is open from 10:00 A.M. to 6:30 P.M. daily; admission is ¥1,000 for adults, ¥500 for children. To get there, take the exit for the Soviet Embassy at Kamiyacho Station and walk for five minutes or take the JR Yamanote Line to Hamamatsucho Station and you'll see Tokyo Tower when you exit the station.

Enoshima Aquarium, Marineland, and Marine Zoo

2-17-25 Katase Kaigan, Fujisawa-shi, Kanagawa-ken
☎ (0466) 22-8111　神奈川県藤沢市片瀬海岸 2-17-25
🚃 Katase Enoshima Station, Odakyu Line; Enoshima Station, Enoshima-Kamakura Kanko Line

The Enoshima Marine Park is actually three outdoor attractions in one. The complex includes a small aquarium, a marineland with dolphin shows daily, and a marine zoo with a sea lion show and other marine life. Located on the beach in Fujisawa, it is open from 9:30 A.M. to 5:00 P.M. Admission is ¥1,700 for adults and ¥750 for children. To get there, take the JR Tokaido Line to Fujisawa Station and transfer to the Enoshima-Kamakura Kanko Line for Enoshima Station. Alternatively, take the Odakyu Line to Enoshima Station. The aquarium is a 10-minute walk from Katase Enoshima Station or Enoshima Station.

Keikyu Aburatsubo Marine Park

1082 Koajiro, Misaki-cho, Miura-shi, Kanagawa-ken
☎ (0468) 81-6281　神奈川県三浦市三崎町小網代 1082
🚃 Misakiguchi Station, Keihin Kyuko Line

This is a 3-hectare park with an aquarium where you can see a dolphin and sea lion show. The park is open February through November from 9:00 A.M. to 5:00 P.M., and December to January from 9:00 A.M. to 4:00 P.M. Admission is ¥1,600 for adults, ¥800 for junior high school students, and

¥430 for children under six. To get there from Misakiguchi Station, take a bus from platform #1 for a 15-minute ride to the terminus at Aburatsubo.

KANSAI AREA

Kobe Municipal Suma Aqualife Park

1-3-5 Wakamiya-cho, Suma-ku, Kobe-shi, Hyogo-ken
☎ (078) 731-7301　兵庫県神戸市須磨区若宮町 1-3-5
🚇 Suma Station, JR San'yo Honsen Line

This is an excellent aquarium with trained dolphins that perform daily. Some consider it to be the best of its kind in Japan, and a visit here is a must if you are near Kobe with the kids. Large indoor tanks, outdoor exhibits, and ¥100 rides make up the park. Open daily from 9:00 A.M. to 5:00 P.M. (6:00 P.M. in summer), the park is closed on Wednesdays except in summer. Admission is ¥800 for adults and ¥300 for children. The park is on Suma Beach—walk from Suma Station or take bus #85 from Kobe Station.

Osaka Aquarium

1-1-10 Kaigan Dori, Minato-ku, Osaka-shi, Osaka-fu
☎ (06) 576-5501　大阪府大阪市港区海岸通り 1-1-10
🚇 Osakako Station, Chuo Line

This spectacular aquarium features water tanks so large that visitors can see fish swimming in a natural-like environment. The Japanese name for this aquarium is "Kaiyukan," and its English nickname is "Ring of Fire," referring to the zone of volcanoes that encircles the Pacific Ocean. Plant and animal life from around the Pacific rim are shown both above and below water. Watching penguins swimming underwater is a fascinating sight for all ages. The aquarium is open daily from 10:00 A.M. to 8:00 P.M., with extended hours in summer. From December through February, the aquarium is closed on the third Wednesday of each month. The aquarium is a 5- to 8-minute walk from Osakako Station on the Chuo Line.

Zoos

KANTO AREA

Ueno Zoo

9-83 Ueno Koen, Taito-ku, Tokyo　東京都台東区上野公園 9-83
☎ (03) 3828-5171
🚇 Ueno Station, Ginza, Hibiya, JR Yamanote, JR Joban lines

This is where the pandas are! Ueno Zoo is the largest zoo in Tokyo, with over 7,000 mammals, reptiles, amphibians, birds, and other animals. A children's zoo and an aquarium are also here. The zoo is open 9:30 A.M. to 4:30 P.M. every day except Monday and holidays. Admission is ¥400 for adults, ¥100 for junior high school students and free for children under twelve.

Tama Zoo

7-1-1 Hodokubo, Hino-shi, Tokyo　東京都日野市程久保 7-1-1
☎ (0425) 91-1611
☗ Tama Dobutsu Koen Station, Keio Line

As many as 210 different kinds of animals roam around in this natural setting. Special attractions include an Insect House with nocturnal animals, a Butterfly House, and a bus ride that, for a small fee, takes you through an area with free-roaming lions. The zoo is open from 9:30 A.M. to 4:00 P.M. every day except Monday and New Year's. Admission to the zoo is ¥400 for adults, ¥100 for middle school children, and free for children under twelve.

Edogawa Ward Nature Zoo

3-2-1 Kita-Kasai, Edogawa-ku, Tokyo　東京都江戸川区北葛西 3-2-1
☎ (03) 3680-0777
☗ Nishi-Kasai Station, Tozai Line

There are twenty-one kinds of animals at this small zoo and it is open every day except Monday and New Year's. Admission is free. To get there, take the Tozai Line to Nishi-Kasai Station and walk for about twelve minutes, or take bus #21 bound for Shin Koiwa or Funabori.

Itabashi Ward Children's Zoo

3-50-1 Itabashi, Itabashi-ku, Tokyo　東京都板橋区板橋 3-50-1 東板橋公園内
☎ (03) 3963-8003
☗ Itabashi Kuyakushomae Station, Toei Mita Line

The Itabashi Ward Children's Zoo has farm animals and pony rides. The zoo is open every day except Monday and New Year's from 10:00 A.M. to 4:00 P.M., December through February, and 10:00 A.M. to 4:30 P.M., March through November. Admission is free, and it is conveniently located a 7-minute walk from Itabashi Kuyakushomae Station.

Hamura City Zoological Park

4122 Hane, Hamura-shi, Nishitama-gun, Tokyo　東京都羽村市羽 4122
☎ (0425) 55-2581
☗ Hamura Station, JR Ome Line

This park is open from 9:00 A.M. to 4:30 P.M. year-round, and admission is ¥200 for adults, ¥50 for children. To get there, take the JR Chuo Line to Tachikawa Station and transfer to the JR Ome Line. From Hamura Station take a bus bound for Hamura Danchi.

Nogeyama Zoological Garden of Yokohama

63-10 Oimatsu-cho, Nishi-ku, Yokohama-shi, Kanagawa-ken
☎ (045) 231-1696　神奈川県横浜市西区老松町 63-10
🚉 Hinode-cho Station, Keihin Kyuko Line

This zoological garden comprises a 3.2-hectare garden and a children's petting zoo. It is open from 9:30 A.M. to 4:30 P.M. except Mondays. Admission is free. The park is a 10-minute walk from Hinode-cho Station.

Saitama Children's Zoo

554 Iwadono, Higashimatsuyama-shi, Saitama-ken　埼玉県東松山市岩殿 554
☎ (0493) 35-1234
🚉 Takasaka Station, Tobu Tojo Line

The zoo is in a 66-hectare park, which is situated in a natural mountain setting. Hours are 9:30 A.M. to 4:30 P.M., December to February, and 9:30 A.M. to 5:00 P.M., March to November; it is closed Mondays. Admission is ¥400 for adults, ¥200 for children. From the station, take a bus bound for Hatoyama New Town for a 5-minute trip to the Dobutsu Koen Mae bus stop.

KANSAI AREA

Oji Zoo

3-1 Oji-cho, Nada-ku, Kobe-shi, Hyogo-ken　兵庫県神戸市灘区王子町 3-1
☎ (078) 861-5624
🚉 Hankyu Oji Koen Station, Hankyu Kobe Honsen Line

Oji Zoo is both a zoo and an amusement park. The zoo is large enough for the kids to get exercise out of doors, and the animals are easy to see and in clean cages. The amusement park is on the small side, but there are enough rides and concession stands to thrill anyone under eight or so. The park is open from 9:00 A.M. to 4:30 P.M. daily except Wednesdays. Children under twelve are admitted free, and those older pay only ¥400. The zoo is in Oji Park, a 3-minute walk from Hankyu Oji Koen Station.

Kyoto Zoological Garden

Hoshoji-cho, Okazaki, Sakyo-ku, Kyoto-shi, Kyoto-fu
☎ (075) 771-0210　京都府京都市左京区岡崎法勝寺町岡崎公園内
🚉 Demachiyanagi and Hankyu Shijo Kawaramachi stations, Hankyu Kyoto Line

When your kids have had enough of shrines and temples in Kyoto, take them to this small zoo for a refreshing break. Located in Okazaki Park just a few blocks from the Kyoto Imperial Palace, this zoo also has a petting zoo where children can listen to talks about the animals and see them up close. Hours are 9:00 A.M. to 4:30 P.M. and they are closed on Mondays. Admission is ¥300; free for children under twelve. To get there, walk five blocks from Demachiyanagi Station or take bus #27 from Hankyu Shijo Kawaramachi Station. An alternative is to take bus #5 from Kyoto Station. The bus trip takes about thirty minutes; get off at the Kyoto Zoological Garden bus stop.

7

Entertaining
the
Kids

NO PROBLEM, DAD!

For kids as well as parents, moving to Japan can seem like accelerating into the fast lane. We have often wondered if we should buy our children their own appointment books to keep track of lessons, play dates, and outings.

There are many opportunities in Japan for parents and children to experience Japanese as well as Western culture in the form of sports, art, and music lessons in a cross-cultural setting. Once children enter the first grade, their free time is at a premium. Therefore, the time to begin taking advantage of these programs is when they are toddlers and preschoolers. Besides teaching your child a new skill, many of these activities will expose him to the Japanese language.

A word about the language difference: when you call to get information about many of the activities listed below, the voice on the other end of the phone will probably be speaking Japanese. Don't let this deter you. If you do not speak Japanese, one of the obvious phrases to try first is, "*eigo ga dekimasuka*?" ("Do you speak English?"). Often the person on the phone does have an elementary English vocabulary, and if you are patient you can get the information you need. Don't be afraid to ask for information to be repeated ("*moichido itte kudasai*") or to ask the person to speak more slowly ("*yukkuri hanashite kudasai*") Other times they will tell you to wait a minute ("*chotto matte kudasai*"), and perhaps someone who speaks English will come to the phone. Whether you end up practicing your latest Japanese lesson or you give someone else a chance to practice his or her English, there are ways to get around the language barrier.

EXTRA-CURRICULAR ACTIVITIES

A wide choice of sports, art, and music classes are available to your children. While you live in Japan your child has a unique opportunity to learn some of Japan's traditional sports in addition to ice-skating, horseback riding, ballet, and other activities. Judo, karate, and many other martial arts teachers hold classes specifically for children. Besides martial arts, the Suzuki music school is here. What better place than Japan for your child to learn by this world-famous music teaching method?

A word of warning about the recitals that go along with some of these classes: Parents are expected to pay a rather exorbitant fee. This large amount of money (often up to ¥100,000 or more) goes toward the cost of renting the performance space and perhaps part of it is the teacher's bonus. Music and dance classes in particular hold such recitals. It would be wise to find out how often recitals would be held and how much money you would be expected to pay before committing yourself to such a class.

The arrangements for many of these classes must be made in Japanese. Often registration forms can be filled out in English, but you must be able to read the questions. If you do not have anyone who can help you with this, ask one of the parents whose children are in the same class or the instructor. This is a great way to meet some of the other parents. You will find that once you break the ice, the parents will be very willing to include you in other activities that their children may be involved in.

Many Japanese children attend private extracurricular classes after school. Abacus, calligraphy, piano, and art are some of the most popular classes. Try to seek out a Japanese neighbor or friend with a child the same age as yours. Chances are that they will know about private schools in your area. An example of one of these private schools is Azabu Art Forum (Yokoyama Bldg. 3F, 4-11-3 Nishi Azabu, Tokyo, (03) 3406-4578). They offer classes such as piano, violin, music listening, penmanship, Japanese painting, and much more. The cost is reasonable at between ¥8,000 to ¥10,000 per month for a two-hour class each week.

Kumon is a private tutorship program that holds lessons year-round throughout the country. Beginning at an early age, children can join these small groups, which often meet in the teacher's home. The fee for these classes is extremely reasonable; for example, in Tokyo ¥5,000 per month would enable a five-year-old to meet twice a week for a 30- to 60-minute class in Japanese language, English language, or math. Older children can choose from a wider variety of subjects.

Many of our friends use this program in the summer months to keep up their children's Japanese-language skills. The atmosphere is relaxed, and because the lessons are brief the children do not feel as if they are attending school.

For more information, call the Kumon Institute of Education, Tokyo Administrative Office at (03) 3234-7011, or write to them at 3-1 Goban-cho, Chiyoda-ku, Tokyo.

SPORTS

Classes for young children in gymnastics, tumbling, ballet, and the various martial arts are available at either private clubs and gymnasiums or through ward or city programs. Each ward and city offers different kinds of activities, and each season the classes usually change. For very young children, there may be a mother and baby class of some sort in swimming or dance, for example. Classes for older children are held on weekends, after school, and during the Japanese school vacation period. For information, contact your local ward or city office.

Private gymnasiums and sports clubs usually hold adult classes, but there are a few that have children's classes as well. Often the international schools offer their space to independent teachers for classes after school hours or on the weekends.

We were disappointed to find no comprehensive listing anywhere of sports organizations or classes for children. Our Japanese friends say that word of mouth is the best resource for finding a class near your home or school. Signboards and advertisements in papers are often written only in Japanese, so don't be afraid to ask if you see something that perhaps would be of interest to your child.

Once in a class, your child may have difficulty understanding the Japanese instructions or feel he is behind at times; but remember that for young children in Japan, the most important thing is not how well the individual performs. In the Japanese classes and schools our children have attended, the spirit of *ganbare*, or "do your best," is by far the outstanding lesson that comes through, and children of all ages can benefit from that.

BALLET AND GYMNASTICS

Formal ballet schools abound in Tokyo and most larger cities in Japan. If you want your child to study ballet, there is a listing of most of the schools in the Japanese-language Yellow Pages. If you are more interested in a fun ballet/tumbling/gymnastics class, contact the Nihon Ballet Kyokai at

1-1-1 Jinnan, Shibuya-ku, Tokyo, (03) 3462-5524 or the Nihon Gymnastics Kyokai at Primera Dogenzaka 1103, 1-15-3 Dogenzaka, Shibuya-ku, Tokyo, (03) 3481-2341 for information on ballet and gymnastics classes for children ages three to fifteen. Only Japanese is spoken. Here we list some schools in greater Tokyo. For class information in Kansai, call the community center nearest you (see chap. 12).

International Gymnastics Club (IGC)

3-45-11 Ebisu 201, Shibuya-ku, Tokyo　東京都渋谷区恵比寿 3-45-11-201
☎ (03) 3440-0384 fax (03) 3440-0628

IGC is run by Lance Lee, an American fitness coach and gymnast. The club holds classes at a number of the international schools after school and on Saturdays. The club's motto, Reaching for the Stars, is embodied in the "I Can!" attitude encouraged in classes to build confidence and a positive attitude. Gymnastics, along with some fitness classes for adults, are the means through which the teachers communicate this message to everyone they come in contact with. IGC also holds summer sessions (see later in this chapter) and birthday parties (see chap. 8).

Ana's School of Dance

2-4-12 West, Kita Senzoku, Ota-ku, Tokyo　東京都大田区北千束 2-4-12 ウェスト
☎ (03) 3748-4639 fax (03) 3748-4839

This school is run by Ana Keates, a British-trained ballerina. She holds ballet, tap, and jazz dance classes at various locations in Tokyo, including several international schools.

Saiga Ballet

2-20 Kagurazaka, Shinjuku-ku, Tokyo　東京都新宿区神楽坂 2-20
☎ (03) 3268-3183

For nearly thirty years Saiga Ballet has offered classes in classical ballet for children aged three and up. The founder of the school, Toshiko Saiga, is a former principal ballerina with the Komaki Ballet. Ms. Saiga speaks excellent English and encourages foreign children to study with her. Saiga Ballet students are invited to participate in the annual Music For Youth (see music section in this chapter) performances of such classics as the Nutcracker.

Yokohama Children's Ballet

2-121-3 Kosugigotencho 105, Nakahara-ku, Kawasaki-shi, Kanagawa-ken
☎ (044) 3711-5653　神奈川県川崎市中原区小杉御殿町 2-121-3-105

The Yokohama Children's Ballet offers classes in the Yokohama area for students starting from the age of three up to adults. The classes emphasize coordination, musicality, and creativity while teaching the basics of classical ballet. The school is directed by Helen Price, a graduate of Canada's National Ballet School.

Chacott

1-20-8 Jinnan, Shibuya-ku, Tokyo　東京都渋谷区神南 1-20-8
☎ (03) 3476-1311

Located directly across from the Seibu SEED store in Shibuya, Chacott is not a ballet school but rather a store for all types of dance supplies. Leotards, tap shoes, ballet shoes—everything for dancers, both adult and children, can be found at this store. The store is also a good resource for brochures from the many ballet schools around town, and they may be able to give you a lead on the right school for your child.

TENNIS

Tennis is taught in Japanese at some of the private sports clubs and at the public courts run by the ward or city offices. To find a class in English, contact the international school or community center nearest you.

In Tokyo, the Krissman Tennis School (founded 1984) holds classes in Roppongi, Setagaya, and some of the international schools. Classes are available for children from the age of five to adults, and both group (six to eight students) and private lessons are available. In 1991, the school introduced Short Tennis to Japan. This is a program for five-year-olds and is available at their schools and also at some of the international schools. Summer programs are also available (see the summer program section in this chapter). For more information, call the office at (03) 3325-0924.

MARTIAL ARTS

The various forms of martial arts all have their origins in the Orient. The most popular and easiest forms are taught throughout Japan in private training halls, or *dojo*, or under the auspices of the wards and cities. Students can begin in some of the classes at the tender age of four, and there are classes for all levels, even for housewives and senior citizens. The brief descriptions below may help you in choosing a class for your child. The information numbers given are the central headquarters—not only the most likely place to find an English-speaker, but also the best place to get information for all of Japan.

Aikido

Call the Tokyo office of the International Aikido Federation at (03) 3203-9236 for information in Japanese or English on aikido classes, or write to them at 17-18 Wakamatsu-cho, Shinjuku-ku, Tokyo. Children may study this martial art form from as early as age five. Aikido was developed in the early part of the twentieth century and is based on an old art form called *aikijutsu*. Its philosophy is based on the idea of overcoming an opponent by using only the minimum amount of force necessary. Known as "the Way of the Spirit and Harmony," aikido is a system of joint locking, throwing, and striking quite different from judo or karate. Practitioners attempt to follow the attacker's line of motion, first overbalancing him and then locking either a wrist or joint to subdue him.

Judo
Call or write the All-Japan Judo Federation, c/o Kodokan, 1-16-30 Kasuga, Bunkyo-ku, Tokyo, (03) 3818-4171 or (03) 3811-7151 for information in Japanese.

Judo is world famous as a system of throwing and grappling with an unarmed opponent. Beginners first learn falling methods, followed by throws, strangles, and hold-downs. Boys and girls from fourth grade and up are eligible for classes in most wards and private facilities. For adults, universities provide excellent training facilities that often nonuniversity members can use. Contact the university nearest you for more information.

Karate
Call or write the Federation of All Japan Karate-Do at Senpakushinko Bldg., 1-15-16 Toranomon, Minato-ku, Tokyo, (03) 3503-6639 for information in Japanese or English. Classes are available for children from the age of six.
Karate, which originated in Okinawa, is a system of empty-hand fighting with the emphasis on punching, kicking, and blocking. Beginners first exercise to improve their fitness and then practice basics in groups, gradually progressing to working with a partner for speed and timing. Karate is split into some twenty different styles, or *ryu*, and you will need to decide which style you prefer to learn.

Kendo
Call or write the Tokyo Kendo Federation at Shinkokusai Bldg. 933, 3-4-1 Marunouchi, Chiyoda-ku, Tokyo, (03) 3211-5967 for information in Japanese. For information in English, call or write Mr. Satoh, c/o Nippon Budokan, 2-3 Kitanomaru Koen, Chiyoda-ku, Tokyo, (03) 3211-5804. Kendo classes are available for children from around the age of eight.
Kendo, or the Way of the Sword, is practiced with both *katana*, the long Japanese sword, and with *shinai*, its bamboo counterpart. Combatants wear protective armor and attempt to strike each other with the *shinai* on

the head, torso, or forearms in imitation of the medieval Japanese art of actual sword fighting. In kendo, the sword is gripped with both hands, as opposed to the one-hand grip used in Western fencing.

T'ai Chi Chuan

For more information on classes for all ages (children can start studying from the age of four), call the Japan T'ai Chi Association at (03) 3371-3362 or write them at 2-32-17 Higashi Nakano, Nakano-ku, Tokyo. Or contact the All-Japan Soft Style Martial Arts Federation (03) 3400-9371. They will answer questions in Japanese.

T'ai-chi chuan, known as *taikyoken* in Japanese, is a martial art form that has been imported unchanged from China. It is probably the softest and least aggressive of the combative sports, consisting of a slow, rhythmic flow of motion aimed at promoting balance, timing, and general good health. It is also designed to promote a balance between the body and the spirit as well as between the yin and yang elements—motion and stillness, emptiness and fullness, hardness and softness. It is distinguished by its unusually slow, circular movements.

HORSEBACK RIDING

Horseback riding is one of the more difficult sports to pursue as a regular hobby, especially in Tokyo. Besides the hefty cost, there is also distance to consider. Most of the horseback riding clubs are an hour or more out of the city by public transportation.

For those who simply want an opportunity for their children to ride on a horse, pony rides are given at several of the large parks (see chap. 5). At Baji Koen (2-1-1 Kamiyoga, Setagaya-ku, Tokyo, (03) 3429-5101), twenty minutes by taxi from Shibuya Station, one Sunday a month is set aside for a horse show at which free horse rides are offered for children age four to ten. The children are allowed to ride the large thoroughbreds with volunteers from the police equestrian unit. This is a very special event; you must pick up your free tickets for the horse rides two hours before the show. The date and time of the event varies from month to month; so call the park at the beginning of the month to find out when the horse festival will take place.

In the Kobe area, riding is available at the Kobe Joba Club, and the Rokkosan Model Pasture Stables. See *Kids in Kobe* (chap. 12) for more information.

GREATER TOKYO RIDING CLUBS

For the serious equestrian, there are horseback riding clubs that you can join. Like other sports clubs, the riding clubs ask for an initial membership fee and then an annual fee. Many of the clubs will provide transportation from the nearest train station to the club if you let them know when you are coming. Boots and riding gear can be rented or purchased at most of the clubs. Visitor passes are available at an hourly rate, and both visitors and members must make a reservation in advance. Below is a short list of some of the larger and more accessible riding clubs available to Tokyo residents.

Avalon Riding Club

3-19-2 Noge, Setagaya-ku, Tokyo　東京都世田谷区野毛 3–19–2
☎ (03) 3702-1770
📞 Futakotamagawaen Station, Shin Tamagawa, Oimachi, Denentoshi lines

Crane Horse Riding Club

286 Kita Yatsu, Chiba-shi, Chiba-ken　千葉県千葉市北谷津 286
☎ (0472) 28-5531
📞 Chiba Station, JR Sobu Line

La Hacienda Riding School

4442 Akuwa, Seya-ku, Yokohama-shi, Kanagawa-ken
☎ (045) 363-2501　神奈川県横浜市瀬谷区阿久和 4442
📞 Mitsukyo Station, Sagamitetsudo Line (from Yokohama Station)

Machida Riding Center

37 Hayamajima, Shiroyama-machi, Tsukui-gun, Kanagawa-ken
☎ (0427) 82-0262　神奈川県津久井郡城山町葉山島 37
📞 Hashimoto Station, JR Yokohama Line

Tokyo Horseback Riding Club

4-8 Kamizono-cho, Yoyogi, Shibuya-ku, Tokyo　東京都渋谷区代々木神園町 4–8
☎ (03) 3370-0984
📞 Sangubashi Station, Odakyu Line

ICE-SKATING

Ice-skating can provide exercise and fun for the entire family. There are many rinks open all year round for those who wish to take lessons or maintain their form. For all the rinks, opening and closing dates and times can vary from year to year, so it is a good idea to call first to be on the safe side. Some rinks are open only in the winter months, others are located within or adjacent to an amusement park (see chap. 6). All of the large rinks have rental skates for adults and children; the rental fee is usually an extra charge above admission. For lessons, call the rink—preferably in Japanese—to inquire. We have many friends who take their children to lessons with a Japanese teacher. Ice skaters face a universal set of challenges, and therefore, the children are able to learn the basics despite the language difference.

If you are outside the Tokyo area, call the Nihon Ice-Skating Renmei at (03) 3481-2351 for information about local rinks.

OUTDOOR SKATING RINKS

Dreamland Skating Rink

700 Matano-cho, Totsuka-ku, Yokohama-shi, Kanagawa-ken
☎ (045) 851-1411　神奈川県横浜市戸塚区双野町700
🚻 Ofuna Station, JR Keihin Tohoku, JR Yokosuka, JR Tokaido lines

Open from mid-November to mid-March. Rates: children ¥900, adults ¥2,000. No lessons available.

Hibiya City Ice-Skating Rink

Hibiya Kokusai Bldg., 2-2-3 Uchisaiwaicho, Chiyoda-ku, Tokyo
☎ (03) 3595-0295　東京都千代田区内幸町2-2-3 日比谷国際ビル
🚻 Uchisaiwaicho Station, Toei Mita Line

Open from mid-November to mid-March. Hours: Monday through Saturday noon to 8:00 P.M. Sunday and holidays 10:00 A.M. to 6:00 P.M. Rates: ¥300. Lessons available for children only.

INDOOR SKATING RINKS

Citizen Skate Rink

4-29-27 Takadanobaba, Shinjuku-ku, Tokyo　東京都新宿区高田馬場4-29-27
☎ (03) 3371-0910
🚻 Takadanobaba Station, JR Yamanote, Seibu Shinjuku, Tozai lines

Open year-round. Hours: Monday through Saturday noon to 7:45 P.M. Sunday and holidays 10:00 A.M. to 7:45 P.M. Rates: children ¥700, adults ¥1,000. Lessons available for both children and adults.

Ikebukuro Ice-Skating Center

2-5-26 Kami Ikebukuro, Toshima-ku, Tokyo　東京都豊島区上池袋2-5-26
☎ (03) 3916-7171
🚻 Ikebukuro Station, JR Yamanote, Tobu Tojo, Yurakucho, Marunouchi, Seibu Ikebukuro, JR Saikyo lines

Open October through April. Hours: Monday through Saturday noon to 8:00 P.M. Sunday and holidays 9:00 A.M. to 8:00 P.M. Rates: children ¥1,250, adults ¥1,950. Lessons available for both children and adults.

Kanagawa Skating Rink

1-1 Hirodai Otamachi, Kanagawa-ku, Yokohama-shi, Kanagawa-ken
☎ (045) 321-3561　神奈川県横浜市神奈川区広台太田町 1-1
🚇 Higashi Kanagawa Station, JR Keihin Tohoku Line

Open year-round. Hours: Monday through Saturday 10:00 A.M. to 9:00 P.M.
Sundays and holidays 9:00 A.M. to 9:00 P.M. Rates: children ¥700, adults
¥1,100. Lessons available for both children and adults.

Korakuen Ice Palace

1-3 Koraku, Bunkyo-ku, Tokyo　東京都文京区後楽 1-3
☎ (03) 3811-2111
🚇 Suidobashi Station, JR Sobu Line; or Korakuen Station, Marunouchi Line

Open October through April (opening time varies from year to year).
Hours: 10:00 A.M. to 8:00 P.M. daily including holidays. Rates: children
under twelve ¥700, students ¥1,000, adults ¥1,300 (including skate rental).
Lessons available for both children and adults.

Meiji Jingu Skating Rink

5 Kasumigaoka-cho, Shinjuku-ku, Tokyo　東京都新宿区霞岳町 5
☎ (03) 3403-3456
🚇 Sendagaya Station, JR Sobu Line

Open October through April. Hours: Monday through Saturday 10:00 A.M.
to 8:00 P.M., Sunday and holidays 9:00 A.M. to 8:00 P.M. Rates: children
under twelve ¥600, students ¥800, adults ¥1,000. Lessons available for
both children and adults.

Shin Yokohama Prince Hotel Skate Center

2-11 Shin Yokohama, Kohoku-ku, Yokohama-shi, Kanagawa-ken
☎ (045) 474-1112　神奈川県横浜市港北区新横浜 2-11
🚇 Shin Yokohama Station, JR Yokohama, JR Tokaido lines

Open year-round. Hours: Monday through Friday 3:00 P.M. to 7:00 P.M.,
Saturday 1:00 P.M. to 7:00 P.M., Sunday and holidays 10:00 A.M. to 6:00 P.M.
Rates: children ¥600 for 1 hour or ¥850 for 2 hours, adults ¥900 for 1 hour
or ¥1,500 for 2 hours (both fees include skate rental).

ROLLER-SKATING

For information on classes and rinks nearest you, call the Zen-Nihon
Roller-Skating Renmei, #3 Lions Mansion 506, 1-31-13 Higashi Ikebukuro,
Toshima-ku, Tokyo, (03) 3983-6335 in Japanese or (03) 3811-2111 (ask for
Ms. Oikawa) in English. Classes are available for children from the age of
two or three.

Boy Scouts and Girl Scouts

Boy Scouts and Girl Scouts are both international organizations concerned with the development and education of young people. Boy Scouts of Nippon is a large organization whose meetings and business are conducted in Japanese. Boy Scouts of America (Japan) is the name under which the international and foreign communities operate their troops. There are more than 100 packs of Boy Scouts in Japan, and they include Scouts from all over the world.

The Boy Scouts of America (Japan) troops are tightly controlled and organized, and there are strict requirements that must be met before a troop may be formed. Children may enter the Scouting program in first grade (age six) and continue to be active in Scouting the rest of their lives. Those who do not live near an organized Scout troop can participate in the Lone Scout program. In this program, the parent and child work together toward the goals and achievements that normally the child would be working on independently. This program also allows children who have been Scouts, or who want to become Scouts when they return to their home country, to keep up with other Scouts their age.

For information on the Boy Scouts of America (Japan) program, contact the Boy Scouts of America, Far East Council, Yokota Air Base, Bldg. 2000, Fussa-shi, Tokyo 197, (0425) 52-2511 ext. 8797/8.

For those interested in the Boy Scouts of Nippon, contact the National Headquarters, Boy Scouts of Nippon, 4-11-10 Osawa, Mitaka-shi, Tokyo 181, (0422) 31-5161 or fax (0422) 32-0010.

Besides the Girl Scouts of Nippon, the Girl Scouts of America are also in Japan. Their organization is not as tightly controlled as the Boy Scouts of America (Japan), making it fairly simple to start up your own troop. Girls from first grade on can become involved. The Girl Scout troops do not need a sponsor in the way that the Boy Scouts do, and so troops often start up and then disband when a particular leader moves away.

The best way to find out about Girl Scouts of America (Japan) programs in your area is to ask at the international schools near you or to contact the West Pacific Girl Scout Council, Yokota Air Base, Bldg. 2000, Fussa-shi, Tokyo 197, (0425) 52-2511 ext. 5880.

For information on the Girl Scouts of Nippon, contact their office at 1-4-3 Nishihara, Shibuya-ku, Tokyo 151, or call (03) 3460-0701 or fax (03) 3460-8383.

Music

Kawai Music Schools

Kawai music schools are located throughout Japan. They offer classes for children from the age of three in both piano and electric piano. For information about classes in your area, contact the Kawai Shibuya Music School at Kawai Sound City Bldg. 5F, 1-11-5 Jinnan, Shibuya-ku, Tokyo 150. The phone number is (03) 3463-7741, and hours are from 11:00 A.M. to 7:00 P.M.

Suzuki Method

The world-famous Suzuki method of teaching music to children began right here in Japan some fifty years ago. The founder, Shin'ichi Suzuki, believed that children can learn to play instruments in much the same way that they learn to speak. This means that beginning at a very young age, perhaps even before the child is born, he or she can be influenced toward becoming a musician.

Lessons for children usually begin around age three. Before age three, the Suzuki method maintains that the child can be prepared for music lessons by listening and observing those around him. Usually the parents of a child under age three are encouraged to learn an instrument themselves by the Suzuki method, to pave the way for the child's lessons. Whenever the child starts lessons, the parent must understand that he or she, too, is going to learn along with the child. A parent must attend all music classes with the child, and in essence learn how to play the instrument with the child. The parent can then direct and observe the child's progress when practicing at home.

Children may start piano, violin, or cello lessons at the age of three and flute lessons at the age of four or five. The Suzuki office in Tokyo, (03) 3295-0270, can provide you with information in Japanese on classes and teachers anywhere in Japan. The Suzuki head office, (0263) 32-7171, can provide you with a contact number, perhaps someone who speaks English. Teachers are available throughout Japan, and many are able to speak a little English.

Yamaha Music Schools

Yamaha music classes are available at numerous locations in Tokyo and other major cities around Japan. For information about class curriculum and school locations in your area, contact the Corporate Public Relations Office of the Yamaha Music Foundation. They are located near the Otori Shrine in Meguro (3-24-22 Shimomeguro, Meguro-ku, Tokyo 153, (03) 3719-3104 fax (03) 3794-1654). English-speaking teachers are available at some locations.

Music For Youth
2-21-2 Nishi Azabu, Minato-ku, Tokyo　東京都港区西麻布 2-21-2
☎ (03) 3400-3386

Music for Youth has been in existence since 1939 and was the first group to introduce educational symphony concerts to Japan. This nonprofit, educational association serves the international community by presenting concerts at low cost for students and family groups. They also provide musical opportunities for handicapped young people, maintain a music lending-library, run a summer music camp at Karuizawa in Nagano-ken, and conduct international music contests.

The force and founder behind this organization is Eloise Cunningham, a remarkable lady who works tirelessly to bring music and education together for children of all ages and races. Music for Youth sponsors a number of concerts by professional and amateur artists and groups (ballet, opera, symphony) each year. They also publish *Forecasts* (see chap. 12), a magazine with Tokyo arts and ticket information, and maps. The group is financed by membership dues, special grants, and sales of tickets.

Call or write if you would like to become a member or want more information.

Theater for Children
1-6-3 Azabu Juban 202, Minato-ku, Tokyo　東京都港区麻布十番 1-6-3-202
☎ (03) 3403-1844

Theater for Children began more than fifteen years ago when a group of foreign women saw a need for children's theater for the English-speaking community. They produce two shows annually, one in the fall in Tokyo and a road show in spring that they take to the major international schools around Tokyo. A volunteer, nonprofit organization, they are always in need of people to help with sets, costumes, music, and, of course, acting. For more information, call Terry Osada at (03) 3403-1844.

MODELING

Upon moving to Japan, many foreigners are told that this may be their golden opportunity to become rich and famous. There are many openings in Japan for both Japanese and foreigners interested in modeling, commercials, and voice work, even for those without prior experience.

For the parents of young children, this poses a curious dilemma. Foreign children are used frequently in advertising campaigns of all types, and even if you do not actively seek modeling jobs for your child, you may be approached with an offer at some time. Most parents' first reaction is, "It is not something I would do in my native country, but since we are here for a couple of years . . ." Modeling can either be an occasional or regular hobby, depending on the level of commitment you choose.

Commitment is a word we often hear from parents who are involved with modeling. The parents are the ones who must take time out of their schedule to accompany children to tryouts, rehearsals, and shootings. Some people are more willing to do this than others, and until you have been to a few jobs you can't really decide how much time you want to commit to your child's modeling career.

Perhaps your child is not really interested in modeling. However, a child often has no interest initially, but after being hired for a job he enjoys it so much he wants to do it again. If you would like to give modeling a try, here are some basic tips on how to get started in Japan.

Choose an agency or two that are conveniently located near you or that have been recommended by friends. Call the agency for suggestions regarding photographs and make an appointment to take your child to see them. Usually for a child under eight or so, it is not worth the money to have professional photos taken. Just take some head and shoulder shots at home and make extra copies for the agencies. Also, it saves time if you know your child's body measurements in centimeters, along with his shoe, underwear, and clothing size in Japanese sizes.

Once you have visited the agency, they will most likely call you for an audition for a job. Many experienced models choose not to go to mass auditions, but when you are starting out it is best to attend all available auditions. If you cannot make it, apologize and thank the agency, but ask them to call you again. Once you are established with one or two agencies, you can let them know what types of jobs you are most interested in and request that they call you only for those.

Many of the agencies listed below handle adults as well as children, and it may be worth your while to sign up with one of them yourself. Even if you don't look like a traditional "model," these agencies handle requests for older adults, average-looking Americans, Italian-looking-males, etc. You never know when you might get your big break. . . .

AGENCIES IN TOKYO

Isop

Imperial Akasaka Ichibankan #317, 8-13-19 Akasaka, Minato-ku, Tokyo
☎ (03) 3405-7151　東京都港区赤坂 8-13-19 赤坂一番館 317
This agency will take foreigners of any age, and they have been in business for eight years.

Carrotte

4-3-1 Azabu Juban #1022, Minato-ku, Tokyo　東京都港区麻布十番 4-3-1-1022
☎ (03) 3453-8251
Carrotte has been representing foreign and Japanese children from new-borns to eighteen-year-olds for fifteen years.

Central

Aoyama Tower Bldg. 3F, 2-24-15 Minami Aoyama, Minato-ku, Tokyo
☎ (03) 3405-5511　東京都港区南青山 2-24-15 青山タワービル 3F
This twenty-five-year-old agency represents newborns to fifteen-year-old Japanese and foreign models.

Cosmic

Eleven Bldg. 3F, 2-19-7 Takadanobaba, Shinjuku-ku, Tokyo
☎ (03) 3232-6604　東京都新宿区高田馬場 2-19-7 タックイレブンビル 3F
Established three years ago, this relatively new agency represents foreigners or Japanese of any age.

Echo

Onosho Bldg. 3F, 8-12-6 Ginza, Chuo-ku, Tokyo
☎ (03) 3542-4731　東京都中央区銀座 8-12-6 小野商ビル 3F
Echo handles foreigners of any age, from babies to their grandparents. They have been in business for twenty-five years.

E Promotions

7-8-703 Daikanyama-cho, Shibuya-ku, Tokyo　東京都渋谷区代官山町 7-8-703
☎ (03) 3770-6191
One of the oldest agencies in Tokyo, E Promotions has been in business for thirty-three years and will represent foreigners or Japanese of all ages.

Free Flight

Meitsufuyoku Nakameguro #202, 3-10-3 Kami Meguro, Meguro-ku, Tokyo
☎ (03) 3760-3733　東京都目黒区上目黒 3-10-3 メイツフヨク中目黒 202
In business for three years, Free Flight handles foreigners and Japanese of all ages.

I.M.O.

1-9-16 Nishi Azabu #1309, Minato-ku, Tokyo　東京都港区西麻布 1-9-16-1309
☎ (03) 3405-0425
Established six years ago, this company represents foreigners of all ages

K and M Promotions

2-10-25 Kita Aoyama #302, Minato-ku, Tokyo　東京都港区北青山 2-10-25-302
☎ (03) 3404-9429
This agency has been representing foreigners of all ages for eight years.

Mickey's Co.

5-1-27 Akasaka #4A, Minato-ku, Tokyo　東京都港区赤坂 5-1-27-4A
☎ (03) 3582-8720
One of the newer agencies in town, they handle foreigners of all ages.

Office Be

3-1-7 Setagaya 303, Setagaya-ku, Tokyo　東京都世田谷区世田谷 3-1-7-303
☎ (03) 3439-4846
This agency handles foreigners of all ages for various movie and TV jobs.

Romeo

Bellza Roppongi Mansion #703, 4-1-9 Roppongi, Minato-ku, Tokyo
☎ (03) 3585-7733　東京都港区六本木 4-1-9-703
This agency handles children and adults for all types of modeling jobs. A fairly new company, it is managed by an American.

Sugar and Spice

5-4-11 Hiroo, Shibuya-ku, Tokyo
☎ (03) 3280-5481 東京都渋谷区広尾 5-4-11
Known for its work with children, this ten-year-old company takes foreign children from newborn to eighteen years.

Tsuboya Enterprises

Noa Dogenzaka #722, 2-15-1 Dogenzaka, Shibuya-ku, Tokyo
☎ (03) 3770-9501　東京都渋谷区道玄坂 2-15-1-722
Young and old alike, all age-groups are represented by this agency. Specializing in foreign models, they have been in business for fifteen years.

KANSAI AREA

Creamy and D Guys

Ekimae Dai 2 Bldg. 2F, 1-2-2 Umeda, Kita-ku, Osaka-shi, Osaka-fu
☎ (06) 347-7705　大阪府大阪市北区梅田 1-2-2 駅前第 2 ビル 2F

Creamy & D Guys has been in business in Osaka for five years, representing both foreigners and Japanese from newborns up to twenty. They will also represent adults who have modeling experience.

PORTFOLIO PHOTOS

Glamour Shots

1-5-10 Azabu Juban, Minato ku, Tokyo　東京都港区麻布十番 1–5–10
☎ (03) 3497-1345

This photography studio is a franchise outfit from the United States and, although they do not specialize in kids' photos, they are the best around for modeling portfolios. Prices are quite reasonable and the picture proofs are instantly visible on a TV monitor within minutes of the session.

See chapter 8 for more information on photography studios.

SUMMER PROGRAMS

Summer programs for children range from intensive language courses to outdoor recreation. Some of the offerings will be in a bilingual setting, others all in English or all in Japanese. Below, we have listed some summer offerings, but there are many more throughout Japan. Often an individual city or prefecture will run what they call a youth symposium, where Japanese and foreign children come together for a weekend of cultural exchange. Sometimes the international schools offer day camp or summer school programs. Large corporations also sponsor camps for children with special interests or needs. The best way to find out about these kinds of activities is to call the international school nearest you, starting in about April. Usually the organizers of these events will send information to the schools for publicity.

During the Japanese school summer holiday, the wards and cities offer special classes in sports, language, and art. The *jido-kan*, or children's centers, and the National Children's Castle in Tokyo (see Rainy Day Activities Section in this chapter) also offer special one- or two-week classes during this time.

YMCA Japan

YMCA head office: 2-3-18 Nishi-Waseda, Shiniuku-ku, Tokyo
☎ (03) 3203-0171　東京都新宿区西早稲田 2–3–18

YMCA Japan runs day camps and overnight camps year-round. There are branches of the YMCA throughout Japan, and each runs its own programs. Most of the summer camps are overnight outdoor camps. Children come for two to five days to a YMCA facility and enjoy outdoor recreation at that location. The YMCA has camp facilities all over Japan. For example, in Okinawa the emphasis is on water sports. In Hokkaido, hiking and skiing are the main activities. Overnight camps are generally for children aged eight to eighteen and are staffed by college-age leaders.

YMCA facilities offer three kinds of camp programs. English-speaking participants and leaders are most likely to be present at the YMCA international programs. YMCA language camps are camps that are run in English to give Japanese children an opportunity to experience an all-English-speaking environment. Native English speakers are welcome at these camps as well. Finally, at the YMCA handicapped camps, programs are run for children with special needs.

Day camps may be held in some areas; these are generally for children age eight to twelve, but some programs may be offered for younger children. To find out about camps and activities in your area, call the head office number listed above or the regional office nearest you. In Tokyo call (03) 3293-1921, Yokohama (045) 662-3721, Osaka (06) 441-0894, Kobe (078) 241-7201, and Kyoto (075) 231-4388.

Nihon UNESCO Kyokai Renmei

P.O. Box 4004, Shinjuku Center Bldg. 38F, 1-25-1 Nishi Shinjuku, Shinjuku-ku, Tokyo　東京都新宿区西新宿 1-25-1 新宿センタービル 38F P.O.BOX 4004
☎ (03) 3340-3921

The UNESCO association seeks to promote international relations and the use of English. It offers a variety of programs, camps, and homestays.

Okutama Bible Camp

3-839 Yugi-cho, Ome-shi, Tokyo　東京都青梅市柚木町 3-839
☎ (0428) 76-0931

This Bible camp facility was founded in 1942. During the summer, the Christian Academy (see chap. 11) runs two one-week Bible camps for international kids. The camp runs from Monday to Saturday, and there are two sessions, one for grades 3 to 5, and one for grades 6 to 8. The camp also runs summer programs for Japanese-speaking children. Activities include hiking, Bible study, and all sorts of outdoor pursuits. The cost is extremely reasonable—below ¥20,000 for the week.

GYMNASTICS SUMMER PROGRAMS

The International Gymnastics Club (see the sports section in this chapter) runs summer programs from June through July. At each location, the program lasts from two to four hours and entails an intensive gymnastic workout. Also in the itinerary is a weekly "meet" where the children are judged and scored by the head instructor. Dates and places for summer sessions are available beginning in April.

TENNIS SUMMER PROGRAMS

The Krissman Tennis School (see the sports section in this chapter) runs four-day summer courses for one hour per day. Geared toward children age five to fifteen.

SUMMER CAMPS ABROAD

If you are interested in enrolling your child in a camp or academic program abroad, try to obtain a copy of Peterson's *Summer Opportunities for Kids and Teenagers*. This sourcebook contains over 1,300 listings in the United States and seventeen other countries. Often the international schools in Japan have a copy of this book for loan, or it can be purchased at most bookstores in the United States.

RAINY-DAY ACTIVITIES AND IDEAS

There are many wonderful things about living in Japan, but the rainy season is not one of them. As the parents of young children, we dread the dreary days of rain, rain, and more rain. This season of precipitation is supposed to fall in June, but the actual time period varies. Some years, we thought we could escape the rain by going on vacation in June, only to find the rainy season beginning in July. Other years, it seems that the rain starts in the spring and continues through August. At any rate, you can count on an extended period of wetness at some point during the summer in Japan.

When the kids cannot go outdoors and play, you will need to find other alternatives to keep them happy. Rainy days can mean visits to museums, movies, or other special indoor outings. If you do not have that kind of energy—you won't after the eighth straight day of rain—then you will need some resources for keeping the kids busy at home.

No matter what you do with the kids, you will want them to have the proper rainwear. Fortunately, Japan has the world's greatest selection of rain gear for kids. You won't be able to resist the adorable boots, hats, coats, and umbrellas in bright colors and cute designs. When the kids want to get out of the house in the summer rain, send them outside with this gear on and let them puddle jump and play to their hearts content—after all, it is only water! One friend pays her kids a few yen to "wash" the windows outside with a spray bottle and towel when it rains. Because of the humidity, it is rare for the children to catch a cold, and if they get really dirty, you can always throw them in the tub when they come inside.

When everybody has cabin fever and you need a break, try taking the kids to a car wash. This probably sounds ridiculous, but ¥1,000 will buy you an exciting trip through the car wash and a clean car as well. There is something soothing to Mom, yet thrilling to the kids about sitting in the car as it gets soaped, sprayed, and shined.

When you decide to brave the weather, plan a special outing to a place where the kids can enjoy indoor activities and burn off some energy. Department stores (see chap. 2), aquariums (see chap. 6), and book and toy stores (see chap. 4) all make great rainy-day outings with the children. The planetariums and museums listed below are of special interest to children and are all good places to visit in any kind of weather.

PLANETARIUMS AND MUSEUMS

There are many excellent planetariums and museums throughout Japan—certainly too many to list here. There are, however, some museums that are more interesting to children than others, and we have listed a few of these. If you have a special interest in a particular type of museum, or want to find one for your children outside of Tokyo, check the English-language newspapers or the listings in *Tokyo Journal* and *Kansai Time Out.*

GREATER TOKYO

Fujisawa Shonandai Bunka Center

1-8 Shonandai, Fujisawa-shi, Kanagawa-ken　神奈川県藤沢市湘南台 1-8
☎ (0466) 45-1500
📍 Shonandai Station (east exit), Odakyu Line

This center houses a small children's museum, a planetarium, and an omnimax theater. Open from 9:30 A.M. to 5:00 P.M. Closed on Mondays.

Goto Planetarium and Astronomy Museum (Goto Planetarium to Tenmon Hakubutsukan)

Tokyu Bunka Kaikan 5F, 2-21-12 Shibuya, Shibuya-ku, Tokyo
☎ (03) 3407-7409　東京都渋谷区渋谷 2-21-2 東急文化会館 5F
📍 Shibuya Station, JR Yamanote, Inokashira, Ginza, Hanzomon, Toyoko, Shin Tamagawa lines

This planetarium, conveniently located across from Shibuya Station, offers a program of shows that is changed regularly. They are often open in the evening for special programs. For up-to-date program information, call the museum or check the museum listings in the monthly city magazines.

Hachioji Children's Science Museum (Hachioji-shi Kodomo Kagakukan)

9-13 Oyoko-cho, Hachioji-shi, Tokyo　東京都八王子市大横町 9–13
☎ (0426) 24-3311
🚉 Hachioji Station, JR Chuo Line

This museum has a planetarium and computers that children can play with. Open from 10:00 A.M. to 5:00 P.M. Closed Mondays. From the north exit of Hachioji Station take a bus to the Fukushi Kaikan stop.

Kamakura Doll Museum (Kamakura Ningyo Bijutsukan)

2-2-18 Yukinoshita, Kamakura-shi, Kanagawa-ken　神奈川県鎌倉市雪の下 2–2–18
☎ (0467) 24-4550
🚉 Kamakura or Kita Kamakura stations, JR Yokosuka Line

This is a new museum that displays European antique dolls and miniature doll furniture. Hours are 10:00 A.M. to 5:30 P.M. and they are closed on Mondays.

National Science Museum (Kokuritsu Kagaku Hakubutsukan)

7-20 Ueno-koen, Taito-ku, Tokyo　東京都台東区上野公園 7–20
☎ (03) 3822-0111
🚉 Ueno Station, JR Yamanote, Joban, Ginza, Hibiya lines

The natural history museum is adjacent to Ueno Park (see chap. 6 under zoos) and has exhibits on astronomy, botany, geology, and much more. If your child wants to see dinosaur bones, this is the place. Open from 9:00 A.M. to 4:30 P.M., the museum is closed on Mondays.

Ome Railroad Park (Ome Tetsudo No Koen)

2-155 Katsunuma, Ome-shi, Tokyo　東京都青梅市勝沼 2–155
☎ (0428) 22-4678
🚉 Ome Station, JR Ome Line

The highlight of the Railroad Park is to see the "trains" run at 10:00 and 11:00 A.M., and at 1:00, 2:00, and 3:00 P.M. You can also play on the locomotives in the park and view the miniature railways panorama. Park hours are 9:00 A.M. to 5:00 P.M., and they are closed on Mondays. To get there, take the JR Chuo Line to Tachikawa Station and change to the JR Ome Line. The park is a 15-minute walk from Ome Station.

Science Museum (Kagaku Gijutsukan)

2-1 Kitanomaru-koen, Chiyoda-ku, Tokyo　東京都千代田区北の丸公園 2–1
☎ (03)3212-8471
🚉 Takebashi Station, Tozai Line

A museum with something for everyone, this large building houses exhibits on electronics, transportation, architecture, space exploration, and much,

much more. Many of the displays are set up so that children can learn "hands on" about the subject. The museum is open from 9:30 A.M. to 4:50 P.M. and is closed on Mondays.

Subway Museum

6-3-1 Higashi Kasai, Edogawa-ku, Tokyo　東京都江戸川区東葛西 6-3-1
☎ (03) 3878-5011
🚇 Kasai Station, Tozai Line

The Subway Museum offers multi-sensory experiences for children and adults—all featuring subways and how they work. There are many things here for children to do first-hand, such as blow train whistles and drive in a subway simulator. The museum is across the street from the subway station exit at Kasai Station.

Sunshine City Planetarium

World Import Mart, 3-1-3 Higashi-Ikebukuro, Toshima-ku, Tokyo
☎ (03) 3989-3466　東京都豊島区東池袋 3-1-3
🚇 Higashi-Ikebukuro Station, Yurakucho Line; or Ikebukuro Station (Sunshine City exit), Yurakucho, JR Yamanote, JR Saikyo, Marunouchi, Tobu Tojo, Seibu Ikebukuro lines

This planetarium (there is also an aquarium, see chap. 6) is the largest in Tokyo. As well as viewing the stars at night, you can have a grand view of the entire Kanto plain from the observatory on the top floor of the building. Call ahead or check the local city magazines for current program information. The planetarium is open daily from 10:00 A.M. to 8:00 P.M.

Tokyo Tower

4-2-8 Shiba Koen, Minato-ku, Tokyo　東京都港区芝公園 4-2-8
☎ (03) 3433-5111
🚇 Kamiyacho Station, Hibiya Line; or Daimon Station, Toei Asakusa Line

Tokyo Tower, the world's tallest self-supporting iron tower, holds a variety of amusements for you and your children. Besides the breathtaking view from the observatory, there is an aquarium (see chap. 6), a wax museum, and something called the Holographic Mystery Zone. There is also a floor full of ¥100 rides and games. The tower is open daily from 10:00 A.M., with extended evening hours in the summer months.

Transportation Museum (Kotsu Hakubutsukan)

1-25 Kanda-Sudacho, Chiyoda-ku, Tokyo　東京都千代田区神田須田町 1-25
☎ (03) 3251-8481
🚇 Kanda Station, JR Yamanote, JR Keihin Tohoku, JR Chuo, Ginza lines; or Akihabara Station, JR Yamanote, JR Sobu, JR Keihin Tohoku, Hibiya lines

This is mainly a rail museum, but you will also find exhibits of cars, bikes, airplanes, and ships. Much of the equipment can be climbed on or operated by children. Open from 9:30 A.M. to 5:00 P.M., the museum is closed on Mondays.

Yokohama Children's Museum

5-2-1 Yokodai, Isogo-ku, Yokohama-shi, Kanagawa-ken
☎ (045) 832-1166　神奈川県横浜市磯子区洋光台 5-2-1
🚆 Yokodai Station, JR Negishi, JR Keihin Tohoku lines

This is a museum with a planetarium, an omnimax theater, and a variety of displays and exhibits that can be used by children. For current program information, call the museum or check the listings in one of the city magazines. Hours are 9:30 A.M. to 5:00 P.M. Monday through Saturday, and 9:00 A.M. to 5:00 P.M. Sundays and holidays. The museum is located behind the Yokohama Bank.

Yokohama Doll Museum (Yokohama Ningyo no Ie)

18 Yamashita-cho, Naka-ku, Yokohama-shi, Kanagawa-ken
☎ (045) 671-9361　神奈川県横浜市中区山下町 18
🚆 Ishikawacho Station, JR Negishi, JR Keihin Tohoku lines; or Yokohama Station, JR Yokosuka, JR Keihin Tohoku, Keihin Kyuko, Toyoko, Sotetsu lines

The Yokohama Doll Museum boasts over 4,000 dolls from around the world, and it also hosts special arts events and performances. For more information, call the museum or check the local arts listings. Hours are 10:00 A.M. to 5:00 P.M. and until 7:00 P.M. in the summer. It is closed on Mondays. From Ishikawacho Station take the south exit and walk toward the Marine Tower. To get there from Yokohama Station, leave by the east exit and take a bus (stop #2) from the bus terminal on the first floor of Sogo Department Store. Get off at the Yamashita Futo Iriguchi bus stop. The doll museum is easily recognizable by its pink, triangular-shaped roof.

THROUGHOUT JAPAN

Here are a handful of museums that for one reason or another are outstanding and should be visited if you live near them or are traveling in the area with your children.

The Hiroshima City Culture and Science Museum

5-83 Motomachi, Naka-ku, Hiroshima-shi, Hiroshima-ken
☎ (082) 222-5346　広島県広島市中区基町 5-83
🚆 Gembaku Dome Mae Station,

This is a science museum that includes a planetarium with seasonal programs.

It is open from 9:00 A.M. to 5:00 P.M. and closed on M
Gembaku Dome Mae Station, turn left and the museum i
down the road past the city's baseball ground.

Japan Toy Museum

671-3 Nakanino, Kodera-cho, Kanzaki-gun, Hyogo-ken
☎ (0792) 32-4388　兵庫県神崎郡香寺町中仁野 671-3
🚇 Koro Station, Bantan Line

The Japan Toy Museum houses changing exhibits of toys from around the
world. Hours are from 10:00 A.M. to 5:00 P.M. and it is closed on Wednesdays. Change to the Bantan Line at Himeji Station for the 20-minute ride to
Koro Station. On foot, it takes about twenty minutes from the station to the
museum.

Himeji Museum of History (Hyogo Kenritsu Rekishi Hakubutsukan)

Honmachi 68, Himeji-shi, Hyogo-ken　兵庫県姫路市本町 68
☎ (0792)88-9011
🚇 Himeji Station, San'yo Honsen, Bantan, Kishin lines

This is an impressive history museum with many exhibits where children
can enjoy "hands-on" experience. Hours are 10:00 A.M. to 5:00 P.M. and
they are closed on Mondays. To get there from Himeji Station, take a
Shinki bus bound for Hiranominamiguchi to Hakubutsukanmae. You will
be on the bus for about fifteen minutes.

Port Island Science Center and Planetarium (Kobe Shiritsu Seishonen Ka-gakukan)

7-7-6 Nakamachi, Minatojima, Chuo-ku, Kobe-shi, Hyogo-ken
☎ (078) 302-5177　兵庫県神戸市中央区港島中町 7-7-6
🚇 Minami Koen Station, Port Island Line

This museum and planetarium occupies a three-story building on Port
Island. Call for special program information. The center is located near
Kobe Portopia Land (see chap. 5). It is open from 9:30 A.M. to 4:30 P.M.
during the week and 10:00 A.M. to 5:00 P.M. on weekends and national
holidays. It is closed on Wednesdays.

Kobe Maritime Museum (Kaiyo Hakubutsukan)

2-2 Hatoba-cho, Chuo-ku, Kobe-shi, Hyogo-ken
☎ (078) 391-6751　兵庫県神戸市中央区波止場町 2-2
🚇 Motomachi Station, JR Tokaido Honsen, Hanshin lines

This is a maritime museum with exhibits of model ships and educational
displays about the geography of the local area and how it was formed.
Hours are 10:00 A.M. to 5:00 P.M. and it is closed on Mondays. Call for

information on summer opening times. The museum is located south of the station, about twelve minutes on foot.

Modern Transport Museum (Kotsu Kagakukan)

3-11-10 Namiyoke, Minato-ku, Osaka-shi, Osaka-fu
☎ (06) 581-5771　大阪府大阪市港区波除 3-11-10
🚉 Bentencho Station, Osaka Loop Line

Conveniently located next to the station, the Modern Transport Museum has real trains and other exhibits that children can climb on and pretend to drive. Hours are from 9:30 A.M. to 5:00 P.M. and it is closed on Mondays.

The World Children's Art Museum

1-1 Toriito, Oka-machi, Okazaki-shi, Aichi-ken　愛知県岡崎市岡町鳥戸 1-1
☎ (0564) 53-3511
🚉 Miai Station, Meitetsu Line

A unique complex adjacent to the Parent-Child Formative Center in Okazaki City, this museum displays drawings by children from all over the world. In addition to the children's art, there are works by world-famous painters that were done in the artists' teenage years. Five permanent exhibits and five special exhibits are presented each year. The museum is open from 9:00 A.M. to 4:30 P.M. every day except Mondays. In summer, hours are extended to 5:30 P.M. To get there, take the Shinkansen (Tokaido Line) to Toyohashi. Change to the Meitetsu Line and get off at Miai Station. The museum is a 5-minute taxi ride from the station.

OTHER INDOOR AMUSEMENTS

National Children's Castle

5-53-1 Jingumae, Shibuya-ku, Tokyo　東京都渋谷区神宮前 5-53-1
☎ (03) 3797-5665
🚉 Omotesando Station, Ginza, Hanzomon, Chiyoda lines

This wonderful establishment in Tokyo was built by the Ministry of Health and Welfare at a cost of ¥32.3 billion in 1985. It was entrusted into the hands of the Child Welfare Foundation of Japan as a place for children to dream, learn, play, and grow together. From its inception, the National Children's Castle has offered an outstanding selection of programs and activities for children and their parents.

To meet the increasing needs of international visitors and members, the castle has an International Division under the direction of an American, Teri Suzanne. Several Japanese staff members can speak English, and English-language information and catalogs are also available. Bilingual family theater programs are also held. For English information about the castle, you are welcome to call or inquire at the International Division. Phone (03) 3797-5665 or write to the above address.

The complex consists of two main buildings that house numerous recreational and educational facilities. On the rooftops of both buildings are outdoor play areas. Our younger children prefer the vast Play Hall on the third floor where they can run and play on the indoor climbing equipment or engage in quiet play in the child-sized kitchen and playhouse. Mothers of crawling babies will appreciate the tatami area and the soft toys provided for little ones.

Across from the Play Hall, the Fine Arts Studio always has art projects going on that the children can participate in. A favorite activity of ours is the long, white drawing board and jars of paint that even the youngest child can use. To the rear of the Play Hall is the Computer Play Room that houses the Computer Challenge Game, the first of its kind in the world. On the same floor there are also bathrooms, a rest area, and vending machines for drinks.

On the fourth floor, the Audio Visual Library has viewing booths for watching a favorite video or cartoon, available from the castle video library, which has over 6,000 titles. Also on the fourth floor are the Music Lobby and Music Studios. Mini concerts featuring international and ethnic music are put on here, and instruments are available for "hands on" experiences.

There are two theaters in the castle. The Aoyama Theater puts on musicals, ballets, concerts, and plays, such as *Annie*, *Big River*, and *Hans*. The Aoyama Round Theater is smaller and more informal.

On the rooftop is an enclosed net area for frisbees and balls and a Playport system jungle gym from the United States.

There is a restaurant on the first floor that offers everything from coffee to breakfast, lunch, and dinner; there is also a sushi bar on the first floor. On the second floor is a coffee shop, and on the eighth floor there is a French restaurant.

Other facilities at the castle include an Olympic-sized indoor swimming pool that is open to the general public. The pool is also used for swimming classes. Also located in this building are a gymnasium, the Child Care Center and Well Child Clinic, a hotel, a personal computer room, gallery for exhibits, and rooms that may be rented for lectures, seminars, dinners, and luncheons.

Classes are offered at the castle in everything from mother and baby swimming to percussion ensemble to recycled art. Unusual offerings also include classes for children with Down's syndrome and counseling for overweight or asthmatic children. You will find many events and classes to occupy the entire family all year round. The class schedule begins in April in accordance with the Japanese school system. When you register for classes, you will be charged a class fee and a ¥1,000 registration fee that is good for three years. While enrolled in a class, you will receive a membership card which entitles you to free admission to the castle. Registration for classes must be done in person, but you may call for class information. All classes are taught in Japanese except for a few that are taught bilingually (in English and Japanese)

Even if you do not take a class, you might consider becoming a member of the Children's Castle by joining the Tomo no Kai membership circle. Initial membership costs ¥1,500 (the application fee), and yearly dues are ¥2,000 per family. Members receive the colorful Castle Newsletter in Japanese six times per year, free general admission tickets, prior notice and early reservation and discount privileges for castle events and theater programs, and discounts on purchases made in the castle shops.

The castle hours are weekdays (Tuesday through Friday) from 12:30 P.M. to 5:30 P.M., Saturdays, Sundays, and holidays from 10:00 A.M. to 5:30 P.M., winter, spring, and summer vacations (Japanese school system) from 10:00 A.M. to 5:30 P.M. The castle is closed on Mondays or Tuesdays when Monday is a national holiday. It is open for all national holidays except at New Year.

Admission is ¥400 for adults and ¥300 for children. When accompanied by an adult, children under three are free. Group rates are available. Special activity programs for school groups are held in the mornings.

Tokyo Metropolitan Children's Museum (Tokyo-to Jido Kaikan)

1-18-24 Shibuya-ku, Shibuya, Tokyo　東京都渋谷区渋谷 1-18-24
☎ (03) 3409-6361
🚉 Shibuya Station, JR Yamanote, Inokashira, Ginza, Toyoko, Shin Tamagawa lines

This is a wonderful place for children and parents to come and play, learn, and explore. The Jido Kaikan is a children's center located near Shibuya Station. Renovated in 1990, this six-story building is overflowing with interesting things to entertain the kids.

There is a small outdoor playground next to the building, but the real fun is inside. Starting in the basement level, there are small rides and electronic games for the children to play. For young children, the wooden toy corner is full of cars, blocks, pretend food, and riding toys, all made of top-quality wood. The first floor is the lobby and information center, and on the second floor is an indoor playground and infant-nursing room. The third floor has science and computer games, and the fourth floor has conference rooms that are used as music space and for lectures. The fifth floor is a small library (most books are in Japanese), and the roof boasts yet another playground.

The layout of the building is easy to figure out, and bathrooms with baby changing facilities are clearly marked on each floor. There are a couple of restaurants in the building where you can get a light meal or snack, and there are plenty of chairs for weary parents to rest in while the kids burn off some energy.

The Jido Kaikan is the only one of its kind in Tokyo. However, many of the wards and cities in Tokyo run local *jido-kan*, or children's halls. Some wards have only one or two, while others, such as Minato-ku, have as many as twelve. These children's centers are smaller in scale than the one in Shibuya and do not offer as many services, but they can be convenient resources if there is one in your neighborhood. Some of them offer after-school programs called "schoolchildren's clubs" for children who come home to an empty house after school.

For information on what programs are run in your area, contact your ward or city office and inquire about the local *jido-kan*.

Kobekko Land

1-3-1 Higashi Kawasaki-cho, Chuo-ku, Kobe-shi, Hyogo-ken
☎ (078) 382-1300   兵庫県神戸市中央区東川崎町 1-3-1
🚃 Kobe Station, San'yo Honsen Line

In 1987, the municipal government built Kobekko Land as a children's indoor center for play and learning. The facilities include not only play and exercise areas, but a performance hall and computer rooms as well. Kobekko Land is free for children up to age eighteen, and accompanying parents or guardians. The center, located in Harbor Land a 7-minute walk from Kobe Station, is open daily except Monday from 9:30 A.M. to 5:00 P.M.

Some of the attractions include video booths where children can select and watch videos; an arts and crafts room with daily supervised projects; a music studio equipped with recording facilities; concerts, films, and plays in the 300-seat Kobekko Hall; and a ham radio corner. For the little ones, there is a play hall with a ball pool that toddlers adore.

On a more serious note, the center also runs a Child Guidance Clinic for parents and children with special needs or behavior problems in school.

CHILDREN'S TELEVISION PROGRAMS

Japanese television programs for toddlers and teens include numerous cartoons of one type or another. Some of these are long-running character cartoons that have spawned all types of accessories featuring the same characters. Others are stories in the Disney style or old Disney cartoons dubbed in Japanese, and still others are Japanese action-adventure with too much violence for our taste. Just be aware that the cartoon scene is a mixed bag, and the smartest thing to do before allowing your children to watch any cartoon is to preview it yourself. One Japanese friend says that maybe half of the cartoons on TV are suitable for young children.

The following are some long-running cartoons that we would recommend for young children.

"Anpan-man"
(Mondays at 5:00 P.M., Channel 4)
This cartoon is about a group of little men made of bread (*pan*). The prefix before *pan* tells you what the little man is full of—i.e., Currypan-man is full of curry, Anpan-man is full of *an*, or bean jam. Kids love the antics of these characters, and for an action cartoon the show is fairly nonviolent. These characters can be found in toy stores as stuffed dolls, finger puppets, in puzzles, on notepaper, etc.

"Doraemon"
(Fridays at 7:00 P.M., Channel 10)
This long-running cartoon stars a robot from the future who comes to earth to help children out of difficult situations. Look for the adventures of Doraemon at movie theaters as well, especially during the Japanese spring school vacation.

"Chibi Maruko"
(Sundays at 6:00 P.M., Channel 8)
An animated story about a third-grade girl named Chibi Maruko, this cartoon has been a huge hit in Japan for a few years now. You will probably recognize the distinctive theme song and the Chibi Maruko character, whose face appears on everything from lunch boxes to bath towels. A charming show that the whole family can enjoy.

"Sazae-san"

(Sundays at 6:30 P.M., Channel 8, and Tuesdays at 7:00 P.M., Channel 8)
This is a long-running program about a typical Japanese family. Although, as with Chibi Maruko, the dialogue is all in Japanese, it is entertaining and interesting to watch. Highly recommended for family viewing.

"Nihon Mukashi Banashi"

(Saturdays at 7:00 P.M., Channel 6)
Old Japanese folktales have been resurrected and animated for this half-hour show. A refreshing break from the average Japanese cartoon programs. For all ages.

In addition to cartoons, there are some excellent educational shows for children. These tend to air early in the morning (starting at 5:45 for English lessons!) and in the late afternoon and evening from approximately 4:30 to 7:00. Recently, the number of shows introducing Japanese children to English and Western culture has increased. We recommend the following educational shows.

"Okasan to Issho"

(Monday through Saturday at 9:30 A.M., Channel 1 and 5:00 P.M., Channel 3)
This show is extremely popular with the one- to four-year-old set. Through the antics of three characters—Porori, Piccolo, and JaJa Maru—"Okaasan to Issho" teaches basic lessons in hygiene, manners, colors, and shapes. The show is produced by NHK, (owner of both Channel 1 and Channel 3) and a different group of children participate on the program each day. All three-year-olds in Japan are invited to enter the lottery to appear in the show. Send a postcard to NHK "Okasan To Issho," 2-2-1 Jinnan, Shibuya-ku, Tokyo 150.

"Eigo De Asobo"

(Monday through Friday at 5:40 P.M., Channel 3)
This show, whose name means "Let's play in English," features both Japanese and foreign children age four to six singing songs, playing games, and dancing. The emphasis is on teaching English songs and games to Japanese children in a fun yet educational setting.

"Sesame Street"

(Sundays at 5:00 P.M. and Fridays at 6:00 P.M., Channel 3)
For most families, "Sesame Street" needs no introduction. A long-running, award-winning program from the United States, "Sesame Street" entertains

and educates children age two to six. The hour-long show is broadcast in English.

"Ponkiki"
(Monday through Friday at 7:45 A.M., Channel 8)
This is a creative and entertaining production, using Japanese children and some foreign children in a variety of settings. There are also dancing and singing segments accompanied by the lovable Ponkiki characters. For children up to eight years old.

Celebrating in Japan

31 DECEMBER

THESE LONG "SOBA" NOODLES
REPRESENT HOPES FOR A LONG LIFE.

For young children, life in a foreign country is a fun-filled adventure. One of the most fascinating aspects of living in a foreign country is the chance to experience the native culture and its traditions. We are continually surprised at how many opportunities there are for our children to participate in Japan's festive offerings. Often, the very fact that we have young children makes it more likely that we will come across these celebrations. There is no better way to get into the spirit of things than to participate in the festivities of your host country with your children.

CELEBRATING JAPANESE HOLIDAYS

Japan has many national holidays. Some, such as the ones listed here, are more meaningful and fun for children than others. For the Japanese, national holidays are often just a day to stay at home and either relax or get some projects done around the house. Other holidays are times for traveling to be with family, while still others are for dressing up and visiting the local shrine for a ceremony or formal portrait to mark the day. When asked about the visits to the shrine, most Japanese will reply that for them it is more of a cultural tradition than a religious rite. You will soon learn which shrines are popular in your area, and which holidays are for traveling or for staying at home.

There are also other holidays that are important in different regions of the country. For example, Tanabata (July 7) is a relatively quiet holiday in most of the country, perhaps marked by a small celebration at home. Sendai (in Miyagi Prefecture), however, is famous for its Tanabata Festival. It is one of the largest festivals of the year, and people from all over the country know that if you want to celebrate Tanabata in a big way, you have to go to Sendai. (However, be aware that in many places, including Sendai, the festival is celebrated on August 7.)

Celebrations may differ from neighborhood to neighborhood as well. During our first year here, on *keiro no hi* (Respect for the Aged Day), all the children in the neighborhood lined up to carry the *omikoshi*, or portable shrine, to the park where the old people in the neighborhood gather. Japanese mothers urged us to join the procession with our children, and upon arrival at the park we were greeted by elderly people from the neighborhood who had prepared bags of goodies for all the children. To this day, *keiro no hi* (September 15) remains our children's favorite national holiday. However, when I told my friends—both Japanese and foreign—about this event near our house, they replied that they had never heard of, or experienced, anything like it in their neighborhood. The best advice we have for you on this matter is just to keep your eyes open!

Many festivities are cause for children—and adults—to dress in traditional costume. Even the international schools have celebrations where Japanese dress is appropriate. Besides being a useful item while you are here, investment in a kimono for your daughter or *hakama* for your son can serve as a memento of your stay long after you have moved on to another country.

There are many opportunities to obtain these traditional costumes at reduced prices. Rental companies often sell off their stock at big discounts in department store sales. Such sales are usually advertised in English newspapers and magazines. Once you attend a sale and register your name, you will receive announcements of upcoming sales. You can also rent traditional clothes for a special occasion from the catalog companies listed in chapter 2.

Another option for purchasing these costumes is the small stores on neighborhood shopping streets, where prices are often lower than at the department stores. If you do purchase an outfit at a neighborhood store, they will show you how to dress your child. For the girls, it's a bit complicated unless you have a Japanese grandmother to teach you! Or you can make an appointment at your local hairdresser or a nearby hotel. They will usually have an employee experienced in the intricacies of putting on a kimono. They will also put up your daughter's hair using exquisite hair ornaments which you can buy to match her costume.

Food plays an integral part in any holiday, and in Japan there are a few basic foods that are prepared for holidays or special events. For example, *osekihan*, a mixture of sticky rice and red beans, is a traditional festive

185

food. The red beans make the rice pinkish red; red is considered an auspicious color and so *osekihan* is served on any festival day or birthday in the family. Many traditional foods can be found ready-made in your local grocery store. Others are easy to make at home, and a basic Japanese cookbook can tell you how.

Every month in Japan brings a new and different holiday or event. To experience Japan through a child's eyes, try to incorporate some of these holidays into your own family traditions.

THE NEW YEAR HOLIDAY (OSHOGATSU)

The first three days of January are all national holidays to celebrate the New Year. On December 31, or *omisoka*, the Japanese hurry about preparing for the new year and participate in events geared to getting rid of all the bad fortune accumulated during the past year. On New Year's Eve, the traditional food is *soba* noodles, eaten around midnight. These long noodles represent hopes for a long life. Homes are decorated with *kadomatsu*, or arrangements of pine branches and bamboo, and ropes hung with white paper strips decorate gateways and doorways to ensure luck in the new year. At midnight, the bells in the shrines and temples toll 108 times to symbolize the banishing of man's 108 sinful desires. The shrines and temples are filled with throngs of people not only at midnight, but for the duration of the holiday. People greet one another with congratulations for the new year, "*akemashite omedeto gozaimasu*" is the greeting you will hear everywhere.

New Year's Day is the most important day for children, although this national holiday is rather solemn compared with some of the other holidays. At New Year's, children receive money from relatives in specially decorated envelopes called *otoshidama*. Although some parents insist that their children save a portion of the gift, many allow them to spend the full amount on whatever their hearts desire. Now you know why kids look forward to the New Year's celebration so much! Other than receiving money and playing a number of traditional Japanese games, there is not much else going on for children at New Year's.

On January 1, the New Year is welcomed by eating *mochi*, a paste made by pounding cooked rice in a mortar with a pestle. Most of the Japanese schools and some of the international schools will have a *mochi*-pounding ceremony at school. If you travel to any of the winter resorts in Japan over the New Year holiday, you will possibly get a chance to experience these foods at the lodge where you stay. *Osechi ryori* is another traditional New Year's food. This *obento* smorgasbord of Japanese delights can be ordered and delivered to your home from many department stores and restaurants, but be sure to place your order early. One of our Japanese friends told us that many people now order from a store and that few people actually make these traditional foods at home anymore.

Most stores and businesses are closed for the first few days of January, and the cities tend to be rather deserted because many families travel to their hometown or ancestral home over the holidays. Once January 3 comes, the stores reopen and all the children rush to department stores and toy stores to spend their *otoshidama*.

FEBRUARY 3 OR 4: BEAN-THROWING FESTIVAL (SETSUBUN)
Although early February still seems like winter in much of Japan, *setsubun* celebrates the first day of the New Year according to the ancient solar calendar and the traditional beginning of spring. This is celebrated by throwing beans and shouting, "*oni wa soto*" ("Out with evil") and "*fuku wa uchi*" ("In with good luck"). This act of purification, said to date from the Muromachi period (1333–1568), was believed to be essential to prepare oneself for the coming year and the spring planting season. You can join the crowds who go to the temple to throw beans, but it's much more fun for the kids to do it at home.

Look in your supermarket for dried soybeans, which are prominently displayed at this time of year. (One mother told us she switched to roasted peanuts in the shell because they were easier to clean up.) Usually children are allowed to throw the number of beans that correlate to their age, which makes the mess minimal for preschoolers.

In most Japanese homes with small children, a devil-like monster mask is made, and the father wears it while the children chase him around the house. Eventually, they chase him outside while they shout "*oni wa soto*" as they throw the beans out of the door or window, and "*fuku wa uchi*" when they toss beans around the house.

MARCH 3: DOLL FESTIVAL OR GIRLS' DAY (HINA MATSURI)
This festival for girls features a set of *hina* dolls arranged on a tier of shelves covered with bright red cloth. We were shocked to find out how expensive these miniature dolls are. Sets in department stores range from ¥50,000 to ¥200,000 and up. Traditionally, when the first daughter is born, she inherits her mother's set of dolls or the grandparents buy a new set. In other cases, girls may receive one doll each year until they have a full set. The basic set consists of an emperor and empress and attendants and musicians

in ancient court dress. Some families opt for just the emperor and empress. Most foreigners decide not to indulge in this expensive souvenir and settle for viewing the lavish displays of dolls at the department stores. Some parents have procured "antique" dolls at flea markets at very little cost. This is perfectly acceptable for foreigners, but you would not find the Japanese using a discarded doll set. The set of dolls can be put out any time beginning in February, but they are always put away on March 3, because of the superstitious belief that a girl won't get married until late otherwise.

It is a real treat to be invited by a Japanese family to view their daughter's doll collection. If you feel that you must have at least one doll to commemorate this special day, look for the dolls at one of the discount stores, or rent the whole set from one of the rental companies (see chap. 3).

On Girls' Day, you will see young girls celebrating with their families, wearing their best kimono or Western dress and eating traditional foods, such as *osekihan.* A special dish for this day is *chirashi-zushi,* or sushi rice with cooked vegetables mixed in. You will also see in the grocery stores the *hishimochi* (diamond-shaped rice cake) colored pink, green, and white, and colorful puffed rice called "*hina* snacks." These pastel colors for Girls' Day are a pleasant reminder that spring is just around the corner.

EARLY APRIL: CHERRY-BLOSSOM VIEWING (OHANAMI)

Perfect pink blossoms suddenly arrive to fill the sky and just as quickly are blown away. This short period of beauty is celebrated by all Japanese in early April or sometimes late March, depending on when the blooms are at their best. Watch the newspapers for reports on the approaching cherry blossom "front."

Children love the cherry blossom season. Favorite places for picnics under the trees in Tokyo are Aoyama Cemetery, Yasukuni Shrine, and Ueno Park. A group of mothers with their children meet for a big picnic in Aoyama Cemetery every year. All you need are blankets and food to make a special outing. The sky is hidden by a cover of blossoms, and toward the end of the peak week they flutter down on your face like snowflakes.

If you are more adventurous, you might want to attempt an *ohanami* party at night. To do this, go to a park early in the morning of the picnic and stake out a spot for your group. Cherry blossoms by moonlight give the picnic another flavor entirely. Be sure to bring enough flashlights or lanterns so you can see what you are eating! There will be a party going on every few feet, but the park is surprisingly dark at night and you won't feel as if you're in a crowd. *Ohanami* is fun to do with several other families.

Just park the car, pile all your gear on the stroller, and head for the site. It is safe, night or day, and you and your children will probably be asked to join in some of the other parties nearby. Everyone is friendly and often a little drunk during the annual week of cherry blossoms.

APRIL 29–MAY 5: GOLDEN WEEK

Golden Week is the name given to the series of holidays that come in quick succession at the end of April and the beginning of May. It is the "spring break" of Japan, and everyone who is able to takes off work and travels. The first day of Golden Week, April 29—formerly Emperor Showa's birthday—is called Greenery Day. At the end of Golden Week is *kodomo no hi*, or Children's Day. In between, there is Constitution Day (May 3) and Citizens' Holiday (May 4). Depending on the days on which the holidays fall, it's possible to take just one day off, combine it with the national holidays, and end up with a week-long break. Bear in mind that most Japanese will also be taking advantage of the holidays to travel; if you plan to take a trip, you will need to make reservations as far in advance as possible. Many people even make reservations a year ahead to be sure of taking a holiday. Recently, companies are tending to shut down for the whole of Golden Week, but the practice has not spread to all Japanese schools yet. Even so, you can be sure that all amusement parks and tourist spots will be very crowded on these holidays.

MAY 5: CHILDREN'S DAY (KODOMO NO HI)

Formerly known as Boys' Day, this national holiday involves some special rites for the sons in the family. Streamers with a carp (*koi*) design are flown from the rooftop, balcony, or flagpole in the garden. The carp is recognized for its strength in swimming against the current and parents hope that their sons will have this same strength and determination.

For May 5, boys sometimes set up a display of dolls on a tiered platform. These dolls are feudal warriors clad in miniature armor. If you decide to invest in a set of these *gogatsu ningyo*, be aware that the red cloth and tiers come together with the dolls. Some people have just one samurai figure as their display. The figures are set up in April and can be taken down anytime after May 5.

Festive food is a big part of the Children's Day celebration. Families serve *osekihan* and *chimaki*, a mixture of *mochi* and rice. Another special dish is *tai* (sea bream), which can be elaborately prepared for you by most department stores. At this time you can easily spot accessories and foods in all the local shops, which makes joining in these celebrations fun and easy.

JULY 7: STAR FESTIVAL (TANABATA)

The celebration of the Tanabata Festival originates in a Chinese legend about two stars who are lovers but separated by the Milky Way. The two stars can meet only once a year on the seventh day of the seventh month. On this day, everyone writes down his wish—it's always fun to see what the little ones have to say—and hangs it on a cut bamboo branch that is placed in front of the house. The wish, or sometimes poem, is written on a strip of paper and hung on the branch together with origami ornaments. At the end of the festivities, the branch is usually thrown into a river to symbolize the ridding of misfortune or sometimes put in a field and used as a scarecrow.

OCTOBER 10: SPORTS DAY (TAIIKU NO HI)

Sports Day in Japan is a national holiday focusing on fitness. Around the time of this holiday, many schools and communities hold their annual field day, or *undokai*. If you live in an area where a community sports day is held, be sure to take part in the fun. The whole family can get involved in races, games, and all manner of good-natured competition.

Most schools hold some form of sports day during the autumn. These competitions often resemble a mini-Olympics with banners, prizes, and the students decked out in team colors. Parents are encouraged to attend these events, so be prepared to do your part in the name of team spirit!

NOVEMBER 15: SEVEN-FIVE-THREE DAY (SHICHI-GO-SAN)

On this day, children all over Japan are celebrated. How wonderful to live in a society where children are so precious! Shichi-go-san literally means "seven-five-three" and describes the day when three- and seven-year-old girls and five-year-old boys are taken to a Shinto shrine by their parents to give thanks to the deities for their children and to pray for their good health.

This is a day that parents mark with a formal photograph. You will see children of all ages dressed in their best on this day. Children of the designated ages in particular are decked out in their finest kimono or Western-style clothes. Most shrines conduct a brief ceremony in which you are welcome to participate. At the larger shrines, pay the fees (¥5,000 or so) at the counter and wait in an adjoining room for your group to be called. After the priest has chanted and waved his wand of streamers across the row of children standing with their parents, it is time to file out. In addition to the ceremony, children receive a good-luck souvenir and *chitose ame*, or 1,000-year candy, to ensure a long life. You can purchase these at one of the counters even if you don't want to take part in the ceremony. At the smaller shrines, the priest is more likely to greet you personally and give your children a private ceremony.

Foreigners in Japan can make this day a memorable one for their children by cooking a favorite food for dinner, baking a cake, or planning a special family activity.

DECEMBER 25: CHRISTMAS IN JAPAN

This holiday is listed under both the Japanese and the Western traditions. Most Japanese families with children celebrate Christmas. The religious aspects of Christmas are nonexistent, however, except for those Japanese who are Christians.

Santa Claus comes to Japan, just as he does to other countries, with a gift for good little boys and girls. Since Saint Nick is a tradition borrowed from Western culture, customs vary from house to house. Instead of coming down the chimney and leaving gifts under the Christmas tree, Santa may leave them outside on the balcony on Christmas morning. One Japanese mother told us that the presents at their house appear on Christmas Eve while the children are having their bath!

As with many other Western customs, the Japanese have tailored Christmas to suit their own lifestyle. The bakeries have come up with "Christmas cakes" that have become an indispensable part of Christmas celebrations. However, you'll be surprised to find that a Japanese Christmas cake is a plain sponge cake covered in cream and decorated with strawberries, which is much more to the Japanese taste than a rich fruit cake. You can order these elaborately decorated (usually with sleighs and Santas) cakes at all bakeries and some grocery stores. Just look for the poster of the cream-covered cake—but be warned that they usually look better than they taste! Also, the Japanese eat roast chicken on Christmas rather than the turkey that is popular in the United States.

In the past few years it has become popular for young couples to make Christmas Eve a romantic night out. Your Christmas Eve date is all-important, and hotels and fine restaurants offer special Christmas Eve packages. Young people make plans early for what is becoming for many Japanese the most romantic night of the year.

Christmas is for children all over the world, and Japan is no exception. However, adults do not often exchange presents, nor is it traditionally a time for a family gathering (this takes place over the New Year). Santa is the primary gift-giver in Japan, and he usually brings one present for each child.

CELEBRATING WESTERN HOLIDAYS IN JAPAN

Before we had children, we never gave much thought as to how traditional Western holidays could be celebrated in Japan. Once we became parents, it suddenly was important to know where we could get Halloween costumes, stocking stuffers for Christmas, valentines, and Easter egg dye. Like most parents, we wanted our children to experience the same holiday traditions we had enjoyed, despite the fact that we were far from our native country. Keeping family traditions alive is important wherever you live. When you live overseas, it takes forethought, time, and money, but the result is worth it.

During the past few years, trendy Tokyo, and much of the rest of Japan, have embraced many popular Western customs. On the majority of holidays, especially the more commercial ones, the Japanese have begun to celebrate in their own way to some degree. Often the celebration is a variation of the holiday we know as Westerners, but at least there is a festive air on that day, and some essential holiday items are available in the stores. The list in the holiday supplies section of this chapter will give you ideas about what can be found in Japan, as well as items available from some mail-order companies to fill the gap.

FEBRUARY 14: VALENTINE'S DAY

Valentine's Day in Japan is one of those holidays with which the Japanese have taken more than a few liberties. In essence, it is the day when women give the men in their lives (boyfriends, co-workers, bosses) a token of their affection, usually candy, called *giri choko*, or "obligation chocolate." Then on White Day, March 14, the men must reciprocate with gifts for the women who gave them candy. Recently, a well-known underwear manufacturer has tried to turn this holiday to its advantage by urging men to buy white lingerie for their loved ones.

From the end of January, you will see valentine candy in many stores in creative styles for everyone in the family. Because in the West, Valentine's Day is for giving candy, flowers, and cards to your sweetheart, this selection comes in handy for foreigners. Its quality varies widely, and as with anything in Japan, you get what you pay for. Chocolate animal, toy, and doll shapes are all available, and they make perfect valentines for children and those young at heart. There are also valentine card displays in some shops, but the cards are usually expensive. We like to let the children make their own to give to friends or to send to relatives overseas. Paper, doilies, heart stickers, and a little glue are all you need.

EASTER

Yes, the Easter bunny does come to Japan. You can buy egg dye here and even cellophane grass for your basket. Most good florists have a selection of straw baskets; this can be the year that you hand-paint your child's basket with his name and some Easter decorations.

For young children, Easter usually means fancy clothes, the Easter bunny, and Easter egg hunts. This is one of those holidays that is extra fun in Japan because of the relative safety of the parks and playgrounds. The weather is usually beautiful at this time of year, and you can gather a group of friends with children and have a real old-fashioned Easter egg hunt in a park. One family we know invites twenty to thirty friends to meet in Yoyogi Park each Easter for a picnic and egg hunt. Any nearby park is suitable for such a gathering, and perhaps this will become an annual tradition for your family, too.

JULY 4: INDEPENDENCE DAY IN THE UNITED STATES

Because we are Americans, we decided to list this holiday for all those who wonder how to celebrate Independence Day while in Japan. In fact, our suggestions can be used to help families from any foreign country understand and participate in their home country's special patriotic day.

In the United States, the Fourth of July involves barbecues, swimming, watermelon, and fireworks. Even though you will miss the picnics back home, if you are like us, you may want your children to experience some of the pride and excitement that goes along with any patriotic celebration. Some of the ways to do this require a little forethought, but they are well worth it. Here are some ideas we have tried: Hang your country's flag around the house or even outside; cook the traditional foods for the celebration during the week and let the children participate, perhaps relating to them stories of your childhood or what their relatives will be doing back home on the day of celebration; read stories about your home country and this particular event in its history; play traditional patriotic music, your national anthem, or other favorite songs, and dance around the house; on the day, have the entire family dress in the colors associated with your country (in the U.S., of course, red, white and blue). Even a two-year-old can learn the name of the country he comes from and enjoy the festivities that you have planned to make this day special.

OCTOBER 31: HALLOWEEN/ALL SAINT'S EVE

Halloween is another Western holiday that is gaining popularity with the Japanese, especially among teenagers and young adults. In the West, the

193

door-to-door quest for treats is the highlight of Halloween for the under-twelve set (and their parents!). In Japan, however, that part of the tradition has not caught on, and the holiday is usually celebrated the weekend before with costume parades, parties, and contests. These are activities the whole family can enjoy. Look for signs on the street and in the paper each year for the annual Halloween festival in Tokyo at Kiddyland on Omote Sando, in Daikanyama/Ebisu, and in Aoyama. Unfortunately, jack-o'-lanterns have not become a common sight during Halloween although pumpkins are available at some supermarkets like National Azabu in Hiroo.

In Japan, door-to-door trick or treating is a safe activity for young children. The foreign community often practices this tradition within their own neighborhoods. If you don't live where there are other foreigners nearby, you can always call a few friends and ask them if you can come by with your ghosts and goblins to give them a chance to pick up a few treats and show off their costumes.

NOVEMBER 23: KANSHA NO HI (LABOR THANKSGIVING DAY)

No matter what country you are from, the harvest season is a good opportunity for children to learn about the traditions and history of their own country, and to learn to give thanks for all they have. Every culture has a harvest celebration in the fall, and Japan is no exception. Japan's harvest celebration, commonly known as Labor Thanksgiving Day, is a Japanese national holiday. Because it falls in late November, when Americans traditionally celebrate Thanksgiving, some expatriate families find it convenient to have their Thanksgiving Day dinner on this Japanese holiday. American Thanksgiving foods are freely available in Tokyo and other large cities. Turkeys, canned or fresh pumpkin, and fall foods such as apples and chestnuts are in abundant supply.

DECEMBER 25: CHRISTMAS

You may be surprised to hear Christmas carols in your supermarket as early as October, but the Japanese merchants go all out for Christmas. When you are downtown shopping, keep your eyes open for some spectacular decorations.

The commercialization of this Christian holiday means that you will have no trouble getting a tree and all the trimmings in Japan. The trees are rather expensive—¥10,000 and up in Tokyo—and they often come as live trees in a pot. Recently, artificial trees have become popular with the Japanese; they are sold in large department stores.

In Tokyo, we take the children to see the lighted tree at Aoyama Gakuin University, where they also have handbell and choral concerts in early December. Refugees International Japan sponsors a large tree at Tokyo Station, and they have special concerts and events there the weeks before Christmas. Hibiya City Ice-skating Rink is Tokyo's version of the Rockefeller Center and is a great outing for the entire family.

Throughout Japan, the Japanese have what they call the season of *daiku*, when groups get together to perform Beethoven's Ninth Symphony. It runs through December and you can choose from a vast number of performances by first-rate orchestras. Other Christmas favorites are the *Messiah* and the *Nutcracker Suite*. Look for listings of these events in English-language newspapers and magazines. When our children were too young to attend these performances, we played recordings of the music around the house at Christmastime to get in the spirit of the season.

Some families take advantage of the long holiday that includes Christmas and New Year's to take a vacation trip to an exotic place in the South Pacific or Asia. The Philippines, being primarily a Catholic country, is a special place to visit at Christmastime. Many resorts offer special Christmas packages for families with children; if you plan on doing this, be sure to make reservations well in advance.

If you decide to stay in Japan over the holidays, there are some special ways to make Christmas without your extended family a memorable occasion. Organize a festive meal with friends and neighbors. Get in the Christmas spirit by spending time together decorating the house and preparing traditional holiday foods

Letters to and from Santa
The International Friendship Association (IFA) in Tokyo has been handling Santa's mail for twenty years. For ¥2,000, they will forward your child's letter to Santa, and he will send a printed reply in four to six weeks. The letters are available only in English, and you must mail your letter by December 10. Only one name is allowed per letter. Put your letter in an envelope addressed to Santa and mail it to International Friendship Association, Chiyoda Seimei Bldg., 1-10 Nampeidai, Shibuya-ku, Tokyo. Pay by check or money order only. For more information, call (03) 3463-4944.

You can also write to Santa Claus at Santa Claus Post Office, 96100 Rovaniemi, Finland, and receive a reply, free of charge.

About Me Books will send a personalized letter from Santa to your child and/or a book all about your child and Santa. Write to: 4 Kids Only, 102 Brentwood, Belle Chase, Louisiana 70037, USA.

Rent-a-Santa

You can rent a Santa in Tokyo from Attractive Zone Media, 301 No. 2 Eiru Bldg., 3-2-9 Azabudai, Minato-ku, Tokyo, phone (03) 3584-2233. They have native English-speaking Santas for rent who will come to your home with a "Ho, Ho, Ho" and a gift for all the good little boys and girls. The standard visit is fifteen minutes, but they also have Santas available for parties and other special events.

Christmas Cards

Each year, Refugees International Japan sells greeting cards designed especially for them by major artists living in Japan. The cards make attractive and original Christmas or New Year's greetings, and the proceeds go to Refugees International Japan, a nonprofit organization run by volunteers. For information, contact Refugees International Japan, Kasumigaseki Bldg. 1922 19F, 3-2-5 Kasumigaseki, Chiyoda-ku, Tokyo 100. Phone (03) 3581-2485 from 10:00 A.M. to 3:00 P.M. UNICEF Japan also has a beautiful catalog of Christmas cards from Japan. For a catalog, call (03) 3355-3255 or write to Dai Ichi Kyocho Bldg. 2F, 31-10 Daikyo-cho, Shinjuku-ku, Tokyo.

If you are looking for personalized Christmas cards from the United States, the company, Contempo Graphics, offers a wide selection at U.S. prices. For more information, contact Rosalie Cicogna at Contempo Graphics, Homat Virginia 305, Minami Azabu, Minato-ku, Tokyo, or call or fax (03) 3440-2181.

Picture Christmas cards can be ordered at a very reasonable rate from Associated Photo Co. in the United States. The cards come with matching envelopes, and there are a variety of Christmas patterns to choose from. This company also prints photo birth announcements, invitations, and We've Moved cards. For information, phone (513) 421-6620 or fax (513) 421-6622 or write them at Box 14270 Dept. R, Cincinatti, Ohio 45250, USA. They accept VISA and MasterCard.

New Year's Cards (Nengajo)

Your local photo shop can make up fairly inexpensive New Year's cards in a week or so. A postcard with your photo on the front, these cards usually say "Happy New Year" in Japanese. However, there is room on the border for you to write your own greeting and sign your name. At larger photo shops, you will find a variety of Christmas and New Year's photo postcards that can be printed for you in English. For a little bit more money, you may have a fully personalized greeting on the card, such as "Merry Christmas and Happy New Year from the Smith Family."

BIRTHDAY PARTIES

When it comes to celebrating birthdays overseas, many parents make an extra effort to make birthdays special for their children. You may miss having relatives around, but even without them there are usually more than enough people to invite to your child's party. School friends, neighbors, just about anyone who knows and cares about your child will want to be invited. This can be a problem if you do not live in a house or apartment large enough for a crowd. We have some alternative locations for you. Of course, for very young children you may want to follow the rule of thumb that says invite one guest for each year of your child's life (i.e., one child guest for a one-year-old's party, two for a two-year-old's, and so on).

Many of the stores listed below will become your sources for all types of birthday party supplies. From paper goods to game prizes, balloons to party hats, these stores have them. Cookie Monster and Superman cakes are more difficult to come by, although you may be able to talk your local bakery into making a cake from a picture you provide. Another alternative is to find a foreigner or a caterer who has made cakes for parties before, or you can buy the supplies to make the cake at home yourself.

Chances are that one of the local McDonald's restaurants has a special room available for birthday parties. Since each restaurant is independently owned, you will have to check on your own. For example, the McDonald's (03-3781-3417) in Musashi Koyama Mall (see chap. 3 under shopping districts) offers the following: For a minimum of six children they will provide a birthday cake (about ¥1,000), and you can enjoy treating the birthday boy or girl and guests to a McDonald's lunch. There are no other charges— except the hamburgers, of course. The big advantage to this plan is that you do not risk demolition of your house, and when the party is over you can get up and go and simply leave the mess behind.

Rooms are available at other restaurants, and the wards usually have some sort of public space available for rent for a small fee. Call your ward office to see what they have and plan on reserving these rooms weeks or even months in advance.

For those of you who are lucky enough to live near a large park, outdoor parties can be easy. That is, of course, unless it rains. Check beforehand to see if the park has covered facilities for reservation or rent. Kinuta Park in Setagaya (see chap. 5) has a large carpeted room available for a small rental fee. You can have the cake and presents inside and if the weather is nice, play games outside.

Other alternative locations are the amusement parks or zoos in your area. This is a big adventure, and if you are paying it can be a big expense. If you do this, enlist the other mothers' help, and put the kids on a budget. For party favors, you could give the kids matching T-shirts or badges to wear on the outing.

PHOTOGRAPHY STUDIOS

During your stay in Japan, you may want to visit a professional studio to have some commemmorative photos taken. The following studios are known for their excellent work.

Igarashi Studio

Hotel Okura South Wing 2F, 2-10-4 Toranomon, Minato-ku, Tokyo
☎ (03) 3586-1690　東京都港区虎の門 2-10-4 ホテル・オークラ
This studio has been a favorite with foreigners in Tokyo for many years. Prices are around ¥10,000 a sitting with special prices for children offered several times a year. Look for their ad in the *Japan Times.*

Clique Productions

Fujiso 2F7, 4-16-12 Tokiwadai, Itabashi-ku, Tokyo
☎ (03) 3936-3943　東京都板橋区常盤台 4-6-12 富士荘 2F7
Neil Krivonak, the professional photographer behind Clique Productions, has gained quite a reputation for his photos of children. His specialty is family portraits, which he will take at any location. The fee of ¥50,000 seems reasonable when you see his exquisite photographs.

HOLIDAY SUPPLIES

There are a few stores that you can always count on to have a supply of seasonal decorations, cards, costume supplies, and gifts. The following list should help you find most of what you will need to celebrate the holidays.

Ito-ya

2-7-15 Ginza, Chuo-ku, Tokyo　東京都中央区銀座 2-7-15
☎ (03) 3561-8311
There are six branches of this stationery shop in Tokyo: the main shop in Ginza and the other branches in Tamagawa Takashimaya Mall (see chap. 2), Shibuya Design House, Marunouchi File Shop, Garden Plaza Hiroo, and the Kasumigaseki Building. Ito-ya has every stationery need you could ever wish for, as well as a good supply of seasonal cards, pins, stickers, and small decorations.

Kiddyland

6-1-9 Jingumae, Shibuya-ku, Tokyo　東京都渋谷区神宮前 6-1-9
☎ (03) 3409-3431
Located on Omote Sando, five minutes from Harajuku Station (see chap. 2 under Harajuku in the shopping districts section), Kiddyland has costumes, gag gifts, kid's toys, and paper products (napkins, plates, streamers, etc.).

Seibu Loft

21-1 Udagawa-cho, Shibuya-ku, Tokyo　東京都渋谷区宇田川町 21-1
☎ (03) 3462-3807
Located in Shibuya and part of the Seibu Department Store, this is a fun store to visit (see chap. 2 under department stores). Year-round you will find goods running the gamut from neon to nice, trendy to traditional. For each holiday, the store carries the cheaper disposable-type decorations, as well as some exquisite handcrafted items. There are also many things that you can put to use for original decorating or gift giving.

National Azabu Bookstore

Located over National Azabu Supermarket in Hiroo, this bookstore-*cum*-gift shop always has a reasonable supply of holiday goods. For a more detailed description, see chapter 4 under bookstores.

Sony Plaza Store

5-3-1 Ginza, Chuo-ku, Tokyo　東京都中央区銀座 5-3-1
☎ (03) 3575-2111
This store has twenty-four branches around town, including stores in the Tamagawa Takashimaya Mall in Setagaya (see chap. 2), the Sony Building in Ginza, and the 109 Building in Shibuya. Sony Plaza stores specialize in imported goods, foods, toiletries, dishes, you name it, from around the world. Many products are from the United States and Europe. Whatever the holiday, the stores always have a large assortment of seasonal goods and decorations on display.

Tokyu Hands

Tokyu Hands is the place to shop for parties in general, and they have lots of supplies for do-it-yourself decorations and gifts (see chap. 2 under specialty shops).

American Balloon Art Company

1-10-6 Higashi Nakanobu, Shinagawa-ku, Tokyo　東京都品川区東中延 1-10-6
☎ and fax (03) 3785-9940

This delivery service offers an extensive variety of balloons for every occasion. Delivery is available in the Tokyo area for a reasonable rate; orders should be placed two days in advance.

Tuxedo Bear Balloon Shop

2-29-18 Dogenzaka, Shibuya-ku, Tokyo ☎ (03) 3463-2525
1-4-1 Minami Azabu, Minato-ku, Tokyo ☎ (03) 3457-5241
Nagata Bldg., 2-30-17 Higashi Kamata, Ota-ku, Tokyo ☎ (03) 3735-2111
This shop can provide helium balloons of all shapes and sizes.

Other outlets for decorations and gifts at great prices are Sanrio stores and the three large shopping districts, Akihabara, Asakusabashi, and Kappabashi (see chap. 2). For costumes, check the resale shops in chapter 2.

MAIL ORDER FROM ABROAD

Unless otherwise specified, VISA and MasterCard are accepted.

All Star Costume

125 Lincoln Blvd., Dept. C-300, Middlesex, New Jersey 08846, USA
☎ (201) 805-0200
This company carries a wide range of costumes for kids and adults. From princesses to ninja warriors, they are all here. You can also order masks, magic wands, and makeup.

Gevette Express

4360 Panorama Dr., La Mesa, California 92041, USA
☎ (619) 460-4335
This company offers inexpensive party kits on a variety of themes, such as Dinosaurs, Sesame Street, Pirates, or Teddy Bears. Halloween and Christmas party kits are also available. The kits include invitations, candles, balloons, plates—everything you need for a successful party. American Express only.

Maid of Scandinavia

3244 Raleigh Avenue, Minneapolis, Minnesota 55416, USA
☎ (612) 927-7996 fax (612) 927-6215
This 200-page catalog is filled with party supplies, such as crepe paper streamers, paper plates and cups, party signs, even piñatas. They also have cake decorating supplies. DISCOVER also accepted.

Stik-ees

1165 Joshua Way, P.O. Box 9630, Vista, California 92083, USA
☎ (619) 727-7011
This company has been in business since we were kids, selling color decals

for all occasions. The designs stick on windows, bathtubs, and most smooth surfaces, and they can be used over and over again. They have packets for sale for all major holidays (cutouts of witches and pumpkins for Halloween, Santa for Christmas, etc.) and children can decorate the windows in the house or their rooms for each season.

Taffy's-By-Mail

701 Beta Drive, Cleveland, Ohio 44143, USA
☎ (216) 461-3360
Although this catalog is known for its dance and cheerleader costumes, they also have butterfly wings, majorette suits, and princess dresses. American Express and DISCOVER also accepted.

The Party Basket, Ltd.

734 Nashville Avenue, New Orleans, Louisiana 70115, USA
☎ (504) 899-8126
This catalog offers the largest selection we have ever seen of children's party goods. From piñatas and party favors to personalized napkins, this company sells everything you need for a perfect party. Besides carrying over fifty choices of table settings and decorations for birthday parties, the Party Basket is full of ideas for major holidays and religious occasions.

PARTY ENTERTAINMENT

Bruce Bryant

c/o ASIJ, 1-1 Nomizu, Chofu-shi, Tokyo 182　東京都調布市野水 1−1
☎ (0423) 33-9507
Bruce puts on one of the best magic acts for children that we have seen. His shows are ideal entertainment for even very young kids and he really knows how to work the crowd. A long-time resident of Japan, Bruce teaches at the American School in Japan during the week. He is available for large stage shows as well as for small parties.

David Letendre

2-2 Fujiya Corpo, 1-32-11 Higashinogawa, Komae-shi, Tokyo
☎ (03) 3489-5330 東京都狛江市東野川 1−32−11 ふじやコーポ 2−2
David has been entertaining kids and families in Tokyo for fifteen years. His show includes comedy, magic, and balloon sculpturing. The entertainment is especially designed for kids and families. We have seen him perform many times and know him to be fun and reliable. Book early for weekend engagements and Christmas parties.

Terry O'Brien

1-8-2 Hyakunin-cho, Shinjuku-ku, Tokyo 160　東京都新宿区百人町 1-8-2
☎ (03) 3209-4319 or (03) 3379-3511

Terry's magic act is very professional, and he performs in major clubs and hotels throughout Japan. If his hectic schedule allows, he also performs for private parties, and he is especially good with children.

Marine Media

2-24-1 Jingumae, Shibuya-ku, Tokyo　東京都渋谷区神宮前 2-24-1
☎ (03) 3403-7190

This company provides various kinds of entertainment for children's parties as well as adult parties. To arrange a birthday or theme party, give them a call.

Unicom

101 Cozy Heights, 5-23-3 Yayoi-cho, Nakano-ku, Tokyo
☎ (03) 3383-6322　東京都中野区弥生町 5-23-3 コージハイツ 101

We first found out about this company when we saw a remarkable one-man band performance by David Budimir at the opening of a children's store. David is part of a coterie of talented performers who can be booked through Unicom. Standing for Universal Communication, Unicom's aim is to expand communication about educational and cultural issues through children's entertainment.

Unicom is run by Colm Largey whose multi-instrumental musical puppet shows are a favorite with kids. Artists working with Unicom include jugglers, mimics, and even a rock musician, Doug Manring, who performs a show specially for kids. All Unicom's performers have experience in working with children, and this friendly group hopes to work more closely in the future with ward and city offices to create special performances around such themes as ecology and third world countries. For information on booking a Unicom performer for a party or school function, ask for Colm Largey at the number listed above.

Del's Delights International

4-18-12 Takanawa, Minato-ku, Tokyo 108　東京都港区高輪 4-18-12
☎ (03) 3447-0627

Del Ferraresi is the talent behind Del's Delights, turning out creative cakes and candies for any occasion. She can concoct just about any fantasy cake your child dreams of, from Ninja Turtles to Barbies. She requests that you place your order at least two weeks in advance.

Brown Rice

3-12-35 Moto Azabu, Minato-ku, Tokyo　東京都港区元麻布 3-12-35
☎ (03) 3408-1424

A source for organic birthday cakes is the Brown Rice bakery, which uses only natural ingredients and sweeteners. Run by Takako Nakamura, this shop will design a special birthday cake in addition to offering such seasonal goodies as wholewheat Halloween cookies.

SPECIAL EVENTS

In addition to national holidays, there are many special events throughout Japan that your children may enjoy. You may find that some of these regional events are worth planning a vacation around.

JANUARY 6: NEW YEAR PARADE OF FIREMEN (DEZOME SHIKI)

There is nothing children like better than firemen, right? Well, this parade is full of them, all dressed in traditional attire and performing acrobatic stunts on bamboo ladders. What a treat! The firemen's parade takes place in Harumi Dori in Chuo-ku. It's a bit crowded but the view from Dad's shoulders is usually pretty good.

EARLY FEBRUARY: SNOW FESTIVAL IN SAPPORO (YUKIMATSURI)

This unique event is well worth the trip to the northernmost island of Hokkaido. Young children delight in seeing elaborate life-size (and larger) snow sculptures. It is a crowded event, and a sturdy backpack helps toddlers get a better view. Strollers are difficult to navigate, and walking the entire route is exhausting even for parents. A better idea is to choose one section of the park and let the kids investigate—the ice slides, sculptures kids can climb on, and their favorite cartoon characters larger than life in ice will captivate the kids for hours.

LAST SATURDAY IN JULY: FIREWORKS DISPLAY ON THE SUMIDA RIVER (HANABI TAIKAI)

From late summer to early fall, fireworks displays are held all around the country. They are traditionally held over water, where their reflection can be enjoyed. For a memorable evening on the Sumida River, rent a cruise boat with other families and watch the magnificent display from the water. You can also watch from the central point, but it is very crowded. The view is exciting even from a distance, however, which is sometimes better for young children who may be frightened by the noise. Also in mid-August there is a fireworks display located in Jingu Stadium. This is visible from many rooftops in the Shibuya area. For more information, watch the papers for details and look out for colorful posters at subway stations.

LATE AUGUST: GOODBYE TO SUMMER RALLY (NORYO TAIKAI)

From late August into early October, neighborhood festivals (*matsuri*) take place throughout Japan. The following description of the Azabu Juban festival in Tokyo is typical of other celebrations at this time of year. At the Juban festival, the crowds have become so huge in recent years that it is best to go in late afternoon just after the stalls have been set up. Dress your children in their cool summer *yukata*, a casual cotton kimono. It is possible to purchase adult and children's *yukata* at a Juban shop in the middle of the festival, which we did one year. The owners were quite gracious about dressing us all up in our finery! Cotton *yukata* are more comfortable than you can imagine in the August heat and humidity.

Even if you don't feel like dressing up, you can still stroll down the long shopping street, which is gaily decorated for the event. There are stalls offering cool treats, such as "ice candy" (popsicles) and *kakigori* (snowballs). Most of the vendors have something especially for children. There are goldfish-catching games and numerous small toys for sale. One of our favorite booths is full of miniature plastic food at bargain prices. A collection of realisitic sushi rolls, soy sauce bottles, and chopsticks is available in addition to fruit, hamburgers, and tiny cartons of milk. We always buy several bagfuls to send back home for children's birthdays, and we keep some for our own grocery shopping games at home.

At the festival, when you hear the drum beat, make your way to the end of the street where a tall platform is erected. On the top you will see a drummer sounding out a traditional beat for the townspeople to dance to. The drummers—young men and women from the neighborhood—are quite impressive to watch. They are accompanied by Japanese folk songs played over the loudspeakers. A procession of locals winds their way around the platform performing simple dances. From grandmothers to toddlers, everyone is welcome to join in the fun. Usually some of the older residents know the dances well, so watch their movements a few times before joining in. Our preschoolers often pick up the dances before we do!

Some of your fondest memories of Japan will be of the nights full of music, food, and fun at your neighborhood festival. There will be some sort of festival in almost every neighborhood either in summer or autumn. The ward office can give you information on your area, but also be on the lookout for signs of preparation. A few days before the festival, the portable shrine (*omikoshi*) will be set up under a tent where people will be making offerings of fruit, sake, and other gifts to the gods. The shopkeepers may also be lining the streets with paper lanterns and streamers. On the day of the *matsuri*, the shrine is paraded around several blocks on the shoulders of the residents. Many neighborhoods also have a shrine for children to carry, and they get a big thrill from being part of the procession. Inquire at the tent about taking part. Usually foreigners are more than welcome. After all, it's your neighborhood too!

EARLY OCTOBER: GINZA FESTIVAL (GINZA MATSURI)

There are several large festivals in the first week of October in Tokyo, including Ginza *matsuri*. These are more commercial and elaborate than the neighborhood festivals, with parades, floats, and streets full of open-air bazaars. Since the main streets are blocked to traffic it is safe to walk with children, but the crowds can be overwhelming on a nice day. For more information about the Ginza *matsuri*, call the festival office at (03) 3561-0919.

EARLY NOVEMBER: AUTUMN FESTIVAL AT MEIJI SHRINE (AKI MATSURI)

This is an excellent opportunity to absorb some of the culture of Japan without buying tickets and sitting in a theater. In the crisp autumn air you can watch Noh plays, see ancient dances, and hear music played on traditional instruments. There is also Japanese archery and a variety of martial arts performances. We have found that these events usually have a special section for children. Some years there is a petting zoo, or appearances by favorite cartoon characters. The Meiji Shrine grounds are quite large, so you might want to bring a picnic and take your time wandering around enjoying the events. For more information about the festival, call the shrine office at (03) 3379-5511.

9

Having a Baby in Japan

AH.... BACH... I HOPE YOU
LIKE HIM TOO.

The idea of giving birth in a foreign country can be unsettling. Fortunately, Japan has one of the lowest infant mortality rates in the world, and those foreigners who have had children here have found that many facilities in Japan do not differ greatly from those in their home country. The Westernization of facilities and practices in the field of obstetrics makes it easy to seek out hospitals with high standards of hygiene and state-of-the-art equipment.

It is interesting to note that the Japanese count the period of pregnancy as ten lunar months of twenty-eight days each, whereas Westerners count nine months of thirty-one days. Home pregnancy tests are available at most drugstores in Japan, although for instructions in English you may have to purchase one from an international pharmacy (see the family planning section in this chapter).

After you have visited a doctor to confirm your pregnancy, you will need to go to your local ward or city office to register the pregnancy. You must take your alien registration card, and fill out a form with your doctor's name and the address of the clinic or hospital with which he or she is associated. You will then receive the booklet, the *boshi kenko techo*, commonly referred to as the *boshi techo*, that will be a record of your health during pregnancy, labor, and delivery and of your child's subsequent development. You will also receive information concerning pregnancy and birth, and a health card entitling you to free checkups at Japanese hospitals during your pregnancy.

The *boshi techo* is an important little book, and you should carry it with you, particularly during your last weeks of pregnancy. The hospital or clinic staff will write in this booklet at each prenatal checkup and many times during your hospital stay. If you take your child to a Japanese hospital or public health center for checkups and shots, or use Japanese National Health Insurance, the *boshi techo* will also serve as your child's record for the first six years. The handbook is also necessary if your child will be registered as a Japanese citizen. A copy of the *boshi techo* in English can be obtained from many of the obstetricians and gynecologists in private practice in Tokyo, and also by writing to the Japanese Organization for International Cooperation in Family Planning Incorporated (see listing under family planning in this chapter). This English-language book is only for your convenience; officially you must register your pregnancy at the ward or city office and receive the Japanese-language *boshi techo*.

MATERNITY CLOTHES

Can't quite zip those jeans? Are your feet starting to swell? You may feel panicked at the thought of finding comfortable and stylish maternity wear in Japan, but we have some suggestions for you. If you need some immediate relief, use the old trick with the rubber band. All you have to do is get a medium-sized rubber band, loop it through the button hole of your pants until it is secure, and then pull the other end over the button on the other side. You can also borrow your husband's old shirts and sweaters for baggy tops. Do not forget the option of asking friends and relatives back home to send you a care package of Western-sized maternity wear for the last mile.

All department stores have a selection of maternity clothes (see chap. 2 under department stores). You can also buy Japanese maternity clothes and undergarments from the Japanese baby equipment catalogs listed in chapter 3. Japanese maternity clothes are, of course, made for Japanese women, and they are often not large enough for Western women, especially after six months of pregnancy. The styles of Japanese maternity clothes are often a bit "fussy" for our tastes, not to mention the outrageous price tag on most items.

You can also make use of bulletin-board ads, newspaper and magazine ads, and friends' maternity clothes if you do not want to spend much money. Another possibility is to look in local resale shops (see chap. 2 under resale outlets) or to mail order from abroad.

MAIL-ORDER MATERNITY AND NURSING CLOTHES FROM ABROAD

The catalogs listed here offer clothes that range from inexpensive, homey fashions to stylish, formal maternity wear. Whatever your style or budget, there is probably something here to get you through those nine long months.

Babe Too!: Patterns

3457 E. K4 Highway, Assaria, Kansas 67416, USA
☎ (913) 667-5125

This company offers patterns for sewing nursing wear. The line includes dresses, blouses, nightgowns, and running clothes.

5th Avenue Maternity

P.O. Box 21826, Seattle, Washington 98111-3826, USA
☎ (206) 343-7046

Fashionable maternity wear from sweat suits to party dresses is available from this company. Bathing suits, underwear, and much, much more are available from this color catalog.

J.C. Penney Company, Inc.

Circulation Dept., Box 2056, Dept. PR22, Milwaukee, Wisconsin 53201-2056, USA

This company has a large selection of maternity clothes and nursing bras in addition to baby furniture and accessories. Prices are extremely reasonable. VISA, MasterCard, and American Express accepted.

La Leche League International

P.O. Box 1209, Franklin Park, Illinois 60131-8209, USA
☎ (312) 455-7730

This group issues a catalog full of material on breast-feeding, nutrition, and childbirth. They also carry a range of accessories for nursing mothers, such as breast pumps, milk storage systems, and breast shields and shells.

Mother's Wear

1738-5 Topanga Skyline, Topanga, California 90290, USA
☎ (213) 455-1426

This company has a good selection of nursing bras in several styles in American sizes from 34C to 40E.

Page Boy Maternity

8919 Governors Row, Dallas, Texas 75247, USA
☎ (214) 951-0055

This company produces seasonal catalogs filled with beautiful maternity wear for all occasions. Black velvet dresses, silk tunics, and T-shirts are featured. VISA, MasterCard, and American Express are accepted.

Reborn Maternity

564 Columbus Avenue, New York, New York 10024, USA
☎ (212) 362-6965

Wonderfully fashionable clothes for pregnant women to wear to the office, to parties, or on casual occasions are available from this company. The glossy color catalog is revised often to include new styles. VISA, Master-Card, American Express, and DISCOVER are accepted.

CHOOSING A PLACE OF BIRTH

Whether you decide to give birth in Japan or in your hometown hospital, the most important thing for expectant couples is to be informed. All options should be considered, and when searching for the ideal doctor or place of birth do not be afraid to get a second opinion. Attending a class on choosing a place of birth is an important first step. There are many options for pregnant women in Japan. A childbirth education class in your area can inform you of possible places of birth and answer many of your questions.

CHILDBIRTH EDUCATION CLASSES

Ward and city offices usually have a series of birth preparation classes taught by a team of nurses, midwives, and at least one doctor. The content and tone of the classes varies tremendously, some being very good and others mediocre. The good thing about these classes is the opportunity they provide for expectant mothers to meet other women and to hear opinions other than those of her doctor. Through the classes, the mother can also become familiar with her *hokenjo* (health department), since it will also be where she will take her child for free immunizations and health checks if she chooses to take advantage of these services. The health department may also have classes on breast-feeding, baby care, weaning, and so on. Many hospitals also offer these types of classes to their patients. Besides these classes, there are often doctors and health-care professionals who give lectures and advice to parents at other centers. Check the department store listings (in chap. 2) for stores that provide this service.

In greater Tokyo and the Kansai area, there are several classes taught in English, and some instructors may be willing to correspond with expectant mothers living in other parts of the country. A short list of independent childbirth education services and programs follows.

GREATER TOKYO

Baby Healthy
1585-17 Yaita Inamachi, Tsukuba-gun, Ibaraki-ken
☎ (0297) 58-3708 茨城県筑波郡伊奈町谷井田 1585-17
Midwife Fusako Sei is experienced in underwater birth.

Tokyo Childbirth Education Association (TCEA), Birth Education and Counseling Associates (BECA)

Homat Virginia 301, 4-11-2 Minami-Azabu, Minato-ku, Tokyo 106
☎ (03) 3440-1657　東京都港区南麻布 4-11-2 ホマットバージニア 301

Founded in 1983 for the purpose of providing quality childbirth education and parenting programs for the foreign community, TCEA offers a comprehensive series of classes on childbearing which are updated regularly. Information on a wide range of childbirth options is available from the TCEA and they will also provide referrals to local resources. Through their program "Birth in Japan," participants are paired up with childbirth educators sensitive to their cultural differences and individual preferences. TCEA is supported by the U.S.-based Birth Education and Counseling Associates (BECA), which provide educational materials for the use of local educators in their classes. A large selection of books and videotapes are available for loan and sale to TCEA participants. Classes are held at Aiiku Hospital in Minami Azabu, Tokyo, and at a number of other locations in the Tokyo area. Call Elena de Karplus at the above number for more information and a brochure containing details of class location and schedule of programs.

Mother Center

3-34-5 Ogikubo 210, Suginami-ku, Tokyo　東京都杉並区荻窪 3-34-5-210
☎ (03) 3391-5642

This center offers classes in active birth preparation and maternity yoga taught by Sakae Kikuchi.

The Childbirth School

1-24-8 Takadanobaba, Shinjuku-ku, Tokyo　東京都新宿区高田馬場 1-24-8
☎ (03) 3232-0006

The director, Tsugiko Sugiyama, started this school in 1979. Classes are taught by independent midwives and doctors who not only train couples in the Lamaze method of childbirth, but also teach them the latest theories of child-rearing and infant care.

The Childbirth Education Service

3-29-20 Shimouma, Setagaya-ku, Tokyo 154　東京都世田谷区下馬 3-29-20
☎ (03) 3410-3737 (in Japanese or English)

Jean Umezu, a registered nurse from the United States, has been teaching childbirth education classes in Japan since 1976. Her classes include information on the Lamaze method, nutrition, exercise, breast-feeding, and choosing a place of birth. Videos and books are available for loan. Jean's classes are taught at the Tokyo Baptist Church in Shibuya. In addition to her childbirth classes, Jean teaches infant and child cardiopulmonary resuscitation (CPR), community CPR, and adult first aid. For more information call the Tokyo Baptist Church at (03) 3461-8439.

Underwater Birth Group (Suichu Shussan Renraku Kai)

1-7-12 Gotenyama, Musashino-shi, Tokyo 180　東京都武蔵野市御殿山 1−7−12
☎ (0422) 47-1444 or (0422) 42-6666
Lessons in preparing for an underwater birth are given by Emi Takada.

KANSAI AREA

Childbirth Education Organization (CEO)　兵庫県神戸市東灘区鴨子原 3−1−5

c/o Kansai CEO, 3-1-5 Kamokogahara, Higashi Nada-ku, Kobe-shi, Hyogo-ken
This service is run by Joan Mason, R.N. and M.S.N. (078-851-6413). Classes are taught in childbirth preparation, covering such topics as exercise, nutrition, breast-feeding, and relaxation during labor. Books and videotapes are also available.

CHILDBIRTH RESOURCES

Louise Shimizu

4-3-4 Minami Ikebukuro, Toshima-ku, Tokyo 171　東京都豊島区南池袋 4−3−4
☎ (03) 3986-3526
A long-time childbirth educator in Tokyo and coauthor of *Childbirth in Japan* (Birth International, Tokyo, 1990), Louise started teaching childbirth preparation classes to foreigners in Tokyo in 1973 and was instrumental in introducing the Lamaze method of childbirth to Japan through classes, lectures, and also by publishing information for Japanese practitioners in their own language. Louise is a valuable contact in Japanese or English for anyone needing information relating to childbirth and infant care in Japan.

MIDWIVES

For generations, midwives have played a valuable role in pregnancy and childbirth in Japan. Today there are more than 23,000 registered midwives, and even in large hospitals midwives may be involved in the majority of deliveries. A home birth is an option considered by some women in Japan because of the access to experienced independent midwives. However, only a small percentage of babies are born at home, with the majority of Japanese women delivering in hospitals and clinics. If you are considering a home birth, be aware that it may be difficult to arrange for emergency backup at a nearby hospital. There are no official support services for midwives although you could arrange for your own transportation.

The following associations can give you information about midwives throughout Japan: Japan Academy of Midwifery, 1-12 Katamachi, Shinjuku-ku, Tokyo 160, (03) 3357-2506; Japanese Midwives' Association, 1-8-21 Fujimi, Chiyoda-ku, Tokyo 102, (03) 3262-9910; Japanese Nursing Association—Midwife Division, 5-8-2 Jingumae, Shibuya-ku, Tokyo 150, (03) 3400-8331.

The childbirth educators in your area may also be able to provide you with some names and phone numbers of midwives. The midwives listed below offer a variety of services in the greater Tokyo area. Some of them work through a clinic, while others will deliver your baby at home.

Name	Place	Telephone	Where	Specialities
Tabata	Yokohama-shi	(045) 751-7685	Home	Lamaze
Mizuochi	Adachi-ku	(03) 3899-5205	Clinic	
Terajima	Shibuya-ku	(03) 3376-5972	Home & Clinic	Lamaze & Active Birth
Kurihara	Saitama-ken	(0492) 31-1046	Clinic	Lamaze
Akutagawa	Taito-ku	(03) 3821-6561	Home & Clinic	Lamaze
Sugiyama	Suginami-ku	(03) 3313-5658	Clinic	
Nomoto	Chofu-shi/ Mitaka-shi	(0424) 82-2973	Clinic	Lamaze
Oshima	Mitaka-shi	(0424) 61-9193	Clinic	Lamaze & Active Birth
Motoyama	Yokohama-shi	(045) 391-1169	Clinic	Lamaze
Fujii	Yokohama-shi	(045) 945-5560	Home & Clinic	
Fukuoka	Sumida-ku	(03) 3611-7563 or (03) 3611-0301	Clinic	Lamaze
Aoyagi	Ota-ku	03) 3761-4138	Clinic	Lamaze
Sei	Ibaraki-ken	(0297) 58-3708	Clinic	Lamaze & Active Birth
Sakuma (no English spoken)	Chiba-ken	(0479) 76-2357	Clinic	Lamaze & Active Birth
Ichikawa	Machida-shi	(0427) 91-1161	Clinic	Lamaze

CLINICS AND HOSPITALS

If you plan to deliver in a clinic or a hospital, take the time to find one whose facilities and philosophies suit you. You will find that most major hospitals have strict birth policies. Some hospitals do not allow husbands to be present at the birth. Others may require a new mother to stay in the hospital for a set period—usually about a week—and also restrict the length of time she can spend with her baby. In general, smaller clinics offer a more personal and flexible service. Of course, your special needs must be taken into consideration. The place of birth that you choose will greatly depend on whether you have a high-risk pregnancy or whether you are expecting your third child.

No matter what the policies are at your place of birth, do not hesitate to question the practices and to request certain changes if necessary. Although doctors are not used to discussing options with Japanese patients, they expect to hear plenty of questions from foreigners. It helps if your doctor speaks English, or if you can communicate in Japanese. If there seems to be a communication problem, try to arrange for an interpreter to come along for at least one visit so that the important issues can be discussed. If you are submitting a birth plan, it is a good idea to have it written in Japanese as well as your native language so that there is no confusion.

Some hospitals are more rigid than others, but we have found that insistence in a firm but polite manner can achieve results. This is especially effective if you are dealing with a situation such as separation from baby at birth. Many mothers enjoy rooming-in with their baby, or at least want unlimited access to their newborn. This is especially important for a breast-feeding mother. Some hospitals have a policy that the baby must be separated from the mother for up to twenty-four hours after birth for observation. Often, with persistence, this rule can be eliminated or at least relaxed.

In Japan today, the trend is toward delivering in large hospitals. Doctors usually have delivery "rights" at certain hospitals, so you should find out which doctors deliver where. Of course, there is often no guarantee at a large hospital that a specific doctor will deliver your baby.

Small ob-gyn clinics are also fairly popular in this country, both with Japanese and with foreigners. Many of these clinics are not luxuriously decorated, but they do offer a cozy environment in which to give birth. A similar atmosphere can be found in maternity homes, which are small clinics run by midwives. Most small clinics have some form of emergency backup, but you should check to see exactly what the situation would be in case of an emergency.

Prenatal and postnatal vitamins are not routinely prescribed in Japan. If you would like to take them, or if you are anemic, your doctor will provide them. Be aware that the iron content—the main reason pregnant and nursing women take these vitamins—may not be as high as even regular multivitamins from the United States. You can also ask your doctor in your home country to give you a supply of prenatal vitamins, or you can order vitamin supplements from the Foreign Buyer's Club (see chap. 10).

Some medical interventions are common in this country both before and during childbirth. For example, ultrasound is frequently used for prenatal exams, and many hospitals require fetal monitors during labor. Induction of labor is not uncommon, especially in small clinics with limited staff. Episiotomies are also quite routine. You will want to discuss these and other issues with your doctor ahead of time. In their birth plan, foreign women sometimes state which interventions they would prefer to eliminate in a normal childbirth.

Many smaller clinics do not offer any pain-relief drugs during childbirth. In some clinics and in the hospitals, an epidural is available, but the majority of Japanese midwives and doctors advocate a "natural" birth without drugs. For true emergencies, a general anesthetic is usually given, but for other situations it is possible to request an epidural. In case of a Cesarean, check to see what anesthesia will be administered and be sure to ask your doctor what sort of incision he will make. A transverse uterine scar is supposedly stronger and will increase your chances of avoiding a Cesarean with your next baby. The 10 percent Cesarean rate in Japan is much lower than in Western countries. Vaginal birth after Cesarean (VBAC) is a new concept here, but some doctors are receptive to the idea.

Amniocentesis, the procedure of drawing fluid from the womb to test for abnormalities in the fetus, is offered by a few specialists, but it is not the common procedure for women over thirty-five years of age that it is in the United States and some other Western countries. If a mother does face some problem in her pregnancy, it is a good idea to contact some of the experts in the field. Several hospitals in Japan are world famous for their work on special problems in conception and childbirth. See the listings of doctors and hospitals later in this section.

Circumcision, the operation in which the foreskin is cut from a male infant's penis, is another procedure that is rarely done in Japan. Because Japanese newborns are not traditionally circumcised, most doctors have rarely performed this surgery. Parents planning to have their infant circumcised should take care to find an experienced doctor. In Japan, this surgery is usually performed by surgeons who specialize in male urinary tract surgery. A good book to read if you want further information on circumcision is *Circumcision* (Edward Wallerstein, Springer Publishing Co., New York, 1980).

Some of the routine procedures administered to newborn babies in Japan are antibiotic eye drops to prevent eye infection, vitamin K shots, screening tests for rare metabolic problems, such as phenylketonuria (PKU), and checks for jaundice. The baby's blood type may not be tested unless specifically requested. Also, an imprint of the baby's footprint is not usually taken as it is in many Western countries. Instead, the baby's dried umbilical cord stub is preserved and sometimes given to the parents in a little box.

We suggest that before leaving the hospital, you ask the doctor or nurse to write down all of the baby's tests and results, in English if possible. This information is not recorded in detail in the *boshi techo*, and you will want to have it for your baby's records.

RECOMMENDED HOSPITALS

Both large and small hospitals with ob-gyn, maternity, and pediatrics departments are listed below. Some of them may be affiliated with a university or teaching facility, while others may have their origins as Christian hospitals. If you visit these hospitals, you will be seen by one of the doctors on the staff there. Usually, it is not possible to make an appointment; you must go and wait your turn. Other doctors may have delivery "rights" at the hospital but see patients by appointment in their own office or clinic.

| KANTO AREA |

Aiiku Hospital

5-6-8 Minami-Azabu, Minato-ku, Tokyo
☎ (03) 3473-8321　東京都港区南麻布 5–6–8

Hiroo Hospital

2-34-10 Ebisu, Shibuya-ku, Tokyo
☎ (03) 3444-1181　東京都渋谷区恵比寿 2–34–10

Jikei University Hospital

3-19-18 Nishi-Shimbashi, Minato-ku, Tokyo
☎ (03) 3433-1111　東京都港区西新橋 3–19–18

Keio University Hospital

35 Shinanomachi, Shinjuku-ku, Tokyo
☎ (03) 3353-1211　東京都新宿区信濃町 35

Red Cross Hospital (Nisseki Byoin)

4-1-22 Hiroo, Shibuya-ku, Tokyo
☎ (03) 3400-1311　東京都渋谷区広尾 4-1-22

Seibo Byoin (International Catholic Hospital)

2-5-1 Naka Ochiai, Shinjuku-ku, Tokyo
☎ (03) 3951-1111　東京都新宿区中落合 2-5-1

Seventh Day Adventist Hospital (Eisei Byoin)

3-17-3 Amanuma, Suginami-ku, Tokyo
☎ (03) 3392-6151　東京都杉並区天沼 3-17-3

Showa University Hospital

1-5-8 Hatanodai, Shinagawa-ku, Tokyo
☎ (03) 3784-8615　東京都品川区旗の台 1-5-8

St. Luke's International Hospital (Episcopal)

10-1 Akashi-cho, Chuo-ku, Tokyo
☎ (03) 3541-5151　東京都中央区明石町 10-1

International Goodwill Hospital

1-28-1 Nishigaoka, Izumi-ku, Yokohama-shi, Kanagawa-ken
☎ (045) 681-0221　神奈川県横浜市泉区西ヶ丘 1-28-1

Kanagawa Children's Medical Center

2-138-4 Mutsukawa, Minami-ku, Yokohama-shi, Kanagawa-ken
☎ (045) 711-2351　神奈川県横浜市南区六ッ川 2-138-4

KANSAI AREA

Kaisei Hospital

3-11-15 Shinohara-kitamachi, Nada-ku, Kobe-shi, Hyogo-ken
☎ (078) 871-5201　兵庫県神戸市灘区篠原北町 3-11-15

Kobe Adventist Hospital

8-4-1 Arinodai, Kita-ku, Kobe-shi, Hyogo-ken
☎ (078) 981-0161　兵庫県神戸市北区有野台 8-4-1

Konan Hospital

1-5-16 Kamokogahara, Higashi Nada-ku, Kobe-shi, Hyogo-ken
☎ (078) 851-2161　兵庫県神戸市東灘区鴨子が原 1-5-16

Ueda Hospital

1-1-4 Kunika-dori, Chuo-ku, Kobe-shi, Hyogo-ken
☎ (078) 241-3305   兵庫県神戸市中央区国香通 1-1-4

Itoh Byoin

3-2 Inokoda-cho, Shimogamo, Sakyo-ku, Kyoto-shi, Kyoto-fu
☎ (075) 781 5188   京都府京都市左京区下鴨狗子田町 3-2

Nihon Baptist Hospital

47 Yamanomoto-cho, Kita-shirakawa, Sakyo-ku, Kyoto-shi, Kyoto-fu
☎ (075) 781-5191   京都府京都市左京区北白川山ノ元町 47

Yoshida Hospital

1-7-1 Saidaiji, Akatamachi, Nara-shi, Nara-ken
☎ (0742) 45-4601   奈良県奈良市西大寺赤田町 1-7-1

Hamada Hospital

1-6-9 Uriwari, Hirano-ku, Osaka-shi, Osaka-fu
☎ (06) 7087-2000   大阪府大阪市平野区瓜破 1-6-9

Iwasa Ladies' Clinic

9-22 Korien-cho, Hirakata-shi, Osaka-fu
☎ (0720) 31-1666   大阪府枚方市香里園 9-22

Morimoto Women's Hospital

4-26-4 Hoshin, Higashi Yodogawa-ku, Osaka-shi, Osaka-fu
☎ (06) 328-6410   大阪府大阪市東淀川区豊新 4-26-4

Santa Maria Hospital

13-15 Shinjo, Ibaraki-shi, Osaka-fu
☎ (0726) 27-3459   大阪府茨木市新庄 13-15

St. Barnabus Hospital (no English spoken)

1-3-32 Saekudani, Tennoji-ku, Osaka-shi, Osaka-fu
☎ (06) 779-1600   大阪府大阪市天王寺区細工谷 1-3-32

Yodogawa Christian Hospital

2-9-26 Awagi, Higashi Yodogawa-ku, Osaka-shi, Osaka-fu
☎ (06) 322-2250   大阪府大阪市東淀川区淡路 2-9-26

PRIVATE OB-GYN CLINICS

The ob-gyn doctors listed below are in private practice, as opposed to
being on the staff at a large hospital. What this means to you as a patient is
that you will most likely be able to make an appointment instead of waiting

your turn at a hospital. These doctors may have delivery "rights" at one or more hospitals, or they may deliver in their own clinic. Private clinics may or may not take Japanese National Health Insurance. This list is by no means complete, but these are doctors who have been recommended by the foreign community and who for the most part have no problem speaking English.

GREATER TOKYO

Dr. Tsuneo Akaeda, Akaeda Roppongi Shinryojo

6-11-35 Roppongi, Minato-ku, Tokyo
☎ (03) 3405-1388　東京都港区六本木 6-11-35

Dr. Ryoko Dozono (female), International Medical Crossing

7-11-16 (2F) Minami Aoyama, Minato-ku, Tokyo
☎ (03) 3499-2665　東京都港区南青山 7-11-16 (2F)

Dr. Sayoko Makabe (female), Kanda Clinic

3-20-14 Nishi-Azabu, Minato-ku, Tokyo
☎ (03) 3402-0654　東京都港区西麻布 3-20-14

Dr. N. Ishizuka, Ishizuka Sanfujinka,

2-3-18 Todoroki, Setagaya-ku, Tokyo
☎ (03) 3703-0114　東京都世田谷区等々力 2-3-18

Naganuma Clinic

1-20-2 Takadanobaba, Shinjuku-ku, Tokyo
☎ (03) 3232-1501　東京都新宿区高田馬場 1-20-2

Dr. Nozue, Dr. Shinno (female), Sanno Clinic

8-5-35 Akasaka, Minato-ku, Tokyo
☎ (03) 3402-3151　東京都港区赤坂 8-5-35

Dr. Hisami Matsumine (female), Toho Fujin Women's Clinic

5-3-10 Kiba, Koto-ku, Tokyo　東京都江東区木場 5-3-10
☎ (03) 3630-0322

Miyamoto Clinic for Women

15-10 Wakamatsu-cho, Shinjuku-ku, Tokyo
☎ (03) 3209-8315　東京都新宿区若松町 15-10

Dr. Hiroko Shinno (female), Tokyo Women's Clinic

Roppongi Denki Bldg. 2F, 6-1-20 Roppongi, Minato-ku, Tokyo
☎ (03) 3408-6950　東京都港区六本木 6-1-20 六本木電気ビル 2F

Dr. Yoichiro Yanagida, Tokyo Maternity Clinic

1-20-8 Sendagaya, Shibuya-ku, Tokyo
☎ (03) 3403-1861　東京都渋谷区千駄ヶ谷 1-20-8

Dr. Yanaihara, Tokyo Medical and Surgical Clinic

2F Mori Bldg. 32, 3-4-30 Shiba Koen, Minato-ku, Tokyo
☎ (03) 3436-3028　東京都港区芝公園 3-4-30 森ビル 32, 2F

Yamanaka Obstetrics and Gynecology Clinic

28-11 Wakamatsucho, Shinjuku-ku, Tokyo
☎ (03) 3200-6913　東京都新宿区若松町 28-11

Yotsuya Obstetrics and Gynecology Clinic,

1-1 Sanei-cho, Shinjuku-ku, Tokyo
☎ (03) 3351-3224　東京都新宿区三栄町 1-1

Dr. Shin Juzoji, Higashi Fuchu Hospital

2-7-20 Wakamatsu-cho, Fuchu-shi, Tokyo
☎ (0423) 64-0151　東京都府中市若松町 2-7-20

Dr. Ryutaro Tojo, Tojo Women's Clinic

2-34-7 Maruyamadai, Konan-ku, Yokohama-shi, Kanagawa-ken
☎ (045) 843-1121　神奈川県横浜市港南区丸山台 2-34-7

KANSAI AREA

Dr. Yuriko Hashimoto (female), Ito Sanfujinka Clinic

5-6-6 Izumi-cho, Suita-shi, Osaka-fu
☎ (06) 388-0141　大阪府吹田市泉町 5-6-6

Dr. Hiroko Kimura (female), Kimura Clinic

4-12-17 Nishitenman, Kita-ku, Osaka-shi, Osaka-fu
☎ (06) 365-9646　大阪府大阪市北区西天満 4-12-17

Dr. Masahiro Nishikawa, Nishikawa Clinic

2-16-10 Tennojikita, Abeno-ku, Osaka-shi, Osaka-fu
☎ (06) 714-5218　大阪府大阪市阿倍野区天王寺北 2-16-10

Tanaka Maternity Clinic

New facilities in Rokko, Kobe-shi, Hyogo-ken available from August 1992
☎ (078) 851-2284

Dr. Miura, Ueda Maternity Clinic

1-4-1 Kunika-dori, Chuo-ku, Kobe-shi, Hyogo-ken
☎ (078) 241-3305　兵庫県神戸市中央区国香通 1-4-1

Dr. Oida, Oida Clinic

Nishihairu Manjuji Dori, Shimogyo-ku, Kyoto-shi, Kyoto-fu
☎ (075) 351-5786　京都府京都市下京区烏丸通万寿寺西入ル

RECOMMENDED READING

We would like to recommend some books that we think cover nearly everything you need to know about the childbirth experience. *A Good Birth, A Safe Birth* (Bantam Books, 1990), by Diana Korte, provides an excellent overview of pregnancy and childbirth, including normal delivery, special situations, and a sample birth plan. We also recommend any of the numerous books by Penelope Leach or Sheila Kitzinger. Most of these are available from the childbirth educators' libraries as well as from La Leche League.

Childbirth in Japan, published in 1990 by Birth International, Tokyo, for an international midwifery conference, contains valuable information about the history of childbirth in Japan as well as modern-day procedures. Birth International is a group of writers and childbirth educators interested in promoting a better understanding of practices and attitudes relating to childbirth. The book may be ordered from Louise Shimizu (see page 211).

BREAST-FEEDING

At one stage, bottle feeding was strongly recommended in Japan, but after peaking in the 1970s it is now on the decline. The vast majority of Japanese women choose to breast-feed their babies, but many have difficulty succeeding due to lack of proper support and information. There are various views about breast-feeding management in this country, so you may hear conflicting advice from doctors, midwives, and well-meaning friends. Breast massage—the Oketani method in particular—is quite popular with the Japanese. This method was started by a midwife who believes that massage can help relieve breast-feeding problems and also increase a mother's ability to produce milk. While in the hospital, new mothers are often offered breast massage by the nurses.

If you are interested in breast-feeding, we suggest that you contact La Leche League International (LLL). This is a nonprofit organization interested in helping mothers to breast-feed their babies. LLL has an international network of trained volunteer leaders who conduct monthly meetings and counsel mothers over the phone. They are backed up by a medical advisory board of doctors and other health-care professionals whose advice is available in case of an unusual problem. There are English-speaking and

Japanese-speaking LLL groups throughout Japan, with at least two groups in the Tokyo area. LLL groups in Japan offer a wide selection of books in English on pregnancy, childbirth, and breast-feeding that are available for loan. To find a leader in the greater Tokyo area, call TELL (Tokyo English Life Line) at (03) 5481-4347. In the Kansai area, contact one of the community centers listed in chapter 12. For a list of leaders in Japan, both English- and Japanese-speaking, write the La Leche League International Headquarters at P.O. Box 1209, Franklin Park, Illinois 60131-8209, USA, or call (708) 455-7730.

AFTER THE BABY IS BORN

Because you live in a foreign country, there are a number of important documents that you will need to obtain after the baby is born. The first item you will want to consider is the child's passport. Most likely you will need to visit your embassy or consulate to find out about the rules and regulations concerning the nationality of your baby. The baby need not be present, but if you want to get a passport for him you will need two identical pictures, just like you would for an adult passport. Some hospitals have access to a photographer who will take your baby's picture while still in the hospital. Children's passports are generally valid for only five years, but it still seems pretty silly to us to have a picture of a two-week-old baby in a passport! The other papers you may need include both parents' passports, parents' marriage certificate (original), parents' alien registration card, and copies of visa applications. Again, the requirements depend on your nationality, so call before you go to make sure that you take all of the necessary documents.

You must also register your child at the local ward or city office within fourteen days of the birth. For this you will need to take both parents' passports and alien registration cards, the original birth certificate (this is a paper in Japanese from the hospital), and the *boshi techo.*

For registration at immigration, you will need to take both parents' passports, the child's passport if he is not registered on a parent's, the alien registration cards of both parents and child, the original birth certificate, and the *boshi techo.*

PARENT SUPPORT GROUPS

There are a number of groups that have met regularly in the past to help parents with special needs. Some of these groups are Adoptive Parents

Support Group, Children of Single and Divorced Parents Group, Family Problem Discussion Group, Parents of Children with Special Needs, and Infant Death Support Group. To find a current contact person for these groups, or to find out if a group for your special need exists, in Tokyo call TELL at (03) 5481-4347 and in the Kansai area call the Community House and Information Centre at (078) 857-6540 or the Kobe International Community Center at (078) 322-0030.

The Association of Foreign Wives of Japanese, the group of Japanese wives of foreign men, and the group, Bicultural Families, may also have up-to-date information about parent support groups. See chapter 13 for more information on these organizations.

Ma-Ma Service

#5 Lions Mansion 314, 1-5-2 Aobadai, Midori-ku, Yokohama-shi
☎ (045) 982-7715 神奈川県横浜市緑区青葉台 1-5-2 第 5 ライオンズマンション 314
Tokyo: ☎ (03) 3496-6515

This company, which offers a new and unique service in Japan, was founded to help new mothers cope with those first few days or weeks at home with a new baby. The employees all have experience with babies, and they also undergo special training before being sent out to work. The helpers will clean, shop, cook, bathe the baby, baby-sit, and do any other baby care that you request. The owner, Katsuko Niwa, intends to employ foreigners in her service in the future, and at present there a few English-speaking helpers available. There is a twenty-eight-hour minimum and a four-hour daily minimum. Requests for help should be made as far in advance as possible. Payments are to be made in advance, and transportation costs are paid directly to the helper.

Birth Stories

Foreign women may well feel apprehensive about giving birth in Japan. To offer encouragement and to allay all fears, three foreign women, Diane, Becky, and Mary, relate their very different experiences of birth in Japan.

CESAREAN SECTION AND VAGINAL BIRTH AFTER A CESAREAN— DIANE

I experienced the births of two children in Tokyo. My first baby was born without complication by cesarean section, and three years later I had an easy vaginal birth with my second baby.

My first pregnancy was uneventful until the last two weeks, when the baby turned into the breech position. My doctor tried to turn the baby, without success, and then suggested a planned cesarean section because of the baby's position and size.

I entered Sanno Clinic on my due date feeling comfortable with the situation. I was introduced to the anesthesiologist, who explained the procedure of the epidural and surgery to me. My husband was allowed into the delivery room and held my hand throughout the operation.

The surgery was performed quickly and expertly. I felt no pain, just a slight grogginess due to the antinausea tranquilizer. A sheet shielded my view of the birth, but as soon as my baby was born he was lifted up for me to see.

My husband carried the baby as I was wheeled back to my room, and there I breast-fed my baby for the first time when he was only forty minutes old. The anesthesia had not worn off, so I was in no pain.

In spite of the initial disappointment over having to undergo a cesarean birth, I was delighted with my healthy son and the warm, friendly surroundings of the clinic. During my recuperative stay of nine days at Sanno, I enjoyed delicious Western meals and was treated very well. Their policy of a twenty-four-hour private nurse and rooming-in for the baby was ideal, particularly after a cesarean birth. (Incidentally, the scar from the surgery is almost invisible, due to a low, horizontal incision.) The staff honored my requests for breast milk only, although some of the nurses suggested sugar water or formula so that I could get some rest.

Two and a half years later I became pregnant with my second child and, after much research, I decided to attempt a vaginal birth. My doctor was not enthusiastic about the idea but, he gradually agreed that I was not a high-risk candidate and that a vaginal birth should certainly be possible. I informed the hospital at this point that I would be bringing a female labor assistant (LA), as well as my husband, to offer support during the birth.

Again, I had a joyous and completely uneventful pregnancy and I gained fifty pounds, exactly the same as with my first baby. It is interesting to note that Japanese doctors seem to be stricter concerning weight gain than their Western counterparts.

Four days after my due date, I went into labor. My LA (who is a trained midwife) and I decided that I should continue to labor at home as long as I felt comfortable, because Sanno is only a 5-minute drive from my house. This was technically my first birth, so there was the possibility of a long labor.

The LA checked my pulse and the baby's heartbeat. I felt excited yet calm, and the contractions continued to be bearable. After three hours, the labor pains accelerated, and I felt that it was time to go to Sanno.

In my birth plan I had specified that I wanted no intervention as long as the birth was progressing normally. With the exception of an external fetal monitor, which was attached to me for only a few minutes upon arrival, there were no interventions or restrictions during the labor.

Specifically, this meant that I continued to wear my favorite cotton nightgown, I was not subjected to a shave or an enema, and I had complete freedom in choosing my labor position. I used various positions that I found comfortable and was not made to lie on my back. Finally, I requested that the midwife break my waters, which she did three hours after I arrived.

Two hours later, I knelt onto the trolley and, leaning on a stack of pillows, was wheeled down to the delivery room. I moved from the trolley onto the delivery table, still in a kneeling position. I'm sure that this was a little unorthodox for the staff, but they continued to allow me to make my own decisions because the birth was progressing quickly and normally.

Still in a kneeling position, I immediately began pushing, and the baby's head popped out before the doctor arrived. Although the head midwife was still washing up, another midwife jumped into position and caught him just in time. There was a little confusion at this point as a kneeling position for birth is not usually encouraged. However, it all happened so quickly and easily that no one was upset. Once the midwife figured out how to flip me over without my sitting on the baby, we cut the umbilical cord and I put the baby to my breast.

The doctor came in to inspect me—I had not had an episiotomy and there was no tear, so I was soon wheeled back to my room. The baby had been washed and weighed and was carried by my husband. Once again we enjoyed the convenience of rooming-in. After such an easy birth, I was discharged after two days, at my own request.

PREMATURE BIRTH—BECKY

My son was born by cesarean section; he was two months premature (gestational age: 29 weeks 5 days) and weighed 1,746 grams (3.85 pounds). At birth he had edema (fluid retention), severe anemia, extremely low immunity (even for a premature infant), and weak respiration.

I first saw him two days after his birth in the neonatal intensive care unit (NICU). I knew nothing about premature babies and was very upset and shocked to see all the medical equipment and my son's scrawny, sickly appearance. He had been given a blood transfusion because of his anemia and was breathing with the aid of a respirator. Two IVs were attached to him—one containing glucose, the other a general antibiotic.

During my first visit to the NICU I met the doctor only briefly because I was too stunned by my baby's condition to ask many questions, and the doctor did not volunteer any information. As the weeks passed I naturally began to have more and more questions about my son's treatment and condition. I had heard that Japanese doctors are far less likely than Western doctors to give detailed information unless specifically asked to do so and I found that I had to work hard at digging the answers to my questions out of my doctor. Especially frustrating was the fact that the doctor seemed more prepared to give information to my husband than to myself.

I found that especially during the crisis points of my son's hospitalization, communication broke down between the staff and myself. Looking back, I realize that part of this was perhaps due to the fact that Japanese and Americans take different approaches to emotional or life-threatening situations.

On the positive side, the doctors allowed me to visit my son at any time, day or night. The studies I have read on premature baby care stress the importance of maternal bonding and touching, even with a very sick premie like my son. In this respect, the NICU was wonderful. I was allowed to hold my son's hand and touch him at any time, although I was not permitted to hold him until he was out of the incubator.

In retrospect, I feel that my son is alive today because of the care he received in the NICU and now that we are back in Tokyo for a second posting, I take my son back to the same doctor for checkups.

HOME BIRTH—MARY

When I became pregnant with my first child, I decided, after much research and reflection, that giving birth at home would offer our baby and myself the best chance of a happy, healthy birth. I wanted a good, safe birth, but I was not able to find a hospital or clinic that I felt good and safe going to. I wanted to have freedom of movement in labor and birth. In particular, I wanted to avoid being forced onto my back and having to push the baby up and out against the force of gravity. Another major factor in the decision process was that I wanted to avoid the unnatural and often unnecessary separation from my baby after birth.

You might think that an awful lot of paraphernalia is necessary to prepare for a birth at home, but in fact relatively little is required. Your midwife or doctor will bring any essential equipment with them, such as a stethoscope, sterile sheets, etc. I decided to try to be as prepared as possible in the highly unlikely event that we would be on our own without anyone to attend to us. I ordered a stethoscope (about ¥1,000), an oxygen kit (about ¥30,000), and postpartum large-sized sanitary napkins from our neighborhood drugstore. Our midwife suggested sterilizing a few squares of white cotton to use to clear away excess fluids and vernix from the baby's face to make breathing easier. As we didn't have a waterproof mattress cover, I used a plastic shower curtain instead.

Through the midwife's contacts, we were able to arrange an ambulance if emergency help was needed. A month before my due date, I visited the hospital to see the facilities and meet the staff. In the end everything went as planned and I gave birth to a healthy girl in the comfort of my own bedroom.

With this happy experience in mind, I decided on a home birth again when I became pregnant with my second child a few years later. Even though I had learned of a couple of maternity clinics that were indeed very good—minimal intervention, no unnecessary separation of mother and baby, visits by children allowed, the possibility of returning home soon after the birth, and so on—this time, however, I had our three-year-old daughter to think about. I didn't want to have to disappear suddenly and then show up a few days later with a stranger in my arms and so I opted for another home birth.

My most recent home birth experience was again positive and without complications. With our wonderful midwife, my sister, and my husband in attendance, I went into labor in our own bedroom. I was able to take a hot bath, which made the rushes of labor easier to take. In bed I felt I had to breathe consciously to "blow away" the pain, but in the warm water I felt far more relaxed. As our three-year-old daughter slept downstairs, I gave birth to her baby brother, and I was able to greet her the next morning in my own bed with her new brother. I was very happy to be able to give our lives a semblance of continuity so that my daughter would feel secure and that her brother's birth would be a joyous rather than traumatic experience for her. I can't help feeling that the kind of birth experience that we have had with our children helps to develop family closeness and stability.

I would urge anyone who is planning on having a baby at home to read any books that they can find on the subject. It is also helpful to interview doctors and midwives before hiring someone to care for you at this most important time. If you are interested in having a home birth in Japan, you can consult the list of midwives in this book. Most of the midwives speak only Japanese, so if you do not, you may want to have a translator accompany you to at least some of your prenatal visits and possibly for the actual birth as well.

FAMILY PLANNING

In Japan, the most popular kinds of contraceptives are condoms, birth control pills, the IUD, and the rhythm method. Other forms of contraception, such as diaphragms, cervical caps, vaginal jellies, and creams, are also available.

Condoms in Japan are unusually thin, yet strong. Since this is the contraceptive of choice for many Japanese couples, you can easily find a selection (in rainbow-colored hues if you wish) in any pharmacy, as well as in supermarkets and vending machines. Size and proper fit may be a problem for some foreigners, in which case you may want to bring a supply with you from home. A source for larger-sized condoms in Japan is the American Pharmacy in Tokyo, Hibiya Park Bldg. 1F, 1-8-1 Yurakucho, Chiyoda-ku, (03) 3271-4034, and in Kobe, Shin Kobe Oriental Hotel, 1-3 Kitano-cho, Chuo-ku, (078) 262-2577.

The Ministry of Health and Welfare in Japan has only recently allowed doctors to prescribe the birth control pill. Previously there were restrictions about the use of the pill, and the government did not consider it to be safe. Now, however, the pill is becoming more acceptable among Japanese women. There is some confusion about the strength of the dosage in the Japanese pill—although some doctors will offer you a "low dosage" pill, it may well be a bit stronger than a similar pill in the United States. However, new varieties of contraceptive pills with lighter dosages have recently been introduced to Japan, and the smaller clinics seem to have the latest information on this. The simplest way to get a birth control pill prescription in Japan is to visit a gynecologist at a small clinic. Of course, if you want to continue on exactly the same pill that you used back home, we suggest that you bring it with you. If you plan to receive birth-control pills through the mail, be aware that the Japanese post office only allows a three-month supply of prescription drugs to enter the country in any one package.

For more information about family planning and contraception, contact the Japanese Organization for International Cooperation in Family Planning Incorporated (JOICFP), Hoken Kaikan Bekkan 6F, 1-1 Sadohara-cho, Ichigaya, Shinjuku-ku, Tokyo 162, (03) 3268-3450. The English version of the Japanese government mother and child health handbook (*boshi techo*) is available from this organization for ¥600.

INFERTILITY

For help and information about infertility, contact Resolve Inc. This support group publishes information on medical issues as well as a directory of infertility specialists. You can write them at 5 Water Street, Arlington, Massachusetts 02174, USA, or call (617) 643-2424.

ADOPTION

Adopting a baby in Japan—indeed in any country—is not without obstacles, but we have heard numerous success stories in the years we have lived here. Although one must be prepared for a long wait, many of our friends have received babies within months of making the commitment to adopt. The key to getting a child seems to be perseverance and a positive attitude. Many of the parents we spoke with mentioned the importance of keeping in regular contact with the adoption agencies. One mother noted that she thought she and her husband were given a baby just so that she would stop calling every week!

An excellent resource in Japan for parents who have adopted children or who wish to adopt a child is the Adoption Support Group at Yokosuka Naval Base. This group meets at the Yokosuka hospital and offers valuable contacts and pertinent information about adopting a baby in Japan. The leaders of the group stress the importance of attending the meetings if at all possible, because this is where new parents can share experiences with couples intending to adopt. The group is willing to send information through the mail for those who live in outlying areas. For more information about the group and their meeting times, call Lorraine Dumas at (0462) 51-1520 ext. 233-6518 or write to her at Beigun Jutaku #448B, 4811 Kamitsuruma, Sagamihara-shi, Kanagawa-ken 228. Information about support groups for adoptive parents can also be obtained by calling either Yokosuka Naval Base (0468) 26-1911 or Camp Zama Family Support Services (0462) 51-1520 (ext. 4572).

The following organizations, both in Japan and overseas, may be able to give you more information about adoption.

International Social Services (ISS)

Koenji Sun Heights 408, 1-5-4 Koenji Minami, Suginami-ku, Tokyo 166
☎ (03) 3312-6661 fax (03) 5377-1348　東京都杉並区高円寺南 1–5–4–408
Adoptions are possible through ISS and they also do home studies and adjustment surveys for babies and children who were adopted overseas and now reside in Japan.

Missionaries of Charity

3-5-24 Honmachi, Nishiarai, Adachi-ku, Tokyo　東京都足立区西新井本町 3-5-24
☎ (03) 3898-3866

This organization, which is affiliated with Mother Theresa, has offices throughout Japan. In addition to helping the poor, they also help unmarried mothers, and sometimes babies are available for adoption.

Adoptive Families of America

3333 Highway 100 N., Minneapolis, Minnesota 55422, USA
☎ (612) 535-4829

This national support organization for adoptive families produces a bimonthly magazine containing descriptions and pictures of children waiting to be adopted, in addition to parenting articles. This group also publishes an annual list of adoption agencies.

Americans for International Aid and Adoption

877 S. Adams, Birmingham, Michigan 48009, USA
☎ (313) 645-2211

This organization places children from Asia and South America in adoptive homes. A free information packet is available.

Families Adopting Children Everywhere

P.O. Box 28058, Northwood Station, Baltimore, Maryland 21239, USA
☎ (301) 239-4252

A bimonthly newsletter and information on domestic and foreign adoptions are available from this support group for people who want to adopt.

Families for Private Adoption

P.O. Box 6375, Washington, D.C. 20014, USA
☎ (202) 722-0338

This support group for parents who wish to adopt or have babies adopted privately issues a quarterly newsletter which is available free to members or for a small charge to nonmembers.

Independent Adoption Center

3333 Vincent Road, Suite 222, Pleasant Hill, California 94523, USA
☎ (415) 944-4744

This organization offers resources and counseling concerning open adoption.

International Concerns Committee for Children

91 Cypress Drive, Boulder, Colorado 80303, USA
☎ (303) 494-8333

This organization helps families interested in adopting children from other countries. Although this group does not actually place children, it provides information and counseling free of charge.

National Adoption Information Clearinghouse

1400 Eye Street N.W., Suite 600, Washington, D.C. 20005, USA
☎ (202) 842-1919
This group refers individuals to organizations and provides a list of adoption agencies.

National Committee for Adoption

1930 17th Street N.W., Washington, D.C. 20009-6207, USA
☎ (202) 328-1200
Many books and pamphlets about adoption are available from this organization for adoptive parents and children, including their own *Adoption Factbook*. A list of publications as well as adoption agencies is also available.

HELPFUL PUBLICATIONS

The Report on Foreign Adoption. Available from the International Concerns Committee for Children, listed above.

The Private Adoption Handbook, by Stanley B. Michelman and Meg Schneider with Antonia Van Der Meer (Villard Books).

A Handful of Hope, by Suzanne Arms (Celestial Arts).

Guide to Adoption Agencies, by Julia Posner. Available from the Child Welfare League of America, 440 First Street N.W., Suite 310, Washington, D.C. 20001, USA.

Birth Announcements

Heralding the arrival of your precious bundle is one of the best parts about having a baby. In Japan, you can either have the announcement made up here, or you can order from an overseas mail-order source. If you choose to have your announcements printed here, check with a well-known stationery company such as Ito-ya (see chap. 8). A small neighborhood printer can probably do the same job for less money, but communication may be difficult.

At Ito-ya you will find a nice selection of fine stationery, such as Crane's, although most are rather expensive. Itoya does not have the variety of personalized birth announcements that are available in similar stores in the United States, but they will try to accommodate your design ideas.

Contempo Graphics (see chap. 8 under Christmas cards) offers one of the widest selections of stationery in Tokyo. Call Rosalie Cicogna to place an order for their catalogs showing their full line of birth announcements, invitations, and personalized stationery from the United States.

If you want a Japanese touch, consider printing the information on *washi* paper, with a matching envelope. Another choice is the blank greeting cards with various Japanese scenes on the fronts available in stationery stores. We once used a greeting card with a picture of a little girl in a kimono for an announcement. You can either have the message inside printed, or you can write it in yourself. Postcards with pictures of children on the front, often available around the Japanese holidays, can be used in a similar way.

Probably the easiest and cheapest method is the one that most of our Japanese friends use. At your local photo shop you can order a postcard with your baby's picture plus a few words about the birth. Most large photo stores will print your announcement in English if you so request. These postcards can be addressed and mailed without an envelope, which saves time and money. You can pick out your style beforehand, and then add the baby picture and the facts later. This kind of birth announcement can usually be ready in a few days. Photo birth announcements at reasonable prices are also available from Associated Photo Co. in the United States (see chap. 8 under Christmas cards).

If you want to order birth announcements from an overseas catalog, plan ahead. You can often order the birth announcement of your choice, and then call or fax the final information after the birth. Ask about this when you write for a brochure. Usually, the company will send you the envelopes ahead of your due date so that you can address them and have them ready to mail when the baby arrives. This method is the least time-consuming—and, of course, it helps to get as many of the little tasks like birth announcements out of the way before the baby arrives.

MAIL-ORDER BIRTH ANNOUNCEMENTS

Babygram Service Center
301 Commerce St., Suite 1010, Fort Worth, Texas 76102, USA
☎ (817) 334-0069
This company produces a photo birth announcement that looks like a real telegram, but with a photograph pasted into the center of the message. They accept U.S. checks or money orders only.

Birthwrites

5 E. Gwynn's Mill Court, P.O. Box 684, Owings Mills, Maryland 21117, USA
☎ (301) 363-0872

Three different styles of birth announcements are available from this company: formal, embossed cards; funny cards with cartoon drawings; and cards with pencil drawings of babies and sentimental messages. Preprinted cards are shipped within twenty-four hours, and five type styles are available. Birthwrites also has a selection of thank-you notes. VISA, MasterCard, and American Express are accepted.

H and F Products Inc.

3734 W. 95, Leawood, Kansas 66206, USA
☎ (913) 649-1444

This company has our favorite selection of baby announcements. You can choose from over thirty different styles of beautiful personalized cards on fine-quality paper. The cards have a unique design, with a small name card attached by a tiny satin ribbon to the larger birth announcement. Photo announcements are also available, and all orders are processed quickly. They also have a good selection of general invitations and thank-you notes. VISA, MasterCard, and American Express are accepted.

Heartthoughts

6200 E. Central, Suite 100, Wichita, Kansas 67208, USA
☎ (316) 688-5781

Birth announcements, thank-you cards, and other greeting cards are available from this company. All cards are illustrated with soft pencil drawings. Special designs are offered for grandparents or the parents of twins. Blank insert cards can be filled in with personal information after the birth.

SPECIAL GIFTS AND MEMENTOS

The birth of a new baby is a blessed event anywhere in the world, but nowhere more so than in Japan. To commemorate your own baby's birth or that of a friend's baby, here are some of our favorite gift ideas.

Japanese baby blankets are made of the softest toweling imaginable. We have not seen these lovely blankets, which are practical as well as pretty, in any other country. For little girls, you may want to start a collection of dolls, and here the selection is vast, from porcelain to plastic to wood. The Japanese teething rings and other plastic toys for young babies are unique and delightful. If you want to buy baby clothes, some of the soft, 100 percent cotton sleepwear is ideal. Another big hit with many of our friends has been the Hard Rock Cafe Tokyo T-shirts or Tokyo Disney-land T-shirts, in baby sizes, of course. Ornate photo albums, embroidered with the baby's name and date of birth, are available in any department store. The style of these albums is uniquely Japanese, and they make a gift that every proud parent can use.

A gift indicating the baby's year of birth in the Japanese zodiac is a good way to commemorate a birth in Japan. These mementos, from statues to soap in the shape of the zodiac animals, are prominently displayed around the New Year, so pick something up then if you will have use for it later in the year.

Even the ward and city offices get into the act when it comes to welcoming a new addition to the household. For example, the Minato-ku office presents potted plants to any household with a new baby. These families are usually notified by postcard as to when they can pick up their plant. Check with your local office to see if any special gift is offered to newborns in your area.

VOCABULARY LIST

Knowing a few key words in Japanese can make all the difference when you are staying in the hospital in Japan, or if you are caught in an emergency situation. The following words and phrases will be helpful during your pregnancy and stay in hospital.

CALLING AN AMBULANCE

The national number for ambulance service is 119. You must give the request and directions in Japanese:

Please send an ambulance: *kyukyusha o onegaishimasu*

I am in labor, please come quickly: *osan desu ga, hayaku kite kudasai*

Please take us to —— hospital: (hospital name) *byoin ni tsurete itte kudasai*

My address is ——: *jusho wa* —— *ku,* —— *cho,* —— *chome*

My name is ——: *namae wa* —— *desu*

GENERAL VOCABULARY

anemia: *hinketsu* 貧血

backache: *senaka ga itai* 背中が痛い

bleeding: *shukketsu* 出血

contraception: *hinin* 避妊

delivery: *osan, bunben* お産，分娩

doctor: *oisha-san, dokuta* お医者さん、ドクター

ectopic pregnancy: *shikyugai ninshin* 子宮外妊娠
endometrium (uterine wall): *shikyu naimaku* 子宮内膜
fallopian tubes: *rankan* 卵管
fetus: *taiji* 胎児
indigestion: *shoka furyo* 消化不良
infection: *kansen* 感染
infertility: *funin* 不妊
menstruation: *gekkei, seiri* 月経、生理
midwife: *osanba-san, josanpu* お産婆さん，助産婦
miscarriage: *ryuzan* 流産
morning sickness: *tsuwari* つわり
nurse: *kangofu-san, naasu* 看護婦さん、ナース
obstetrics and gynecology: *sanfujinka* 産婦人科
oral contraceptive pills: *keiko hininyaku, piru* 経口避妊薬、ピル
ovarian cyst: *ransoo-noshu* 卵巣のう腫
ovary: *ransoo* 卵巣
ovulation: *hairan* 排卵
pelvic examination: *naishin* 内診
pelvis: *kotsuban* 骨盤
placenta: *taiban* 胎盤
pregnancy: *ninshin* 妊娠
swelling: *hare* はれ
toxemia: *ninshin chudokusho* 妊娠中毒症
uterus: *shikyu* 子宮

vagina: *chitsu* 膣
vaginal discharge: *taige, orimono* 帯下、おりもの

GENERAL HOSPITAL VOCABULARY

What are you doing?: *nani o shitemasu ka?* 何をしてますか
Who are you?: *donata desu ka?* どなたですか
Please call the doctor: *oisha-san o yonde kudasai* お医者さんを呼んで下さい
Please call the nurse: *kangofu-san o yonde kudasai* 看護婦さんを呼んで下さい

LABOR

breaking of waters: *hasui* 破水
breech birth: *sakago* 逆子
cesarean section: *teio sekkai* 帝王切開
contraction: *itami, shushuku* 痛み、収縮
fetal monitor: *taiji kanshi sochi* 胎児監視装置
induced labor: *yuhatsu bunben* 誘発分娩

pain or discomfort: *itami, itai desu* 痛み、痛いです
shaving: *teimo* 剃毛
labor has begun: *jintsu ga hajimarimashita* 陣痛が始まりました
labor pain: *jintsu* 陣痛
labor room: *jintsu shitsu* 陣痛室
How many minutes apart are your contractions?: *nanpun oki ni itami ga arimasu ka?* 何分おきに痛みがありますか
one minute apart: *ippun oki desu* 1分おきです
two minutes apart: *nifun oki desu* 2分 ″
three minutes apart: *sanpun oki desu* 3分 ″
four minutes apart: *yonpun oki desu* 4分 ″
five minutes apart: *gofun oki desu* 5分 ″
six minutes apart: *roppun oki desu* 6分 ″
seven minutes apart: *nanafun oki desu* 7分 ″
eight minutes apart: *happun oki desu* 8分 ″
nine minutes apart: *kyufun oki desu* 9分 ″
ten minutes apart: *juppun oki desu* 10分 ″

enema: *kanchoo* 浣腸
episiotomy: *ein sekkai* 会陰切開
medicine: *kusuri* 薬
injection: *chusha* 注射
general anesthetic: *zenshin masui* 全身麻酔
local anesthetic: *kyokubu masui* 局部麻酔
epidural anesthetic: *komakugai masui* 硬膜外麻酔
spinal anesthetic: *sekizui masui* 脊髄麻酔

DELIVERY
delivery room: *bunben shitsu* 分娩室
delivery table: *bunben dai* 分娩台
pillow: *makura* 枕
dilation: *kakucho* 拡張
full dilation: *zenkaidai* 全開大
transition: *ikoki, henka* 移行期、変化
I feel like pushing, or I want to push: *ikimitai desu* いきみたいです
bag of waters: *yomaku* 羊膜
afterbirth: *atozan* 後産
placenta: *taiban* 胎盤
umbilical cord: *heso no o* へその緒

POSTPARTUM

bowel movement: *otsuuji, haiben* お通じ、排便
catheter: *kuda, kateteru* 管、カテーテル
constipation: *bempi* 便秘
diarrhea: *geri* 下痢
lochia or normal bleeding after delivery: *orimono* おりもの
heavy bleeding or hemorrhage: *shukketsu* 出血
laxative: *shikanzai, kangezai, bempi yaku* 弛緩剤，緩下剤，便秘薬
perineum: *einbu* 会陰部
sanitary pads: *napukin* ナプキン
stool: *ben* 便
urine: *o-shosui* お小水
I want to go to the toilet: *toire ni ikitai*
Please may I get up?: *okitai no desu ga ii desu ka?*

THE BABY

baby: *akachan* 赤ちゃん
birth certificate: *shussei shoomeisho* 出生証明書
circumcision: *katsurei* 割礼
jaundice: *odan* 黄疸
meconium: *taiben* 胎便
May I see my baby?: *akachan ni attemo ii desu ka?*
May I hold my baby?: *akachan o daitemo ii desu ka?*
Please bring my baby: *akachan o tsurete kite kudasai*
nursery: *shinseiji shitsu* 新生児室

BREAST-FEEDING

breast: *oppai, o-chichi* おっぱい、お乳
breast-feeding room: *junyu shitsu* 授乳室
breast massage: *o-chichi no massaji* お乳のマッサージ
breast milk: *bonyu* 母乳
breast pump: *sakunyuki* 搾乳器
colostrum: *shonyu* 初乳
glucose water: *budoto eki* ブドウ糖液
nipples: *chikubi* 乳首
I am going to breast-feed: *o-chichi o agetai desu*
May I feed my baby?: *akachan ni o-chichi o agetemo ii desu ka?*
My breasts are full: *o-chichi ga hatte imasu*

10

Kids' Health

In

Japan

THE DRINKING WATER IN JAPAN
DOES NOT CONTAIN FLUORIDE.

Nothing is more important to parents than their children's general health and well-being. Living in Japan is becoming a healthier prospect all the time as hospitals and emergency services continually update equipment and modernize procedures. Once you become accustomed to Japanese medical procedures and medications, and find out what is and what is not available here, you will be able to feel confident that you are doing all you can to keep your kids healthy.

TAKING CARE OF THE KIDS' HEALTH

Many Western pharmaceutical goods are available in this country, but there are a few products that the parents of young children should bring from home. The first is Children's and Infant Tylenol or a similar acetaminophen product to reduce fever and discomfort in a sick child. We suggest that you bring a year's supply of the drops or chewable tablets. Remember that Japanese post office regulations prohibit sending more than a three-month supply of a prescription drug through the mail. Tylenol is not considered a prescription drug in other countries, but as it is not available over-the-counter here, it may be considered one by the post office. Have your contact person send it in small amounts to be on the safe side.

The second medicine-cabinet essential that we miss is teething gel. Anabasol, Orajel, and other brands of teething gel are a great help when babies are cutting teeth. Some infants do not care for the stuff, while others just about live on it for their first two years of life. Borrow some from a friend or fly it in just in case your child is of the latter persuasion. Also worth bringing is a children's decongestant for colds, expectorant for coughs, and a sudafed (pseudoephedrine) product for adults.

FEEDING THE KIDS

Recently, many mothers are wisely choosing to breastfeed their babies. For information and support about breastfeeding, call La Leche League International. There are English- and Japanese-speaking groups throughout Japan. For further information, see chapter 9. Mothers who plan to feed their babies formula can choose from several Japanese brands. There is one American brand, SMA, that is available at large supermarkets. The instructions for mixing the formula are all in Japanese, but you can ask your doctor which formula he would recommend and how to mix it. Unfortunately, formula in Japan, as in other countries, is often made with palm and coconut oils so it is high in saturated fat, as well as being expensive. Soy formula is available at a few stores for those children who are allergic to milk products. If you decide to use formula, you will need to use bottled or purified water to mix it with.

For bottles and nipples, check any department store or baby supply store. The Nuk brand nipples are sold here, and the Playtex disposable bottles are available at the American Pharmacy listed in this chapter and at some of the international supermarkets.

The drinking water in Japan does not contain fluoride, so some parents opt for supplementing it with fluoride drops or tablets. If you want your children to have fluoride supplements, you will have to buy them overseas because they are not available in Japan. Check with your doctor back home for his advice on fluoride supplements.

Children's multivitamins are available in stores, but all the information is in Japanese and the dosage may not be what you are accustomed to in your home country. The Foreign Buyers' Club has a catalog for vitamins and health food products from the United States (see the listings in this chapter).

When it comes to baby food, you won't run into many problems finding good-quality, healthy food to feed your baby in Japan. Jars of Gerber prepared baby food are sold in large supermarkets. Even if the label is in Japanese, you can tell what is in the jar by the picture on the front. There is another good alternative to Gerber, however, from a Japanese company. Wakodo makes freeze-dried baby food to which you add hot water to reach the desired consistency. The food comes in packets just large enough for one serving, with fish and vegetables being predominant. Look for the white box with "Wakodo" written on it in English. Kewpie Co. has recently started making their own freeze-dried baby food that is packaged in a box similar to Wakodo. Look for the Kewpie baby food in jars as well.

Other nutritional favorites of little ones in Japan are *yakiimo*, or sweet potatoes, that we buy from vendors on the street. Kids also enjoy strips of *nori* and *shirasuboshi*, the tiny fresh fish you see in the refrigerated section of grocery stores. Get a rice cooker and cook rice; you can mix it with any number of dishes and your children will enjoy it.

MAINTAINING THE KIDS' APPETITES

Whether you are looking for food products from abroad, no-pesticide produce, a special treat from home, gourmet delicacies, or just a supermarket that takes phone orders and will deliver, you can find it here. Many of these companies are run by foreigners, therefore language is not a problem. Call or write the companies below for their catalogs, and you should never have to go too long without that important something from home.

Benten Supermarket

16-2 Wakamatsu-cho, Shinjuku-ku, Tokyo　東京都新宿区若松町 16-2
☎ (03) 3202-2421

No home should be without a Benten catalog. This supermarket has Western food products similar to those available at supermarkets catering to foreigners like National Azabu or Kinokuniya, but at somewhat lower prices. Price is not the only reason for shopping at Benten's, however. Just the fact that you can look in the catalog and place an order for your week's groceries and have them delivered the next day—free of charge if you spend over ¥5,000—makes the catalog a necessity for every household. There is no membership fee, and deliveries in metropolitan Tokyo are daily, except for the Fuchu, Mitaka, and Kurume areas, where delivery is only on Wednesday and Friday afternoons. For long-distance deliveries, you can place your order by mail, and it will take one to two weeks to arrive. There is a packing charge of ¥1,500, and you pay the shipping charges on delivery.

Chikyujin Club System

4-1-19 Chigasaki Minami, Kohoku-ku, Yokohama-shi, Kanagawa-ken
☎ (045) 942-3288　神奈川県横浜市港北区茅ヶ崎南 4-1-19

Chikyujin Club is more of a food co-op than just a mail-order company. Once a week, you will receive an order list in the mail. There are over 500 items available, from nonhomogenized milk and low-pesticide produce to whole grains and bakery goods. The fruits and vegetables are harvested the day before delivery, so freshness is assured. The order form itself is in Japanese, but there is a computer printout of all the products in English, so

242

all you have to do is match the number on the order form to the item on the printout. The 2,000-member club is based in Yokohama, and they deliver once a week to the Tokyo-Yokohama area free of charge with a minimum order of ¥3,000. There is a membership fee of ¥5,000.

Farmland Freezer Club

1-27-11 Higashi Tamagawa, Setagaya-ku, Tokyo　東京都世田谷区東玉川 1–27–11
☎ (03) 3720-4651

Farmland Freezer Club is a great resource for those of you who like to shop ahead, or who have a large freezer! Most of their offerings are frozen, and imported meats and seafood make up the majority of the list. Also available are some frozen fruits and vegetables. The meats are offered at lower prices than you would pay elsewhere, and there are many types of meat not available in your local stores. Ground lamb, whole bone-in hams, and a wide variety of fresh sausages are just some of the "not available in Japan" items you can order. To order from the club, you must become a member. The nonrefundable membership fee is ¥10,000 for one year or ¥5,000 for six months. You can also shop at the store itself in Setagaya, or they will deliver to your home free of charge.

Japan-Europe Trading Company

PMC Bldg. 3F, 1-23-5 Higashi Azabu, Minato-ku, Tokyo
☎ (03) 3588-6386 fax (03) 3583-9060　東京都港区東麻布 1–23–5 PMC ビル 3F

This company offers an exclusive catalog of imported goodies for the gourmet. Many of the items are of the hard-to-find variety, and often they are discounted below retail price. If you have a craving for fine cheeses, wines, or specialty meats, this is the catalog to have. There is no membership fee, and you pay the delivery costs.

Foreign Buyer's Club 兵庫県神戸市東灘区向洋町中 1–14 イーストコート 2 番 307

East Court No. 2/307, 1-14 Koyochonaka , Higashinada-ku, Kobe-shi, Hyogo-ken
☎ (078) 857-9001 fax (078) 857-9005

The FBC is a wonderful co-op run by a foreign couple in Kobe. It is a nonprofit organization, and they import goods from the United States through a large wholesale house. What that means to you and me is that we can get almost any item we want from the United States delivered to our door, and at a reasonable price. Orders must be made by the case, so unless you have adequate storage space, get together with a friend to order. For ¥200 each, FBC also offers specialty catalogs for baby goods, health food, coffee and teas, and vitamins. There is a ¥1,000 membership fee, and you pay delivery charges. Usually delivery takes four to five weeks.

Natural House

6-14-15 Akasaka, Minato-ku, Tokyo　東京都港区赤坂 6–14–15
☎ (03) 3589-1070

Natural House is a large chain of stores that offers an assortment of "healthy" products. There are eleven Natural House stores in the Tokyo area and eight in the Kobe-Osaka region, and since it is such a large operation, the controls on all of their products may not be as strict as some of the smaller companies. Natural House does not deliver, but stores centrally located in Tokyo are at 3-6-18 Kita Aoyama, Minato-ku, phone (03) 3498-2277, and at Sun Road 6F, 1-1-3 Nishi Shinjuku, Shinjuku-ku, phone (03) 3349-5787

Radish Bohya

☎ (03) 3258-5630 for catalog and to place orders.

Radish Bohya will deliver chemical-free vegetables anywhere in the country. For more information, call (0483) 22-4000.

Seikatsu Club Kyodokumin

☎ (03) 3425-0111

For those days when it's difficult to get out of the house or when you're tired of carrying home heavy bags along with those screaming children, why not become a member of your local cooperative and have goods delivered to your door? For more information on the cooperative nearest you and how to join, call the Seikatsu Club.

Tengu Natural Foods

11-14 Inari-cho, Hanno-shi, Saitama-ken　埼玉県飯能市稲荷町 11–14
☎ (0429) 74-3036 fax (0429) 72-6979

Tengu Natural Foods is a company that offers healthy foods imported from the United States and Canada at reasonable prices. Granola, wholewheat flour, and an assortment of whole grain breads are just some of the goodies offered that are also good for you. The company has been in business for over five years and is constantly expanding its line of health-food products. There is no membership fee, and shipping is free if you order over ¥12,000 worth of goods. Delivery is made to your home, usually within a few days of placing your order.

VACCINATIONS AND JAPAN

"Vaccines and vaccinations have some side-effects and unknown factors related to them and are therefore controversial."

This quotation was taken from a paper, "Immunizations in Japan." This section is not intended as a recommendation, but rather as a resource to help you understand what vaccinations are available in Japan, compared with those available in some other countries. The final decision on when and which vaccinations should be given to your child should be taken after you consult with your doctor.

Because of the Vaccinations Law and the Tuberculosis Prevention Law, the Japanese government implements vaccinations "in order to protect society from communicable diseases" (quoted from the *boshi techo*, the mother and child health record). All babies resident in Japan are entitled to free polio, TB, DPT (diptheria, pertussis, and tetanus), and measles immunizations. To receive your free immunization coupons, contact the Health Department (*hokenjo*) of your ward or city office, and you will receive a *boshi techo* if you do not already have one (see chap. 9 for information on obtaining the *boshi techo* during pregnancy if your baby is to be born in Japan).

The DPT and measles injections must be done by a doctor in your ward; polio and BCG must be administered at the Health Department. The vaccinations are administered on designated dates, and because some vaccinations are given in a series, none of the vaccinations should be missed. If your child cannot make one of the designated dates, it may be necessary to make special arrangements to receive them. Call your Health Department in Japanese to check the dates.

Of course, you do not have to use the coupons for free vaccinations. You may go to a private doctor and pay for the vaccinations with cash or by using whatever foreign insurance coverage you would normally use.

The BCG, the vaccination for tuberculosis, is one of the most controversial vaccinations because it provides only limited protection against acute TB and no protection for the ordinary, most common, adult TB. It is generally recommended for areas with low overall hygiene. Presently, in Europe a BCG vaccination is administered after birth; in Japan and Britain, it is given later in childhood. The United States does not ordinarily give the vaccination. However, at public schools in the United States, skin tests are done annually for TB. If a child has had a BCG, he may then test positive for TB and will then have to have a chest X-ray and possibly have further tests for TB.

The common vaccinations are DPT, DT (diptheria and adult tetanus), MMR (measles, mumps, and rubella), TB (tuberculosis), and BCG (for increased resistance to tuberculosis).

SCHEDULE OF VACCINATIONS

	JAPAN	USA	UK
DPT	3 times between 3 months and 4 years (2 to 3 years) booster, 12 to 18 months after initial series	2, 4 & 6 months 18 months 5 years	3 months 4¹/₂ to 5 months and 6 to 8 weeks later
DT	12 years	15 years and every 10 years throughout life	with polio at 4¹/₂ to 5 years
POLIO	twice between 3 months and 4 years (4 to 18 months) at 6-week intervals	2, 4 & 18 months 5 years	with tetanus 15 years
MEASLES	once from 1 year to 6 years (recommendable at 18 months)	——	at 1 year
MUMPS	once at 12 months	——	15 months & above
RUBELLA	females only, once 14 to 15 years	——	females only 11 to 13 years
MMR	Once from 12 months to 6 years (recommendable at 18 months)	15 months	——
BCG	birth to 4 years (3 to 12 months if prior TB skin test is negative	not recommended	11 to 13 years if prior TB skin test is negative
CHICKEN POX	once after 1 year	not available	not available
HEPATITIS B	given to newborn of carrier mothers	——	——
INFLUENZA	3 to 15 years		
HEMOPHILUS INFLUENZA	——	3 times in the first 12 months	

(The years in parentheses refer to the age at which vaccinations are given at public health centers.)

The schedule for administering the various kinds of vaccinations and serial vaccinations differs from country to country. The general trend, however, is to cut down the number of vaccinations given. It is less important which schedule you follow; *completing the vaccinations on schedule is what is important.* If you plan to leave Japan while in the process of getting your child vaccinated, it is advisable to follow a schedule most adaptable to your move.

The schedule of vaccinations (from *Accessible Medical Services for Foreign Residents of Tokyo,* Dai-Ichi-Hoki Shuppan Co., Ltd., 1988) is used with permission from the Kansai Childbirth Education Organization, with the guidance of Dr. G. Barraclough.

BE PREPARED

During your stay here, you will want to have your own library of medical and developmental books in your native language, and many of the best books in English are available from the mail-order sources discussed in chapter 4. Especially useful is a help-at-a-glance reference book on medical emergencies. The National Safety Council in the United States publishes two books on emergency medical treatment, one for infants and one for children. The books *Emergency Medical Treatment: Infants* and *Emergency Medical Treatment: Children* are available through the Chinaberry Book service listed in chapter 4. The books are made of thick paper with tabs for quick reference in case of emergencies and give large-print, step-by-step instructions and pictures of what to do in case of injuries, such as choking, poisoning, burns, broken bones, and more.

We list here a few books that have been written to assist foreigners with medical procedures in Japan. Everyone should read them and keep them on their shelves in case of an emergency.

Accessible Medical Services for Foreign Residents of Tokyo (Dai-Ichi Hoki Shuppan Co., Ltd., 1988)

This book was compiled by the Metropolitan Tokyo Research Team to Study the Medical System for the Foreign Community. It gives clear and concise answers to many questions about the Japanese medical system and how it relates to foreigners. We suggest it not only for Tokyo residents but for anyone who wants an easy reference book for emergencies. The book can be obtained at some Tokyo English-language bookstores or from the publisher for ¥800, at Dai-Ichi Hoki Shuppan, 2-11-17 Minami Aoyama,

Minato-ku, Tokyo 107, phone (03) 3404-2251.

Staying Healthy in Japan (Elyse Rogers, Tokyo Weekender, 1985)

Kansai Medical Directory (Kobe Community House)
This handbook full of useful information is available from Community House in Kobe for ¥500 plus ¥260 postage.

Living in Japan
See the reference in chapter 14.

Most doctors recommend that parents take an infant CPR course when they have a baby. Infant and adult CPR courses and basic first-aid courses are offered in English through the community centers (see chap. 12), churches, private clubs, and some of the childbirth educators (see chap. 9).

It is wise to plan what you would do in case of an emergency—when you move to Japan, locate the hospital nearest you that has a 24-hour emergency room. There are three levels of emergency room care, and you should find out what is available in your area. Tertiary emergency facilities can handle life-threatening emergencies, secondary emergency care hospitals can care for serious but not life-threatening emergencies, and primary emergency care is available at a large number of hospitals and clinics.

CALLING AN AMBULANCE

The ambulance and emergency procedures and services in Japan are most likely not what you are used to in your home country. Ambulance drivers in Japan are not trained paramedics as in the United States and other countries, and often foreigners are advised to get to the nearest emergency hospital on their own if the situation is not a true emergency. Your doctor can also arrange for an ambulance to pick you up and take you to the hospital of his choice.

Throughout Japan, 119 is the emergency number for fire and ambulance services. Call 110 for police. You must be able to give the information in Japanese.

For ease in calling during an actual emergency, it is a good idea to place a memo near your telephone with the emergency phone numbers and Japanese-language phrases for stating your address, phone number, and name written down.

To call an ambulance, dial 119.

Please send an ambulance: *kyukyusha onegai shimasu*

My address is ——: *jusho wa* —— *ku,* —— *machi* —— *chome,* ——
banchi, —— house name and ——*go* (apartment or house number)
My name is ——: *namae wa* ——*desu*
My telephone number is ——: *denwa bango wa* ——
I live near (some landmark): (——) *no chikaku*

Once you have telephoned, the ambulance will be dispatched even if
you stay on the line. If you are not able to make yourself understood, do
not hang up. In many areas, they will be able to direct an ambulance to
you by tracing your call.

POISON CONTROL CENTERS

In case of accidental poisoning, call the following numbers for help in English.
U.S. Air Force Hospital at Yokota (0425) 52-2511 ext. 7740 or 7852
U.S. Navy Hospital at Yokosuka (0468) 26-1911 ext. 5137 or 7141
New York Poison Control Center 212-340-4494
Los Angeles Poison Control Center 213-664-2121

In Japanese, there are two 24-hour phone numbers for poison information: the Tsukuba Chudoku Center at (0298) 52-9999 and the Osaka
Chudoku Center at (06) 451-9999.

PEDIATRIC CARE

Finding a reliable doctor who makes you and your child feel comfortable is
important to all parents. In Japan, there are many pediatricians and general
practitioners with training and experience overseas, and many who speak
English. You can visit a nearby hospital and see any one of the doctors in
the pediatrics department, or you can go to a private clinic by appointment. Be aware, however, that, as with the ob-gyn doctors in chapter 9,
you will not usually be able to make an appointment, and you may have to
wait until a doctor is available to see you. At the private clinics, Japanese
National Health Insurance may or may not be accepted.

There are a number of doctors that we know of—both pediatricians
and general practitioners—in the Tokyo-Yokohama area and in the
Kobe-Osaka area who have been in private practice for years. Many of
them are foreigners, and they all have experience in helping foreigners in
Japan with their medical problems. If you live in an outlying area and need
advice or referral, most of these doctors will be happy to assist you. For a
list of maternity/children's hospitals frequented by foreigners and where
you are likely to find English-speaking pediatricians, see chapter 9.

Dr. Annerosa Akaike

OAG House, 7-5-56 Akasaka, Minato-ku, Tokyo
☎ (03) 3584-1727　東京都港区赤坂 7-5-56 OAG ハウス

Dr. Norio Endo, Endo Clinic

Meguro Nishiguchi Mansion #305, 2-24-13 Kami-Osaki, Shinagawa-ku, Tokyo
☎ (03) 3492-6422　東京都品川区上大崎 2-24-13 目黒西マンション

Dr. Aksenoss, Dr. Shane, International Clinic

1-5-9 Azabudai, Minato-ku, Tokyo
☎ (03) 3582-2646　東京都港区麻布台 1-5-9

Dr. Theodor King, King Clinic

Olympia Annex, 6-31-21 Jingumae, Shibuya-ku, Tokyo
☎ (03) 3400-7917　東京都渋谷区神宮前 6-31-21 オリンピア アネックス

Konno Clinic (English-speaking doctor mornings only)

7-21-7 Nishi Shinjuku, Shinjuku-ku, Tokyo
☎ (03) 3371-5813　東京都新宿区西新宿 7-21-7

National Medical Clinic (over National Azabu Supermarket)

4-5-2 Minami-Azabu #502, Minato-ku, Tokyo
☎ (03) 3473-2057　東京都港区南麻布 4-5-2-502

Shinjuku Clinic

Arai Bldg, 1-24-3 Kabukicho, Shinjuku-ku, Tokyo
☎ (03) 3360-3306　東京都新宿区歌舞伎町 1-24-3 新井ビル

Shiraki Clinic (English-speaking doctor mornings only)

4-1-3 Nishi Ochiai, Shinjuku-ku, Tokyo
☎ (03) 3951-3070　東京都新宿区西落合 4-1-3

Dr. Michiko Suwa (female), Sanno Clinic

8-5-35 Akasaka, Minato-ku, Tokyo
☎ (03) 3402-3151　東京都港区赤坂 8-5-35

Dr. G. Symonds, Dr. Fair, Dr. Marshall, Dr. Fuji
Tokyo Medical and Surgical Clinic (across from Tokyo Tower)
32 Mori Bldg. 2F, 3-4-30, Shiba Koen, Minato-ku, Tokyo
☎ (03) 3436-3028　東京都港区芝公園 3-4-30 32 森ビル 2F

Dr. A. Altinbay

254 Yamashita-cho, Naka-ku, Yokohama-shi, Kanagawa-ken
☎ (045) 681-2113　神奈川県横浜市中区山下町 254

Bluff Clinic

82 Yamate-cho, Naka-ku, Yokohama-shi, Kanagawa-ken
☎ (045) 641-6961　神奈川県横浜市中区山手町 82

Dr. George Mikasa

101 Yamashita-cho, Naka-ku, Yokohama-shi, Kanagawa-ken
☎ (045) 641-6991　神奈川県横浜市中区山下町 101

Dr. Hideki Mukaiyama

90 Honmoku Sannotani, Naka-ku, Yokohama-shi, Kanagawa-ken
☎ (045) 623-7311　神奈川県横浜市中区本牧三ノ谷 90

Dr. Joseph Sato

1-18 Honmoku, Naka-ku, Yokohama-shi, Kanagawa-ken
☎ (045) 621-4403　神奈川県横浜市中区本牧 1-18

Dr. Yoshiro Shioda and Dr. Chieko Shioda

6224-6 Izumi-cho, Izumi-ku, Yokohama-shi, Kanagawa-ken
☎ (045) 804-6655　神奈川県横浜市泉区和泉町 6224-6

KANSAI AREA

Dr. Masanori Kyogoku's Clinic

8-13 Kusunoki-cho, Ashiya-shi, Hyogo-ken
☎ (0797) 31-2735　兵庫県芦屋市楠町 8-13

Dr. Shigeto Aoyama

4-2-11 Hachiman-dori, Chuo-ku, Kobe-shi, Hyogo-ken
☎ (078) 221-8623　兵庫県神戸市中央区八幡通 4-2-11

Dr. G. Barraclough

4-23-11 Ninomiya-cho, Chuo-ku, Kobe-shi, Hyogo-ken
☎ (078) 241-2896　兵庫県神戸市中央区二ノ宮町 4-23-11

Dr. Watanabe

5-2-16 Sakaguchi-dori, Chuo-ku, Kobe-shi, Hyogo-ken
☎ (078) 221-5111　兵庫県神戸市中央区坂口通 5-2-16

Dr. Yukio Sona

3-13-16 Nishimidorigaoka, Toyonaka-shi, Osaka-fu
☎ (06) 848-0057　大阪府豊中市緑ケ丘 3-13-16

Special Needs

For those children with learning or physical disabilities, contact the Tokyo International Learning Community (see chap. 11) for referral or advice.

VOCABULARY LIST

First of all, the phrase — *ga itai* (my — hurts) will work wonders in communicating the nature of your problem to the doctor.

arm: *ude* 腕

broken leg: *ashi no kossetsu* 足の骨折

bronchitis: *kikanshien* 気管支炎

chicken pox: *mizuboso* 水疱瘡

a cold, catch a cold: *kaze, kaze o hiku* かぜ，かぜをひく

constipation: *benpi* 便秘

convulsions: *hikitsuke* ひきつけ

cough: *seki* せき

diaper rash: *omutsu kabure* おむつかぶれ

diarrhea: *geri* 下痢

earache: *mimi ga itai* 耳が痛い

eczema: *shisshin* 湿疹

fever: *netsu* 熱

food poisoning: *shokuchudoku* 食中毒

German measles: *fushin, mikkabashika* 麻疹，三日ばしか

headache: *atama ga itai* 頭が痛い

jaundice: *odan* 黄疸

leg: *ashi* 足

measles: *hashika* はしか

mumps: *otafukukaze* おたふくかぜ

pediatrician: *shonika i* 小児科医

pediatrics: *shonika* 小児科

polio: *porio, shonimahi* ポリオ，小児麻痺

pneumonia: *haien* 肺炎

rash: *hosshin* 発疹

roseola: *toppatsusei hosshin* 突発性発疹

stomachache: *onaka ga itai, fukutsu* おなかが痛い、腹痛

sprained finger: *tsukiyubi* 突き指

sneeze: *kushami* くしゃみ

scarlet fever: *shoko netsu* 猩紅熱

sore throat: *nodo ga itai* のどが痛い

tetanus: *hasshofu* 破傷風

tonsils, tonsilitis: *hentosen, hentosenen* 扁桃腺，扁桃腺炎

tuberculosis (TB): *kekkaku* 結核

whooping cough: *hyakunichizeki* 百日ぜき

11

Educating the Kids

Preschools

Preschools are big business, especially in Tokyo, and the number of these schools serving the international community continues to grow each year. Often it is hard to determine what is meant by the name "preschool." Preschool as most Westerners know it means a preparatory program for the first grade. This traditional preschool education is available at a number of schools listed here. Many of the international schools have pre–school/ kindergartens affiliated with them. All the Japan Council of International Schools (JCIS) member preschool/kindergarten programs will prepare students for first grade in any international school.

All the international schools run from September to June, and often preschool/kindergartens run a summer school program in June and July. The admission process for the fall semester usually begins in February of the previous school year, and screening of the child is often involved. In Tokyo, most of the schools save a few openings for those people moving to Japan during the summer, and there are always openings during the school year because many families are transferred in the middle of the year.

For information about day-care centers and nurseries see chapter 12.

TOKYO PRESCHOOLS
For descriptions of JCIS preschool/kindergarten programs that are affiliated with or are part of one of the larger international schools, see the listings in the international schools section of this chapter.

Tokyo Union Church Preschool/Kindergarten

3 to 5 years
5-7-7 Jingumae, Shibuya-ku, Tokyo 150　東京都渋谷区神宮前 5-7-7
☎ (03) 3400-1579
🚉 Omotesando Station, Ginza, Hanzomon, Chiyoda lines; Harajuku Station, JR Yamanote Line

Tokyo Union Church Preschool operates both morning and afternoon half-day programs for three- to four-year-olds and a full-day kindergarten program for five-year-olds. Children may attend two, three, or five days a week. The underlying aim of the school is to foster growth according to Christian principles, and the program is designed for international families. Both Japanese language and culture are part of the curriculum, and special instructors are brought in for physical education and music classes. The teacher-student ratio is 1:6 for the three-year-olds and 1:10 for the four- and five-year-olds.

Global Garden

2 years 9 months to 5 years
3-25-11 Ebisu, Shibuya-ku, Tokyo 150　東京都渋谷区恵比寿 3-25-11
☎ (03) 3449-8060
🚉 Ebisu Station, JR Yamanote, Hibiya lines

Global Garden is the brainchild of Maureen Ilg, a self-styled global citizen who has been teaching in Tokyo for several years. Recognizing the problems faced by children speaking two (or more) languages, Ms Ilg decided to set up the Global Garden while in the process of completing graduate studies in preschool teaching at the University of British Columbia.

One of the first priorities of the Global Garden was to create a multicultural curriculum, respecting and supporting the cultures and languages of the students enrolled. Consequently the curriculum at the Global Garden reflects the diverse backgrounds of the children attending and all activities are presented in both English and Japanese by two teachers who are always present. By creating a balanced learning environment in which children can develop both languages equally through play and learning projects, Ms Ilg believes not only that the children's language skills improve but also that the children display greater self-awareness and increased social competence.

The play-based curriculum, which aims to teach communication skills and build self-confidence, is played out in projects that very often develop from the children's own initiative. Classes are kept small and the play area is well supplied with bright and colorful child-oriented toys and equipment, from which the children learn through interaction and direct encounter.

Parents are extremely welcome at the Global Garden: they can watch educational videos in an adjoining room or help with the children's activities until they are reassured that their children are comfortable with being left in this microcosm of our multicultural society.

Child's Play

2 to 3 years
1-3-11 Nishihara, Shibuya-ku, Tokyo 151　東京都渋谷区西原 1-3-11
☎ (03) 3460-8841
🚇 Yoyogi Uehara Station, Chiyoda, Odakyu lines

Child's Play calls itself a play group, but it also acts as a preschool education center. Children may attend two, three, or five days a week. Three-year-olds are eligible for a full-day program three days a week. The staff for each session consists of one fully qualified kindergarten/nursery school teacher and two qualified teaching assistants. The day is scheduled into segments for free play, crafts, music, tumbling, rest time, and other activities.

Cooperative Playgroup, Franciscan Chapel Center

4-2-30 Roppongi, Minato-ku, Tokyo　東京都港区六本木 4-2-30
☎ (03) 3401-2141
🚇 Roppongi Station, Hibiya Line

The Cooperative Playgroup is a private nonprofit organization that meets in the Franciscan Chapel Center hall in Roppongi. The group's organization is left entirely to the committee of mothers whose children are enrolled in the group each year. To be eligible, a child must be an English speaker with an English-speaking mother, and the child must be two years old by the New Year. The contact person for this group changes from year to year; call the Franciscan Chapel Center to get the current phone number.

Gregg International Kindergarten

2¹/₂ to 6 years
1-14-16 Jiyugaoka, Meguro-ku, Tokyo 152　東京都目黒区自由が丘 1-14-16
☎ (03) 3725-6495
🚇 Jiyugaoka Station, Toyoko, Oimachi lines

Gregg International Kindergarten is a part of the Gregg International College of Languages that is headquartered in Tokyo. They offer full- or half-day programs for two-and-a-half- to four-year-olds. The kindergarten program is full-day. Classes are conducted in English, and the teacher-student ratio is 1:6. Art, music, and gym are included in the weekly schedule of games, crafts, stories, and free time.

Junior Athletic Club (JAC) Prekindergarten

1¹/₂ to 6 years
5-3-20 Minami Azabu, Minato-ku, Tokyo 106　東京都港区南麻布 5–3–20
☎ (03) 3473-2161
🚇 Hiroo Station, Hibiya Line

JAC Prekindergarten is a community of children from all over the world. The school attempts to give an international and bilingual education that emphasizes social skills. The school is run in a Montessori-like fashion in that children are encouraged to pursue activities which best suit their own personality. All the teachers and assistants are trained and have teaching experience. The school is divided into two groups, a junior group with children age one and a half to three years and a senior group with children age three to six. The school runs from 10:00 A.M. to 1:00 P.M. daily, with options for two-, three-, four-, and five-day programs. Also available at the school are afternoon activities in language, gymnastics, and exercise. It is located near Arisugawa Park in Hiroo.

Kids House

2 to 4 years
c/o Sanshu Club, 1-20-27 Kami Osaki, Shinagawa-ku, Tokyo 141
☎ (03) 3447-6776　東京都品川区上大崎 1–20–27 三州倶楽部内
🚇 Meguro Station, JR Yamanote, Mekama lines

Kids House is a bilingual preschool—English and Japanese are used interchangeably, depending on the particular activity. The school offers a morning program for two-year-olds and an afternoon program for three- and four-year-olds. They advertise a relaxed and friendly environment in which children can learn and play. The teacher-student ratio is 1:7 for the three- and four-year-olds, and 1:5 for the two-year-olds.

Maria's Babies Society

2 months to 6 years
3-36-20 Jingumae, Shibuya-ku, Tokyo 150　東京都渋谷区神宮前 3–36–20
☎ (03) 3404-3468
🚇 Gaienmae Station, Ginza Line; Omotesando Station, Ginza, Hanzomon, Chiyoda lines

Billed as Japan's first bilingual and bicultural institution for children, Maria's Babies employs mostly British women to teach proper English, games, and etiquette to babies and children up to age six.

There are mother-and-child programs in addition to classes geared toward a group of children only. Lessons in teaching English to your child are available for mothers whose children are students. This school emphasizes exposure to Western culture through music, language, art, and culture classes.

RLC Playgroup

2 to 4 years
Roppongi Lutheran Church,
6-16-43 Roppongi, Minato-ku, Tokyo　東京都港区六本木 6–16–43
☎ (03) 3406-0671
📞 Roppongi Station, Hibiya Line

The RLC Playgroup was started over ten years ago by Elsa Muller as a play-group to serve the international community in Tokyo. The school is now located in the Roppongi Lutheran Church (a Japanese-speaking church) and runs from 9:30 A.M. to noon five days a week. Children from two to four years of age are welcome to attend as many days a week as their parents desire, and there is one qualified teacher and one assistant. Parents are not required to stay and participate. The school is conducted in English, and the students are mainly from international families.

Saint Alban's Nursery Program

2 to 4 years
3-6-25 Shiba Koen, Minato-ku, Tokyo 105　東京都港区芝公園 3–6–25
☎ (03) 3431-8534
📞 Kamiyacho Station (exit 1), Hibiya Line

The nursery program at Saint Alban's Anglican Church is part of the church's group of community programs. Designed to provide educational activities for children in the two to four age group, it is not technically a preschool, but rather a pre-preschool, helping to prepare children for a more formal preschool/kindergarten education elsewhere. There are two teachers in charge of the morning program. Two-year-olds may come two mornings a week, three-year-olds may come three or five mornings, and four-year-olds attend five mornings a week.

Saint Cecilia Preschool

3 to 5 years
4-7-23 Shirogane, Minato-ku, Tokyo 108　東京都港区白金台 4–7–23
☎ (03) 3446-9884
📞 Shibuya Station, JR Yamanote, Ginza, Hanzomon, Inokashira, Shin Tamagawa lines

Saint Cecilia is a Catholic, Japanese-speaking preschool that operates six days a week. In past years, they have had a number of international students. Fees are very reasonable compared with international schools. Children are at school from 9:00 A.M. to 1:30 P.M., and they must bring their own lunch. Saturday is a half day, and the school follows the Japanese school year schedule. They have an outdoor play area. They are affiliated with another preschool called Seishin Gakuen, (03)-3312-5701, in Suginami Ward. From Shibuya Station take bus #87 bound for Tamachi.

Shirogane International School

3 to 5 years
5-5-2 Shiroganedai, Minato-ku, Tokyo 108　東京都港区白金台 5-5-2
☎ (03) 3442-1941
📞 Meguro Station, JR Yamanote, Mekama lines

Shirogane International School offers full-day programs, five days a week for three- to four-year-olds and four- to five-year-olds. Teaching is all in English, and the teacher-student ratio is 1:7. Besides regular classroom activities, outside teachers are brought in for music and gymnastics classes each week.

Sunshine Preschool

$2^1/_2$ to $4^1/_2$ years
3-8-8 Hiroo, Shibuya-ku, Tokyo 150　東京都渋谷区広尾 3-8-8
☎ (03) 3400-2559
📞 Hiroo Station, Hibiya Line

Established in 1983 by Sandy Uri, (03) 3487-8680, a qualified preschool teacher from the United States, the Sunshine School is a nonsectarian preschool located in the Jewish Community Center (JCC). The school is not affiliated with the JCC, and has a curriculum much like an American preschool. The staff consists of two fully qualified teachers, and to keep the student-teacher ratio low, they only accept an average of twelve students per year. Although all classes are taught in English, nonnative English speakers are welcome. The school encourages parental involvement and sponsors many field trips as well as an annual mother-and-child workshop.

Unida International School

2 to 6 years
3-25-2 Ebisu, Shibuya-ku, Tokyo 150　東京都渋谷区恵比寿 3-25-2
☎ (03) 3443-6850
📞 Ebisu Station, JR Yamanote, Hibiya lines

Unida offers full- and half-day classes for children from two to six years old. Preschool activities are conducted in English, with fifteen minutes of Japanese or English lessons daily. Both native and nonnative English speakers are on the staff, and the teacher-student ratio is 5:24. The curriculum includes art, music, dance, exercise, reading, writing, and speaking.

KANSAI AREA PRESCHOOLS

Ashiya International Cooperative Playgroup

18 months to 4 years

Contact Community House, (078) 857-6540, for current phone number.

Ashiya International Cooperative Playgroup has been serving the international community in Kobe for about twelve years. The playgroup accepts up to fourteen children from the age of eighteen months to four years. A teacher is hired who is responsible for the planning and implementation of the program, and all mothers (who must be able to speak English) stay and help supervise and interact with the children at every session. The playgroup is held twice weekly at the Ashiya Luna Hall, and children may attend once or twice a week.

Aotani International Preschool

3 to 4 years

1-3-10 Kagoike-dori, Chuo-ku, Kobe-shi, Hyogo-ken 650

☎ (078) 221-3805　兵庫県神戸市中央区篭池通 1–3–10

The Aotani International Preschool was founded in 1984 by Sole Bruggemann. She is an accredited teacher with many years of teaching experience in the international schools in the Kobe area. Three-year-olds may attend either three or five days a week, and four-year-olds attend five days. The curriculum is designed to help prepare students for kindergarten at any of the international schools, and there are many extracurricular activities and outings during the school year.

INTERNATIONAL SCHOOLS

English-speaking international schools have been serving the foreign community in Japan since 1872. In 1965, these schools met formally to discuss matters of administration and curriculum and formed the Japan Council of International Schools (JCIS). This body facilitates open communication between the schools and provides the teaching and administrative staff with in-service and professional growth opportunities.

There are twelve JCIS international schools in Tokyo and twelve more throughout Japan. Most of these schools have a kindergarten (usually for ages four to five) and offer education through grade 12.

There are also a number of smaller international schools that are not affiliated with JCIS. These schools usually represent a particular nationality (e.g., the German schools in Tokyo and Kobe) and were founded for the purpose of educating those foreign nationals who intend to continue their education in their home country after a stay in Japan. Classes at these schools are conducted in the native language, and the lessons usually follow the national curriculum of the related country. Some of the schools accept students who are not of that nationality, but the student must be able to speak the language of the school fluently. To find out more about these schools, contact the embassy of the country you are interested in.

Because of the concentration of international schools in Tokyo, we have chosen to describe the JCIS schools in the city in detail. We have visited the administrators and staff at these schools and have spoken with parents of children who attend. Perhaps the best recommendation for any of these schools is the fact that each parent insists that their child's school is the best in town!

JCIS schools located outside the greater Tokyo area are listed at the end of this section.

Each school has a distinct personality, the result of the school's founding principles, the current administration, and the philosophy of education. The best method to use when deciding which school best suits your child is to go and visit the school personally. You will find that the school administrators welcome the parents of prospective students and encourage interested parents to learn more about all the schools before choosing one for their child. Some schools have large, modern facilities; others have small classrooms and a more informal feel. For some parents, accessibility (location near a subway or the use of a school bus service) is an important criterion. Still other parents are swayed by the quality of the playground equipment. It all depends on your priorities and what you and your child feel is important at this time in your child's life. Finally, whatever school your child attends, you can rest assured that all JCIS schools offer a high standard of education.

A word about admissions. Rumors fly fast and furious about the difficulty of being admitted to this or that school. It is true that these schools have a limited number of places for new students each term. They may also have quotas for the number of nonnative English speakers allowed in each class, and the boy-girl ratio may also be fixed. As a parent, such variables may be beyond your control, and all you can do is follow the admission process carefully and keep your fingers crossed.

For more information on a particular school, call the school directly or consult the American Chamber of Commerce publication *Living in Japan*, available at English-language bookstores.

Unless otherwise noted, the schools do not provide a private bus service.

The American School in Japan

Kindergarten to grade 12/coed
Founded 1902
1-1-1 Nomizu, Chofu-shi, Tokyo 182　東京都調布市野水 1-1-1
☎ (0422) 31-6351 fax (0422) 33-0608
Nursery School/Kindergarten Campus
2-15-5 Aobadai, Meguro-ku, Tokyo 153　東京都目黒区青葉台 2-15-5
☎ (03) 3461-4523

The American School in Japan (ASIJ) offers students a long and rich heritage of educational excellence. ASIJ is home to students from over thirty countries; one of the school's goals is to prepare these students to be citizens of the world.

The school is under the administration of a headmaster and is overseen by a board of directors. The large campus in west Tokyo offers an abundance of fresh air and open spaces. The campus houses modern school buildings as well as a sports complex and playing fields. There is a private bus service to the Chofu campus, and the average bus ride is forty-five minutes from central Tokyo. There is no uniform requirement.

Students from kindergarten to grade 12 may attend the Chofu campus. The school also has a small campus in Meguro that is home to the nursery school and kindergarten program. Children from age three to five are eligible to attend the Meguro campus (children must be three by September 1). All nursery/kindergarten programs are full-day. There are six classes at the Meguro campus, each staffed by one teacher and one assistant teacher. The number of pupils per class ranges from eighteen to twenty-two, depending on the age. All classes are conducted in English, and if the child is not a native English speaker, the parents must be able to speak English. Parent involvement is encouraged at all levels of the nursery/kindergarten program.

The kindergarten program at the Chofu campus is similar in content to the one in Meguro. Children must be five years old by September 1 to qualify. As at the Meguro campus, each class has approximately eighteen to twenty-two pupils and is taught by one teacher and one assistant. Some parents say that the Chofu campus has a more mature feel to it, perhaps because of the proximity of the older children in the elementary school. The children at the Chofu campus also have access to the music, library, sports, and computer facilities at the elementary school. If your child is of kindergarten age and you are not sure which campus you would prefer, the best thing to do is to visit both schools and talk with the teachers.

The elementary, middle, and high schools at the Chofu campus all offer a wide range of academic and extracurricular activities. Japanese language classes are required for all students from grades 1 through 5, and in the middle and high school Japanese is offered as part of the foreign language program. Students at both campuses are given numerous opportunities to experience Japanese culture and to interact with Japanese schoolchildren. Instruction in English as a second language is available for children in all grades of the elementary school.

Many elective and summer educational opportunities are offered through the school and summer school is available for children at the nursery/kindergarten levels. ASIJ also offers a postgraduate year for serious students who desire an extra year of personal enrichment or intensive preparation for college.

The British School in Japan

Ages 3 to 8/coed
Founded 1989
1-21-18 Shibuya, Shibuya-ku, Tokyo 150　東京都渋谷区渋谷 1-21-18
☎ (03) 3400-7353 fax (03) 5485-5340

Since opening its doors, the British School has expanded from three grades to four, and they have tentative plans to expand to include pupils up to age eleven. The school's main objective is to prepare British nationals to return to the British school system. In order to meet this objective, the school closely follows the British national curriculum and hires all of its teachers from Britain.

In its first year, 66 percent of the students were British, with the remaining students representing eleven different countries. The school is run by a board of trustees and is under the administration of a headmaster. All students must wear the prescribed uniform, and all classes have a full-day program.

The British national curriculum stresses reading, writing, and arithmetic in the first year (four- to five-year-olds), which is known as Primary 1 in the British system. Students must be fluent in English, and it is recommended that at least one parent be fluent as well.

Nominal time is spent on lessons in the Japanese language, as the national curriculum does not leave a lot of time for alternative lessons in the classroom. Non-denominational Christian religious studies are part of the program, and those students not from a Christian background may be exempted from such classes at the discretion of the headmaster.

The Christian Academy in Japan

Kindergarten to grade 12/coed
Founded 1950
1-2-14 Shinkawa-cho, Higashi Kurume-shi, Tokyo 203
☎ (0424) 71-0022 fax (0424) 76-2200　東京都東久留米市新川町 1-2-14

The Christian Academy in Japan is located on a four-acre campus in Kurume and provides a Christian-based education in English for the missionary community and other international families. The school is owned and operated by a twelve-member board of directors selected from six sponsoring evangelical mission organizations.

Two-thirds of the student body are the children of missionaries, and the school has an average enrollment of 300 students. Kindergarten applicants must be five years old by September 1.

The school accepts students from non-English-speaking homes, but the children must be able to pass an English-language screening test. Enrollment of students from non-English-speaking homes is limited to a maximum of 20 percent in each year. Non-Christian enrollment is also limited to 20 percent per grade.

The majority of the faculty members are hired from the United States, and the curriculum is also from the United States. Participation in Bible studies is required of all students, and non-Christian students make a commitment to comply with this rule at the time of registration. Other religious activities include devotions during the day and weekly chapel meetings. The school offers a wide variety of other extracurricular activities, and the sports teams compete with other international schools in the Tokyo area.

International School of the Sacred Heart

Kindergarten coed; grades 1 to 12 girls
Founded 1908
4-3-1 Hiroo, Shibuya-ku, Tokyo 150　東京都渋谷区広尾 4-3-1
☎ (03) 3400-3951 fax (03) 400-3496

The International School of the Sacred Heart is a girls' school that is directed by the Catholic Sisters of the Worldwide Society of the Sacred Heart and provides an education in English for children of the international community. Located near the Azabu district in central Tokyo, Sacred Heart's student body is made up of approximately 650 students of diverse faiths from over fifty countries. From the first grade, the school uniform is compulsory.

The kindergarten program is open to both boys and girls from ages three to five, although the program for three-year-olds is only available for children who have siblings attending the school. All kindergarten programs are full-day, and emphasis in the kindergarten is on developing the whole personality and helping children to become self-learners.

All classes at Sacred Heart are taught in English, and in general parents of students are expected to be fluent English speakers. The school accepts some nonnative English speakers who are not Japanese, and the number changes from year to year. Enrollment of Japanese nationals is usually limited to returnees from an English-speaking country who do not wish to reenter the Japanese school system.

Sacred Heart hires native English-speaking teachers who are qualified in their home countries. The curriculum and materials used are primarily from the United States and Great Britain. Sports teams from Sacred Heart compete in the league with the other international schools and occasionally with Japanese schools as well. Extracurricular activities are offered for students in grade 2 and above. Also from grade 2, Catholic students begin preparation for confirmation. At grade 5, students are offered a program of religious studies and can choose to study Christianity (Catholicism or Protestantism) or other world religions.

Japan International School

Grades 1 to 9/coed
Founded 1980
2-10-7 Miyamae, Suginami-ku, Tokyo 168　東京都杉並区宮前町 2-10-7
☎ (03) 3335-6620 fax (03) 3332-6930
Affiliated kindergarten: Aoba International School
1¹/₂ to 6 years
Founded 1976
2-10-34 Aobadai, Meguro-ku, Tokyo　東京都目黒区青葉台 2-10-34
☎ (03) 3461-1442

Japan International School is a nonparochial, bilingual, and multicultural elementary and middle school. Affiliated with the school is Aoba International School, a four-year kindergarten. Both schools were founded by Regina Doi, who now acts as headmistress, to offer an international education to all children, especially nonnative English speakers.

There are no quotas at the schools for the number of Japanese students accepted, and although all classes are taught in English, Japanese is often the language used among students. Both schools welcome students who want to experience Japanese culture on a daily basis.

At the four-year kindergarten in Meguro, children are prepared to enter a first-grade class in either a Japanese or an international school. The children come from a wide variety of backgrounds, and all of the classes are taught in English. At both schools, those students whose English is not up to standard are given special help and are offered a Saturday program of English instruction.

The Japan International School is located in a five-story building in the heart of Shibuya. There is bus transportation to and from school, and students are required to wear uniforms. The curriculum is basically from the United States but it is oriented toward Japan and the world at large in social studies, history, and geography. The school prides itself on its advanced math program, and children are instructed in the abacus up to grade 3. Qualified teachers and staff are hired from around the world, and most of them have a strong background in teaching students whose native tongue is not English.

There are approximately 280 students in the elementary and middle school, and all children go to various locations each week for sports and outdoor recreation. The school does not compete in sports with other schools but aikido is taught to students from third grade.

The school places many students in boarding schools abroad for high school studies upon completion of middle school. Help with placement in other international schools in Japan is also available.

Nishimachi International School

Kindergarten to grade 9/coed
Founded 1949
2-14-7 Moto Azabu, Minato-ku, Tokyo 106　東京都港区元麻布 2-14-7
☎ (03) 3451-5520 fax (03) 456-0197

Nishimachi International School's mission since its founding has been to educate children so that their thinking "embraces the world." Today, the school is among several international schools serving not only foreigners but also the Japanese community. The school is located in the Azabu district of central Tokyo and has an enrollment of approximately 400 children. All grades attend a full-day program.

The core group of students at each level are native English speakers. There are also large numbers of international students whose native tongue is a language other than English or Japanese. Yet a third group is made up of Japanese students, many of whom do not speak English at the time of entry. English as a second language programs are available beginning in kindergarten. Over the years, the staff at Nishimachi has discovered the right mix of native tongues that works at each grade level, and their admission tests and screenings help to maintain this balance. Nishimachi is not a bilingual school; all classes are taught in English except for language classes. The goal of the teachers and administration is to teach Japanese to all their students, and the school attempts to give the children as many opportunities as possible to both speak and listen to the Japanese language. Beginning in kindergarten, all students attend Japanese lessons, and more than half of the students are bilingual. The course structure of the school is basically American, but resources from Great Britain, Canada, and Australia are also used. The school is not affiliated with any church or country.

As a school that strives to give students a cross-cultural education, Nishimachi offers many extracurricular activities that are Japanese in nature. Sports teams from Nishimachi compete with other international schools as well as with local Japanese schools.

Nishimachi International School prides itself on its familylike atmosphere and small classes. The faculty consists of teachers from around the world, the majority of whom are from the United States, Japan, and Great Britain.

Saint Mary's International School

Pre-first grade to grade 12/boys
Founded 1954
1-6-19 Seta, Setagaya-ku, Tokyo 158　東京都世田谷区瀬田 1-6-19
☎ (03) 3709-3411 Fax (03) 707-1950

Saint Mary's International School is located near Seisen International School (see page 268) in the residential area of Setagaya. Saint Mary's is run by a Roman Catholic order, the Brothers of Christian Instruction. The school includes boys of all faiths and nationalities and strives to blend these diverse backgrounds to give students a worldwide perspective and to teach respect for one another. All students at Saint Mary's wear school uniforms.

As Seisen is nearby, many boys attend the kindergarten program there before moving to Saint Mary's in the first grade. Saint Mary's elementary school has its own Reading Readiness program for five-year-olds, but boys must be five years old on or before September 1 to be eligible. Extracurricular activities are offered at all grade levels.

All classes are taught in English, but special efforts are made to meet the needs of all students. Non-English-speaking students receive special instruction in English as a second language. As a school serving the international community, Saint Mary's limits acceptance of Japanese students to those returning from living abroad. The school curriculum is basically American, and the majority of the teachers come from North America. For high school students, Saint Mary's offers classes leading to an international baccalaureate diploma. This course consists of a two-year (grades 11 and 12) course leading to a diploma that qualifies students for admission to universities throughout the world. Advanced college standing is offered in many U.S. colleges for those holding this diploma.

Saint Mary's shares a private bus service with neighboring Seisen.

Santa Maria School

Kindergarten to grade 6/girls; Kindergarten to grade 5/boys
Founded 1959
2-2-4 Minami Tanaka, Nerima-ku, Tokyo　東京都練馬区南田中 2-2-4
☎ (03) 3904-0509

Santa Maria School was established by a Roman Catholic order—The Sisters Adorers—at the request of parents from the nearby U.S. military facility. Since then, the school has grown and it now serves both the military and civilian communities near Yokota Air Base and in the Tokyo area. In total, the school enrolls approximately 140 students from kindergarten to grade 6.

The curriculum at Santa Maria is typical of a parochial school in the United States. There are American and Japanese faculty members, and English as a second language instruction is available for those students who need it.

All students attend classes full-time, and are required to wear school uniform from first grade. Regular religious training is part of the curriculum, and Catholic students are prepared for first communion in the second grade.

The school observes some American and some Japanese holidays and encourages all parents to participate in the PTA.

Seisen International School

Kindergarten to grade 12/girls
Founded 1962
1-12-15 Yoga, Setagaya-ku, Tokyo 158　東京都世田谷区用賀 1-12-15
☎ (03) 3704-2661 fax (03) 3701-1033

Seisen International School is a Roman Catholic girls' school run by the Handmaids of the Sacred Heart of Jesus. The school serves a truly international student body with over 500 students representing some sixty countries. The school's educational program is based on reverence for God as the basic attitude of humanity. The faculty at Seisen strives to realize the full potential of its students and to help them come to an understanding of the essence of humanity uniting world cultures.

The coed kindergarten follows the Montessori system of education. Children age three to six are grouped together, and three-year-olds are only eligible for half-day programs. Two-and-a-half-year-olds may be eligible depending on their level of maturity, and those older than three may choose half- or full-day programs. There is also a pre-first grade class to prepare five-year-olds for first grade.

Religious instruction is compulsory for all students at Seisen. Classes in Catholic instruction are available, as well as other world religions. All classes are taught in English, and English as a second language courses are available for international students who are nonnative English speakers. Although Japanese children whose parents are both Japanese are generally not eligible for acceptance at Seisen, as with many other international schools, those Japanese children who are returning from a long stay abroad may be accepted.

From grade 1 of elementary school, Japanese language classes are given twice a week. Extracurricular activities are available for students in all grades. Seisen's sports program offers a wide range of sports for girls, and they compete with the other international schools as well as with U.S. military and Japanese schools.

Seisen International School shares a private bus service with nearby St. Mary's International School.

Tokyo International Learning Community

Ungraded/coed
Founded 1987
Tokyo Baptist Church, 9-1 Hachiyama-cho, Shibuya-ku, Tokyo 150
☎ (03) 3780-0030　東京都渋谷区鉢山町 9-1
Additional campus: 6-3-50 Osawa. Mitaka-shi, Tokyo 181
☎ (0422) 31-9611　東京都三鷹市大沢 6-3-50

The Tokyo International Learning Community (TILC) is a unique school for international children of all ages with special needs. Founded by a group of concerned parents and professionals, this school meets the previously unmet needs of English-speaking children with developmental disabilities. For the most part, the international schools in Tokyo offer no special services or integration programs for children with any type of developmental disability. In addition, TILC has seen the need for services above and beyond a special school for children and has expanded its services to meet these needs.

The staff at the school includes fully qualified special education instructors and a full-time administrator. The enrollment in the first three years grew from four children to nearly twice that many. The school is given space in the Tokyo Baptist Church free of charge, but it is not otherwise affiliated with the church. Funding comes from community and corporate sources, and the school is run by a board of directors made up of parents and educators.

The school incorporates specialists in many fields into their family of educators dedicated to the international community and its children. Besides operating the school, TILC also sponsors a support group for parents of children with special needs and two resources for the screening and evaluation of children with learning problems.

The Child and Adolescent Guidance Services (CAGS), phone (03) 3773-9552, is one of these resources. Services including psychological assessment, treatment, and consultation are available to families and educators of the English-speaking community in Tokyo and Yokohama.

Along with CAGS, TILC also offers an Early Childhood Program for children from birth to age five with developmental disabilities and other learning problems. Services include screening, case planning, individual learning sessions, consultation with schools, and infant and preschool services. To date, the Early Childhood Program has been able to integrate the children who have used this service in existing preschool programs, and it is the desire of all those involved with TILC that integration programs with the other international schools may some day be possible for children of all ages. For further information, call (03) 3224-6946, afternoons only.

TILC sponsors a toy library, also located in the Baptist Church (for more information, see chap. 4).

JICS MEMBER SCHOOLS OUTSIDE TOKYO

Canadian Academy

Preschool to grade 12/coed
Founded in 1950
4 Koyo-cho Minami, Higashi Nada-ku, Kobe-shi, Hyogo-ken 658
☎ (078) 57-0100 fax (078) 57-3250　兵庫県神戸市東灘区向洋町南 4

Fukuoka International School

Grades 1 to 9/coed
Founded 1972
3-18-50 Momochi, Sawara-ku, Fukuoka-shi, Fukuoka-ken 812
☎ (092) 8641-7601　福岡県福岡市早良区百道 3–18–50

Hiroshima International School

Kindergarten to grade 9/coed

Founded 1962
3-49-1 Kurakake, Asakita-ku, Hiroshima-shi, Hiroshima-ken 739-17
☎ (082) 843-4111 fax (082) 843-1111　広島県広島市安佐北区倉掛 3-49-1

Hokkaido International School

Grades 1 to 9/coed
Founded 1951
2-5-35 Sanjo, Fukuzumi, Toyohira-ku, Sapporo-shi, Hokkaido 062
☎ (011) 851-1205 fax (011) 855-1435　北海道札幌市豊平区福住三条 2-5-35

Kyoto International School

Kindergarten to grade 8/coed
Founded 1957
Shishigatani, 29-1 Kamimiyanomae-cho, Sakyo-ku, Kyoto-shi, Kyoto-fu 606
☎ (075) 771-4022 fax (075) 771-4022　京都府京都市左京区鹿が谷上宮の前町 29-1

Marist Brothers International School

Preschool to grade 12/coed
Founded 1951
1-2-1 Chimori-cho, Suma-ku, Kobe-shi, Hyogo-ken 654
☎ (078) 732-6266 fax (078) 732-6268　兵庫県神戸市須磨区千守町 1- 2-1

Nagoya International School

Nursery to grade 12/coed
Founded 1963
2686 Minamihara Nakashidami, Moriyama-ku, Nagoya-shi, Aichi-ken 463
☎ (052) 736-2025 fax (052) 736-3885　愛知県名古屋市守山区中志段味南原 2686

Osaka International School

Kindergarten to grade 12/coed
Founded 1991
4-4-16 Onohara-Nishi, Minoo-shi, Osaka 562
☎ (0727) 27-5050 fax (0727) 27-5055　大阪府箕面市小野原西 4-4-16

Saint Joseph International School

Pre-kindergarten to grade 12/coed
Founded 1901
85 Yamate-cho, Naka-ku, Yokohama-shi, Kanagawa-ken 231
☎ (045) 641-0065 fax (045) 641-6572　神奈川県横浜市中区山手町 85

Saint Maria International School

Nursery to grade12/coed
Founded 1872
83 Yamate-cho, Naka-ku, Yokohama-shi, Kanagawa-ken 231
☎ (045) 641-5751 fax (045) 641-6688　神奈川県横浜市中区山手町 83

Saint Michael's International School

Pre-kindergarten to grade 6/coed
Founded 1946
3-17-2 Nakayamate-dori, Chuo-ku, Kobe-shi, Hyogo-ken 650
☎ (078) 231-8885 fax (078) 231-8889　兵庫県神戸市中央区中山手通 3-17-2

Yokohama International School

Nursery to 13 years/coed
Founded 1924
258 Yamate-cho, Naka-ku, Yokohama-shi, Kanagawa-ken 231
☎ (045) 622-0084 fax (045) 621-0379　神奈川県横浜市中区山手町 258

OTHER EDUCATIONAL ORGANIZATIONS

Tokyo Association for the Education of Young Children (TAEYC)

TAEYC is the Tokyo branch of a national organization that works to facilitate the professional growth of people working with or for young children. The organization is made up of teachers, administrators, educators, and trainers working with future teachers, social workers, health specialists, and others.

As a parent with a young child, you may obtain a regular or student membership to this organization and receive a magazine that keeps you in touch with the latest developments and concerns in early childhood education. For a current phone number, call Tokyo English Lifeline (TELL) at (03) 5481-4347.

JAPANESE YOCHIEN AND SHOGAKKO

In addition to the international private schools, you may want to consider the Japanese public schools, which are accessible to any resident of Japan. Not only are they affordable, but they also give foreign residents the opportunity to learn Japanese-language skills, experience Japanese culture, and meet Japanese people. Some foreign residents choose to send their children to Japanese private schools, which are more costly than the public ones.

Children who attend Japanese schools go to school five and a half days a week, including Saturday morning. There are three semesters in the school year, which begins in April, and vacation times are usually from July 20 to August 31, and from December 26 to January 8. There is a short (ten days or so) break in late March between the end of one school year and the beginning of the next.

YOCHIEN

Yochien are Japanese preschool or kindergarten programs, which may be public or private. Public *yochien* start at the age of four, whereas private *yochien* offer programs from the age of three or even earlier. Public *yochien* costs are extremely reasonable. For example, in Minato-ku in Tokyo, the registration fee is ¥500, and monthly tuition is ¥4,000. Some private *yochien*, on the other hand, come close to rivaling international schools in cost, so this may help determine where you send your child.

Because the school year begins in April, the child must be of the proper age by April 1. Usually, applications for April can be picked up from the school from about November.

For young children, most Japanese *yochien* emphasize games, play, and cooperation. Academics are usually not introduced until the age of five. Many foreigners send their preschoolers to *yochien* because it provides an excellent opportunity for their children to learn the Japanese language. The programs usually run through lunch. (8:30 A.M. through noon is average although until 2:30 P.M. is not uncommon. On Saturdays and one other day, usually Wednesday, *yochien* end at 11:30 A.M.). Some *yochien* have lunch programs but usually each child must take his own *obento* (box lunch).

Our personal experience with *yochien* was extremely positive. The only problem we encountered was the language difference, not for the children so much as for us, the parents. We were given many information sheets in Japanese each week, and although there were a few English-speaking teachers who would translate the important information, it was still frustrating for us. On the whole, the other mothers as well as the teachers were willing to assist us when we needed help. There are many opportunities for parents, mothers in particular, to become involved at the *yochien*. Field trips, parties, and special events all require parental involvement.

For more information on the *yochien* in your area, contact the education committee of your local ward or city office. Also, be aware that each ward or city is allotted a certain amount of money to help defray preschool costs for families who send their children to private *yochien*, even if the parents are sending a child to a *yochien* outside their ward. Many foreign families are not aware that they may qualify for this stipend, so inquire at the school at the time of registration, and they will give you the required forms to fill out.

SHOGAKKO

Japanese elementary school, or *shogakko*, runs from grade 1 through grade 6. To attend a public elementary school, a child must meet the following requirements. First, the parents must be residents of the ward where the school is located. Second, the child must be age six by March 31. Third, the parents must have proof of residence in Japan (Alien Registration Card).

If you and your child meet these requirements, you can go to the education section of your ward or city office with your proof of residency and fill out an application form. It is a good idea to take along a Japanese-speaking person because the forms must be filled out in Japanese. A school will be chosen according to where you live, and a meeting will be set up with the principal of the school. According to law, all residents of a ward or city are entitled to send their children to local public elementary schools. This means a school must automatically accept you. If you are interested in a private elementary school, you should go directly to the school to request an application form. Some of these schools have a few spaces set aside for foreign students, and so even if the school has no openings at the time for Japanese students, they may make an exception for foreigners.

Your child will then be registered in the grade appropriate to his age. If his language skills are not adequate, he will actually be placed in a lower class until he is ready to join his peers, although he will be registered in the higher grade.

Also important in the registration process is the physical examination. The checkups are given free by school-approved pediatricians and must be done in November of the year before the child is to begin school. Forms for the physical can be picked up at the ward or city office after October 1. If the November deadline is missed, a physical should be arranged with the school doctor, because no student can begin school without this completed form.

HOME SCHOOLING IN JAPAN

Although Japan's international schools are all first-rate and Japanese schools are a viable alternative, home schooling is an option that more and more foreign parents are choosing in order to meet their children's educational needs. The families that decide on this option are as diverse as the home schooling approaches themselves. Some of these families are:

Bicultural families who don't feel comfortable in either the Japanese or a Western school system.

Expatriate, military, and diplomatic families who are frequently transferred.

Japanese families who feel that the Japanese school system is too rigid, but whose children cannot enter an international school because of the language requirements.

Families who find the tuition fees at the international schools too expensive.

Families who live too far away from any acceptable school.

Families whose children are not particularly happy in school.

Families whose religious beliefs or philosophies differ from their children's school.

Home schooling is legal in Japan. The Ministry of Education, Mombusho, treats home schools in the same category as the international schools. To make sure that your child's education meets government standards, it is recommended that you file basic information about your child's schooling with your local ward office or city hall each year. State that you have found a suitable educational program for your child and that he or she has been "registered" for the year with whatever program you have chosen (see the sample list of programs later in this chapter). Have all of the above information translated into Japanese and submitted to the proper authorities.

When considering home schooling, you will want to find out about the numerous accredited programs available. Often parents are overwhelmed at the thought of being totally responsible for their child's education, but with a fairly structured program a parent need not act as the sole teacher. Depending on the ages and needs of your children, you can choose either a program that includes every material you could possibly need, from textbooks and maps to the pencils and paper, or a program that gives you only general guidance. Of course, a home schooler benefits from the involvement of at least one parent. We know families where each parent brings his own strong points to the program. For example, in one family the Japanese father works on language, calligraphy, and math, while the American mother uses her talent in carpentry, cooking, and music to offer her children an education in those areas.

If there are certain subjects that children cannot master at home, parents are encouraged to make use of the programs and facilities at nearby schools, if possible, or to engage a tutor. One of the biggest advantages of home schooling is the opportunity it gives children to develop their own talents and interests. A budding tennis champ or concert violinist can devote a larger proportion of time to these pursuits than enrollment in the regular school system would allow.

Socialization is a major concern of parents when they begin a home schooling program. Those who have educated their children at home for years note, however, that these fears are usually unfounded. Because the child is not in school all day, he has many opportunities to visit with people of various ages. These parents have found that by exposing their children to a wide range of activities, and by opening their home to frequent visits from friends and relatives, their home-schooled children learn to communicate and socialize with all ages and types of people.

In order to foster interaction with their child's peers, home schoolers often use the morning as their "class" time and go on outings or enroll the children in music or art lessons in the afternoons. This schedule gives children the opportunity to learn from a teacher other than the parents, as well as to meet children their own age. Other suggestions from parents who educate their children at home include joining an international school library, participating in intramural sports, and asking if your children can take part in special events at the local schools. It may be possible to make use of nearby *yochien* playgrounds and empty classrooms in the afternoons, by asking the school and explaining your intentions and goals for your child.

Many resources are available to help parents who are interested in the home-schooling option. In Japan, Gail Asano has offered to be a contact person for interested parents. She is willing to lend her copies of the 1986 and 1987 directories, *The Big Book of Home Learning* and *The Next Big Book of Home Learning*, both by Nary Pride. You can contact Gail at (0486) 51-7334 or write to her at Century Omiya Koen 202, 1-338-2 Uetake-cho, Omiya-shi, Saitama-ken. If you would like your own copy of one of these directories, write to the publisher at Crossway Books, 9825 W. Roosevelt Rd., Westchester, Illinois 60154, USA.

Another book for home schoolers, put out by *Mothering Magazine*, is *Schooling at Home*, which contains both listings of resources and informative articles about home schooling. It can be obtained by writing to John Muir Publications, Box 613, Santa Fe, New Mexico 87504-0613, USA, or call (505) 982-4078.

Dr. Raymond Moore, an advocate of home-schooling, is director along with his wife Dorothy of the Christian-based Moore Foundation. Dr. Moore periodically visits Japan to give lectures. The Moore Japan Association puts out a newsletter in Japanese every month. For more information about the Moore Foundation, write to Mrs. Iibuka, c/o Akagiyama Gakuin, 4192

Kashiwakuda, Miyagi-mura, Seta-gun, Gunma-ken. Call the U.S. Moore Foundation at (206) 835-2736, or write Box 1, Camas, Washington 98607, USA.

Although the home-schooling movement originated with religious organizations, its horizons have broadened tremendously over the past ten years. Most of the overseas programs used here in Japan are from the United States. One of the best sources for information is the John Holt organization. John Holt was an American elementary school teacher who eventually became a strong advocate of home learning. He is the author of several well-known books, such as *How Children Fail* and *Teach Your Own*. These publications are available through John Holt's Music and Book Store, 2269 Massachusetts Ave., Cambridge, Massachusetts 02140, USA. Their superb catalog carries many educational materials, including books, tapes, and musical instruments. An international newsletter, *Growing Without Schooling*, was founded by John Holt in 1977. Containing pertinent and practical information, this newsletter is a valuable forum for home schoolers around the world. An annual subscription to Japan is US$20 for six issues by sea mail. For airmail add US$10.

The Waldorf school program is used extensively by home schoolers. Anthroposophic Press offers a comprehensive selection of books about Waldorf education, as well as books and lectures by Rudolph Steiner, the founder of the school. For their address, see chapter 4 under mail-order companies. A Waldorf newsletter, *Childhood: The Waldorf Perspective*, is published by Nancy Aldrich, R.R. #2, Westford, Vermont 05494, USA.

For information on the Montessori technique for home schoolers, write to American Montessori Consulting, at P.O. Box 5062, Rossmoor, California 90721-5062, USA, or call (213) 598-2321. They offer a home learning kit in addition to the book *Montessori at Home*.

The following is a short list of some of the most popular home-learning programs in the United States and other countries.

Clonhara

1289 Jewett, Ann Arbor, Michigan 48104, USA
☎ (313) 769-4515
This well-balanced program offers a flexible yet standard approach.

Oak Meadow

P.O. Box 712, Blacksburg, Virginia 24060, USA
☎ (703) 552-3263
This company offers home-study courses for kindergarten to grade 12 and also a course for parents called "Parent Sensitivity Training."

The Calvert School

Dept. GW, Tuscany Road, Baltimore, Maryland 21210, USA
☎ (301) 243-6030
High-quality home-study courses developed by certified teachers for use in kindergarten through grade 8.

Les Enfants D'Abord

Contact Dolores Foin-Sanchex, 18 Grande Rue, 26000 Valence, France
This is a newly formed group that also publishes a newsletter with the same name.

Quebec Home Schooling Advisory

4650 Arcadia, Lachine, Quebec HA2 IN5, Canada

Alternative Education Resource Group (AERG)

39 Williams Street, Hawthorne, Melbourne 3122, Victoria, Australia

Education Otherwise

25 Common Lane, Hemingford Abbotts, Cambridge PE18 9AN, England

For more international information, contact World Wide Educational Services, Strode House, 44-50 Osnaburgh Street, London NW1 3NN, England, or write to Holt Associates and request a copy of their directory issue of *Growing Without Schooling*, which contains the names of over 2,000 home schoolers around the world.

The following books are recommended for families contemplating home schooling:
Home Schooling: Taking the First Step, by Borg Hendrickson, is available from the Chinaberry Book Service (see chap. 4).

Better Than School, by Nancy Wallace, *School's Out*, by Jean Bendell, and *The Three R's at Home*, by Howard and Susan Richman, are all available from John Holt's Music and Book Store (see above).

12

The Care and
Nurturing of
Parents

TIME TO SHAPE UP

Besides the normal wear and tear of raising small children, in Japan there is the added stress of living in both a foreign culture and one of the most work-oriented countries in the world. Any parent who has successfully raised children will tell you that one of the most important things to do while the children are small is to carve out a little time for yourself. This is also one of the most difficult things to do, and in Tokyo it is nearly impossible. With long work hours, business and social obligations, club or group functions, and playgroup or school activities, there is very little time left for either parent to spend alone or together. For your physical as well as mental health though, it is important to make the effort to take time out.

PHYSICAL HEALTH

If you thrive on regular exercise and plan on continuing a regime while in Japan, there are a few important things to consider. Parents with small children may not want to take the time to go to a club for exercise, but instead may want to work out at home. Because of limited space in most homes, a weight or workout room may not be possible. If you need to exercise, push back all of the furniture and go for it! Another idea is to invite some other mothers over during the day and let the kids play while you exercise together.

One of the advantages of living in Japan is the relative safety of walking or jogging alone on the streets. If you are lucky enough to live near a large park, temple, or shrine, you can walk or run in the beauty of the trees and gardens. Be aware, however, that only walking, not running, is allowed on the paths in many shrines. Check with the authorities before you start out. One man we know ran every morning for weeks in the grounds of a shrine unaware that he was being told over the loudspeakers—in Japanese, of course—to stop running.

Private fitness centers and spas abound in Japan. They are popular with young Japanese, but because of work schedules, the clubs can be crowded during the evening hours and on weekends. This can work to your advantage if you have flexible hours that allow you to use the club during the day. Many clubs have a special day rate—often just a monthly fee and no registration charge. Other clubs have restricted membership and charge an annual subscription as well as outrageous registration fees. Club styles range from European-type spas, to overdecorated gyms, to clubs with state-of-the-art weightlifting equipment and personal trainers who speak three languages. The one you choose may depend more on location and cost than decor.

Most wards and cities also have public sports centers, with low entrance fees and many types of facilities. If you do not speak Japanese, you may need to take a Japanese-speaking person with you the first time you go to fill out forms and translate the various rules and regulations.

Call your local ward or city office for more information.

Mental Health

Many organizations exist throughout Japan solely for the purpose of helping foreigners cope with life. Besides providing basic information on life in Japan, these centers may offer cultural and orientation classes. The cultural classes range from Japanese flower arranging (ikebana) to basic language and cooking courses. Orientation sessions often include local tours and guest speakers.

Many cities are now funding what they call "international associations" to run such centers, not only for foreign residents, but for Japanese citizens as well. The Nagoya International Center, 1-47-1 Nagono, Nagoya-shi, Aichi-ken, (052) 581-5678 was one of the first and serves as a model for the rest of the country. If you are new to an area, or simply want to learn a little more about your neighborhood and perhaps meet some new people, check out what is being offered by the groups in your area by contacting your local ward office, city hall, or community center.

In Tokyo, the churches, international schools, and private clubs offer similar services and opportunities for the foreign community, so the need for government-funded community centers has not been as great as in the outlying areas.

COMMUNITY AND INFORMATION CENTERS

KANSAI AREA

Community House and Information Centre (CHIC)

East Court No. 2, Business Center 203, 1-14 Koyo-cho, Higashinada-ku, Kobe-shi, Hyogo-ken

☎ (078) 857-6540　兵庫県神戸市東灘区向洋町中 1-14 イーストコート 2 番 203

Hours: 9:30 A.M. to 4:30 P.M. Monday through Friday. Summer until noon. Closed in August.

This volunteer organization exists to help foreigners who live in the Kobe-Osaka area. Besides the orientation and cultural classes they offer, they publish two books that are a must for foreigners living in the area. *Living in Kobe*, a sourcebook for information and services in the area, costs ¥2,000 plus ¥260 postage from CHIC. Another useful book, *Kids in Kobe*, has numerous listings of places of interest and services that parents need to know about. *Kids in Kobe* includes information about Kyoto and Osaka, so before you travel that way make sure to get a copy. It is available only through the Community House and Information Centre for ¥1,000 plus ¥260 for postage.

Kobe International Community Center

Edo-machi SK Building 5F, 92 Edo-machi, Chuo-ku, Kobe-shi, Hyogo-ken

☎ (078) 322-0030　兵庫県神戸市中央区江戸町 92 江戸町 SK ビル 5F

Hours: Monday through Friday 10:00 A.M. to 8:00 P.M., Saturday 10:00 A.M. to 5:00 P.M.

Established in 1990, this center is run by Kobe International Association (a governmental body) for all residents. They offer Japanese-language and cultural classes free of charge and give information by phone or in person. At the center there are foreign magazines and newspapers, an English typewriter and word processor available for use, satellite TV, and a message board.

Kyoto International Community House

2 Awadaguchi Torii-cho, Sakyo-ku, Kyoto-shi, Kyoto-fu

☎ (075) 752-3010　京都府京都市左京区粟田口鳥居町 2

Hours: 9:00 A.M. to 9:00 P.M. Tuesday through Sunday. If Monday is a holiday, they are open that day and closed the next day.

Sponsored by the city government, Kyoto Community House opened in September 1989 to assist the needs of the foreign community and to serve as a cultural exchange center for Japanese citizens. Among their programs are traditional Japanese culture courses (in English), a home-visit program, lectures about Asia (in Japanese), foreign movies, and classical concerts. There is a library with foreign newspapers, magazines, and books and also live CNN television in the information area in the lobby.

Osaka International House (OIH)

8-2-6 Uehonmachi, Tennoji-ku, Osaka-shi, Osaka-fu
☎ (06) 772-5931　大阪府大阪市天王寺区上本町 8-2-6
Hours: Daily from 9:00 A.M. to 9:00 P.M.

OIH is a conference and international exchange center built by the city of Osaka to provide a place for cultural exchange for all residents. Besides information in English, International House provides a number of services and facilities, including cultural classes about Asia for a minimum charge, a reading corner with foreign newspapers and magazines, a library with books in English and Japanese (books must be read on-site), live CNN television in a comfortable lounge, a message board, and conference and hotel facilities for use at a reasonable cost.

COUNSELING SERVICES

Besides these community centers, there are counseling services for foreigners that provide individual or family counseling, and others that can give assistance over the telephone, either by supplying basic information or by helping in a crisis situation. They are nonsectarian and are staffed by both trained volunteers and professional counselors.

IMMEDIATE HELP OVER THE PHONE
Japan Helpline
Phone toll free 0120-461997 anywhere in Japan, 24 hours a day, for counseling advice or help.

TELL (Tokyo English Lifeline)
☎ (03) 5481-4347 for phone counseling, referrals, or crisis intervention.
Hours: 9:00 A.M. to 4:00 P.M. and 7:00 P.M. to 11:00 P.M. daily.

COUNSELING SERVICES—KANTO AREA

TCCS (TELL Community Counseling Service)
9-1 Hachiyama-cho, Shibuya-ku, Tokyo 150
☎ (03) 3780-0336　東京都渋谷区鉢山町 9-1
Hours: 9:00 A.M. to 5:00 P.M. Monday through Friday.

Connected with TELL (Tokyo English Lifeline), TCCS provides individual, group, and family therapy by trained counselors. Fees are assessed on an ability-to-pay basis. They also hold workshops and employee assistance programs.

Tokyo International Learning Community (TILC)
☎ (03) 3780-0030
See chapter 11 for information on all their services.

COUNSELING SERVICES—KANSAI AREA

International Counseling Center (ICC)
☎ (078) 856-2201
Hours: 9:00 A.M. to 5:00 P.M. Monday to Friday
ICC provides counseling services by qualified counselors for the foreign community in the Kansai area. The center can provide long- and short-term counseling as well as give referrals to other counselors. Call for an appointment.

SUPPORT GROUPS

Numerous support groups for people with special needs, such as Alcoholics Anonymous or Overeaters Anonymous, have English-speaking chapters throughout Japan. These groups meet regularly, and to find out what groups meet in your area and when, contact the organizations listed here—in particular, TELL for the Tokyo area and the Community House and Information Centre for the Kansai area—or check the English-language newspapers and journals (parent support groups for special needs are listed in chap. 9). If you cannot find a group to meet your needs, consider forming your own support group.

INFORMATION NETWORK

One of the most important things to have while living in Japan is information, not just information about the world, but about those things that are of special concern to parents.

INFORMATION BY PHONE

Each month it seems that there are more services that give information by phone, not only in English, but in several other languages as well. Keep these numbers by the phone as these agencies can provide answers to questions on almost any subject. If they do not know the answer, they will steer you to someone who does.

NTT Town Network Service

☎ (03) 3201-1010
Directory assistance and answers to questions about daily living.

English Directory Assistance (NTT)

☎ (03) 3277-1010 or (06) 313-1010
Hours: 9:00 A.M. to 5:00 P.M. Monday through Friday, and 9:00 A.M. to noon Saturdays. They are closed Sundays and on national holidays.
Call NTT for phone numbers anywhere in Japan.

International Directory Assistance (KDD)

From anywhere in Japan call 0051 for phone numbers abroad.

Japan Hot Line (KDD/NTT)

☎ (03) 3586-0110
Information on anything, Monday through Friday 10:00 A.M. to 4:00 P.M. (except holidays).

Tourist Information Center

☎ (03) 3502-1461 in Tokyo, (075) 371-5649 in Kyoto, and 0120-444-800 toll free elsewhere
Call for information on just about anything. You can also arrange to visit a private Japanese home through their Home Visit System.

Teletourist Information

☎ (03) 3503-2911 in English, (03) 3503-2926 in French
Recorded information on cultural events.

Tokyo Metropolitan Government Foreign Residents Advisory Service

Information in English, Monday through Friday 9:30 A.M. to noon and 1:00 P.M. to 4:00 P.M. (03) 5320-7744
Information in Chinese on Tuesday and Friday (03) 5320-7766
Information in French on Thursdays (03) 5320-7755

Tokyo Bar Association Information Center for Legal Affairs

☎ (03) 3581-2201
Call for an appointment.

NEWSPAPERS

The following newspapers are printed in Asia and can be delivered to your door at a relatively low cost. Other major newspapers from around the world can be airmailed to you in Japan, but the cost may be prohibitive.

Dailies:

Asahi Evening News: (03) 3543-3321
Asian Wall Street Journal: (03) 3292-1458
The Daily Yomiuri: (03) 3242-1111
The International Herald Tribune: (03) 3216-3358
The Japan Times: (03) 3453-5311
Mainichi Daily News: (03) 3212-0321
Shipping and Trade News: (03) 3542-6511
U.S.A. Today: (03) 3270-8650

Weeklies:

The Nikkei Weekly: (03) 3270-0251
The Japan Times Weekly: (03) 3453-4350

FREE NEWSLETTERS

A number of free newsletters are published in English for foreign residents and tourists. Most of them can be picked up in supermarkets and shops that foreigners frequent, as well as in the major hotels. Some of the newsletters can be subscribed to for a small fee and delivered to your door. All of these publications are full of timely and valuable information, such as phone numbers for services, articles on new businesses, and movie and concert information. Many of these newsletters also contain personal and classified ads that are a good place to find used items or to sell something. This listing is by no means complete, since every six months it seems a new publication pops up and another one dies. The following are newsletters that have been around for a while.

| TOKYO AREA |

City Life News

Kita Bldg. 2F, 2-8-13 Shiba, Minato-ku, Tokyo　東京都港区芝 2–8–13 キタビル 2F
☎ (03) 3457-7541 or fax (03) 3457-7544
Monthly, general interest newsletter, available around Tokyo or by subscription.

Nippon View

2-8-6 Shiroganedai, Minato-ku, Tokyo　東京都港区白金台 2–8–6
☎ (03) 3442-0211 fax (03) 3442-0217
Similar to *City Life News*, this monthly publication has a full page of important phone numbers to tear out and keep by the phone. Delivered with the *Japan Times* and available around Tokyo at select locations.

Tokyo Weekender

Tuttle Bldg. 2F, 1-2-6 Suidobashi, Bunkyo-ku, Tokyo
☎ (03) 5689-2471 fax (03) 5689-2474　東京都文京区水道 1-2-6 Tuttle ビル 2F

In Tokyo for twenty years, this newspaper is full of interesting tidbits and informative articles for the foreign community. Available every Friday at major supermarkets, hotels, and restaurants; or have it delivered to your door.

Tokyo City Guide

OS Bldg. 5F, 4-4-12 Tsukiji, Chuo-ku, Tokyo
☎ (03) 3542-5027 fax (03) 3546-1480　東京都中央区築地 4-4-12 OS ビル 5F

Specifically for tourists, but great for residents because of the excellent maps and comprehensive movie and restaurant listings. Delivered to all major hotels each Sunday or to your home by subscription.

KANSAI AREA

Kinki Nippon Tourist　　　　東京都千代田区神田松永町 19-2 近鉄ビル 2F

Kintetsu Bldg. 2F, 19-2 Kanda-Matsunaga-cho, Chiyoda-ku, Tokyo ☎ (03) 3253-6131 or Nikko Bldg. 7F, 2-11-8 Sonezaki, Kita-ku, Osaka ☎ (06) 313-6868

A monthly paper with basic tourist information for the Kansai area. Available at major hotels and tourist locations and from Kobe Community House and Information Centre.

MAGAZINES

Like any major city, Tokyo has a number of city magazines, full of information on what's happening around town. They fill the same void as the free newsletters, but are more comprehensive in the information that they give, and they are full of interesting features on a potpourri of subjects. There are also some journals that are written for foreigners living in Japan, which contain cultural and regional articles. Again, the ones that have passed the test of time are listed here.

Eye-Ai

Sennari Bldg. 5F, 5-6-20 Minami Aoyama, Minato-ku, Tokyo
☎ (03) 3406-7373　東京都港区南青山 5-6-20 千成ビル 5F

Published monthly, full of news and information regarding the traditional culture, entertainment, and popular music and arts of Japan.

Forecasts

2-21-2, Nishi Azabu, Minato-ku, Tokyo 106
☎ (03) 3400-3386　東京都港区西麻布 2-21-2

An excellent resource for Tokyo concert and arts information, theater maps and tickets. Published by Music For Youth (see music section in chap. 7).

Gochiso-Sama!

13-2 Yagoto Fujimigaoka, Tenpaku-cho, Showa-ku, Nagoya-shi, Aichi-ken 466
☎ (052) 835-4458　愛知県名古屋市昭和区天白町八事富士見丘 13-2
A quarterly culinary newsletter, full of recipes, cookbook and restaurant reviews, regional food close-ups, and much, much more. Available only by subscription.

Hello Friends

Kanagawa International Association, Sangyoboeki Center Bldg. 9F, 2 Yamashita-cho, Naka-ku, Yokohama-shi, Kanagawa-ken
☎ (045) 671-7070　神奈川県横浜市中央区山下町 2 産業貿易センタービル 9F
This is not actually a magazine, but a twice-yearly newsletter in English with helpful information for foreigners living anywhere in Japan. To receive the newsletter free of charge, call the association (they are closed on Mondays).

Insights

c/o IRF Labs. Inc., Takaoka Bldg. 4F, 2-22-2 Yushima, Bunkyo-ku, Tokyo
☎ (03) 3831-8717 fax (03) 3832-5429　東京都文京区湯島 2-22-2 高岡ビール 4F
This quarterly magazine is full of all kinds of interesting articles, essays, and interviews focusing on the New Age movement in Japan. The free bulletin board listings are a great way to find out about anything from meditation workshops to macrobiotic chefs.

Kansai Time-Out

1-1-13 Ikuta-cho, Chuo-ku, Kobe-shi, Hyogo-ken 651
☎ (078) 232-4516　兵庫県神戸市中央区生田町 1-1-13
A monthly publication with feature articles and arts and entertainment information for the Kansai area. A must for foreigners living in the area.

Tokyo Journal

Wako No. 5 Bldg. 5F, 1-19-8 Kakigara-cho, Nihombashi, Chuo-ku, Tokyo
☎ (03) 3667-7397　東京都中央区日本橋蠣殻町 1-19-8 和考第 5 ビル 5F
Trendy and colorful, full of Tokyo film, festival, and exhibition listings, as well as a number of feature articles each month.

Tokyo Time Out

Kamiyama Ambassador 2C, Kamiyama-cho, Shibuya-ku, Tokyo
☎ (03) 3460-8195　東京都渋谷区神山町神山アンバサダ 2C
A relatively new city magazine that has up-to-date listings for theater and

arts events, TV, and radio. One or two feature articles are also included each month.

Tokyo Today

3-14-12 Roppongi 505, Minato-ku, Tokyo
☎ (03) 3423-0660   東京都港区六本木 3-14-12-505
Monthly listings for Tokyo cultural events, television, arts features, etc.

PARENTING INFORMATION FROM ABROAD

Without news from your home country on a regular basis, you may begin to feel "out of it." As a parent, this problem is magnified. You need up-to-date information on current trends in health, nutrition, and education, which could have some bearing on your child's development.

We have compiled a list of popular parenting magazines from the United States, with brief descriptions and the addresses to which you can write for subscription information. Most magazines require payment before they will begin overseas delivery, and it takes six to eight weeks to process a new subscription. Unless otherwise noted, major credit cards (Visa, Master-Card, etc.,) are accepted, as are U.S. dollar checks or money orders.

Baby Magazine

636 Avenue of the Americas, New York, New York 10011, USA
☎ (212) 989-8181
Monthly magazine covering topics of interest to expectant and new parents, such as baby care and child development. U.S. check or money order only.

Child

New York Times, Magazine Division, 110 Fifth Ave., New York, New York 10011, USA
☎ (315) 247-7500
A glossy, fashion-oriented magazine with information on the latest trends for kids as well as helpful articles on parenting.

Growing Child

22 N. 2nd St., Box 1100, Lafayette, Indiana 47902, USA
☎ (317) 423-2624 fax (317) 423-4495
A monthly newsletter focusing on the issues, problems, and choices that parents face as their children grow. Most useful for first-time parents who want month-by-month information on the mental and physical development of their children.

Mothering

P.O. Box 1690, Santa Fe, New Mexico 87504, USA
☎ (505) 984-8116 fax (505) 982-6790

A quarterly publication dealing with all aspects of parenting, from infancy through the teenage years. Of special interest is the readers forum and the international focus of the magazine.

New Beginnings

P.O. Box 1209, Franklin Park, Illinois 60131-8209, USA
☎ (708) 455-7730 fax (708) 455-0125

An inexpensive bimonthly publication from La Leche League International. In addition to breastfeeding information, you will find articles on child-rearing, nutrition, and more.

Parenting

P.O. Box 52424 Boulder, Colorado 82321-2424, USA
☎ (303) 447-9330

A magazine with a fresh layout and glossy photographs and articles addressing parenting issues in the world today.

Parents

P.O. Box 3055, Harlan, Iowa 51593-2119, USA
☎ (515) 247-7500

A wealth of information about every stage of development. This is one of the longest-running popular magazines for parents in North America.

Pediatrics For Parents

358 Broadway, Suite 105, Box 1069, Bangor, Maine 04401, USA
☎ (207) 942-6212

A monthly newsletter covering medical aspects of rearing children and educating parents about children's health.

The Exceptional Parent

1170 Commonwealth Ave., Boston, Massachusetts 02134, USA
☎ (617) 536-8961 fax (617) 730-8742

A magazine covering issues of concern to parents of disabled children.

Twins

P.O. Box 12045, Overland Park, Kansas 66212, USA
☎ (913) 722-1090 fax (913) 722-1767

A magazine for parents of multiples offering support and interesting and informative articles.

Working Mother

Box 53861, Boulder, Colorado 80322, USA
☎ (303) 447-9330

A magazine for working mothers but with information of interest to all parents on child care, health, and fashion.

WHO'S MINDING THE KIDS?

Baby-sitters in Japan come in all shapes, sizes, and nationalities. There are many options for creative child care that are affordable. It is also possible to hire live-in help from abroad by becoming a sponsor.

BABY-SITTING SERVICES

There are a number of baby-sitting services in Japan that serve both the Japanese and the foreign community. These services are numerous and competitive in the Tokyo area. To find help in your area, check at the bulletin boards where foreigners post messages and exchange information. If you live elsewhere in Japan, you may have to search for a service that will meet your needs, especially if you require an English-speaking baby-sitter or maid.

The companies offering baby-sitting services are usually more expensive for a one-time job than if you have a regular, independently hired baby-sitter. Often a company will refuse to send you the same person more than once for fear that you will hire her away from the service or use her during off hours. If you want to build a relationship with one or two sitters, check with the company to see if this is possible.

Most of the services listed below have a minimum charge for a certain number of hours, for example, ¥4,500 for a minimum of three hours, and then an hourly rate after that. You usually pay for transportation as well. Some of the services charge a registration fee that you pay upon joining, others charge an annual fee. Along with the names and phone numbers, we have specified below what kind of help each service offers, whether or not English is spoken, and additional comments as necessary.

| THROUGHOUT JAPAN |

Tom Sawyer Agency

Grandspot 105, 22-17 Sakuragaoka-cho, Shibuya-ku, Tokyo ☎ (03) 3770-9530
Centerpoint 3F, 1-3-4 Uchihirano-cho, Chuo-ku, Osaka-shi, Osaka-fu ☎ (06) 943-4530
Kobe ☎ (078) 221-6530; Kyoto ☎ (075) 371-1530

Branches of Tom Sawyer Agencies are located throughout Japan. They provide baby-sitting service twenty-four hours a day for children from birth to twelve years of age. The charges are reasonable at ¥3,000 for the first two hours and ¥1,200 per hour after that. You can become a member by paying a fee, and then your hourly rates will be lower. For reservations, you must call by 8:00 P.M. the day before you require service. Generally, no English is spoken.

GREATER TOKYO AREA

Homeaid

2-1-7 Ebara, Shinagawa-ku, Tokyo
☎ (03) 3781-7536　東京都品川区荏原 2-1-7
Homeaid has been in business for four years providing both maid and baby-sitting services. It is a small agency; baby-sitters are part time in most cases and maids work only on a regular basis. You need to call a couple of days beforehand to reserve baby-sitters. The owner, Mrs. Tajima, speaks English and only hires people with experience. Although she can provide baby-sitters who speak English, Mrs. Tajima stresses care over language, especially with infants. There is no membership fee, but there is a four-hour minimum charge for a maid and a three-hour minimum for a baby-sitter.

Japan Baby-Sitter Service

Shuwa Jingu Residence 405, 3-3-16 Sendagaya, Shibuya-ku, Tokyo
☎ (03) 3423-1251　東京都渋谷区千駄ヶ谷 3-3-16 秀和神宮レジデンス 405
This is a baby-sitting service that sends older, experienced women to baby-sit in your home. There is a three-hour minimum, and the rates are very reasonable. There is an additional fee for more than one child, or baby-sitting early in the morning, overnight, or in the evening after seven o'clock. Only Japanese is spoken.

Kinder Network

1-3-18 Shibuya B503, Shibuya-ku, Tokyo
☎ (03) 3486-8278　東京都渋谷区渋谷 1-3-18 B503

Kinder Network is strictly a baby-sitting service—they do not offer to clean your house. What they will do, however, is play with your child, give piano lessons, help with homework, and give all of their attention to the happiness and security of your little ones. There is an annual membership fee, and then an hourly rate (three-hour minimum). Call three days in advance for a reservation, Monday to Friday from 10:00 A.M. to 6:00 P.M. The office has only Japanese-speaking personnel; some sitters may speak English.

Nihon Baby-Sitter

Sun Palace Minami Urawa 206, 3-7-10 Minami Urawa, Urawa-shi, Saitama-ken
☎ (03) 3822-8058　埼玉県浦和市南浦和 3-7-10 サンパレス南浦和 206
Strictly a baby-sitting service, sitters are available for part-time or regular sitting. They can pick up children after school. Only Japanese is spoken.

Poppins Service

Hasebe No. 2 Bldg., 5-21-2 Hiroo, Shibuya-ku, Tokyo
☎ (03) 3447-2100　東京都渋谷区広尾 5-21-2 長谷部第 2 ビル
Poppins will provide baby-sitters for newborns to twelve-year-olds. The staff is made up of female college students with education in early childhood development, and older women who have experience as teachers or in the nursing field. They not only baby-sit, but also engage the children in activities throughout the day—they list twenty possibilities in their pamphlet. The service maintains a hot line to a doctor twenty-four hours a day from their main office. They will also clean and shop if necessary. There is a two-hour minimum charge. Only Japanese is spoken at the office, but your baby-sitter may speak some English.

Reiyukai

1-7-8 Azabudai, Minato-ku, Tokyo
☎ (03) 3586-7852　東京都港区麻布台 1-7-8
This service provides experienced sitters for newborns to nine-year-olds and the elderly. Only Japanese is spoken.

Takara Pink Unicorn, K.K.

Dai Ichi Tani Bldg. 7F, 1-18-6 Kandasuda-cho, Chiyoda-ku, Tokyo
☎ (03) 3255-0007　東京都千代田区神田須田町 1-18-6 第一谷ビル 7F
Takara Pink Unicorn is a members-only baby-sitting service. Their sitters are all licensed nursery school teachers or nurses. There is a registration fee of ¥15,000, and an annual membership fee of ¥15,000 which covers the cost of an A.I.U. insurance policy for the child. There is an hourly fee, and a three-hour minimum. Reservations must be made one week to ten days in advance. They will baby-sit children from birth to twelve years old.

Tokyo Domestic Service

6-10-42 Akasaka, Minato-ku, Tokyo
☎ (03) 584-4769　東京都港区赤坂 6-10-42
The granddaddy of hired help in Tokyo, this service has been in business for thirty-five years. Bilingual maids and baby-sitters are available. There is no membership fee; help is available weekly, on a regular basis, or part time.

PUBLIC DAY CARE CENTERS

Every ward or city sponsors its own day-care centers (*hoikuen*), and as a resident of that ward or city, you are entitled to use them. These centers provide good care at a very low cost and are specifically for families with two working parents or a disabled parent. Aside from the public *hoikuen*, run by the ward or city, there are private *hoikuen* that are licensed by the ward or city. Public *hoikuen* accept children from four months of age, although some may only accept them from one year. Private *hoikuen* may accept children under four months.

The *hoikuen* schedule follows the Japanese school system in that age requirements must be met as of March 31. Your ward or city office will usually accept applications or they will direct you to your nearest welfare center (*fukushi jimusho*). A Japanese-speaking person is often useful when making your application. You will need to show proof that both parents are employed full time or that the primary care-giver is disabled or sick. After applying, you will be called in a couple of weeks for an interview with you and your child. To apply to a private *hoikuen*, go to the facility directly and ask about applications. All children must have a physical exam before entering a *hoikuen*. You should apply before the middle of January for April entrance. If you apply during the middle of the year, there may be a waiting list, and you will be accepted when there is an opening. Standard hours for *hoikuen* are 8:30 A.M. to 5:00 P.M., and at licensed centers meals are provided. The employees will most likely speak only Japanese, but these day-care centers are an economical and convenient solution for many parents throughout Japan.

PRIVATE DAY-CARE CENTERS

In the private sector, day-care centers tend to look like international preschools. They charge large fees and have a schedule that they follow throughout the day to keep the children happy and entertained. The concept of a "nursery," to which you can take your child and leave him for a few hours, is new to Japan. As more mothers find themselves without grandparents and relatives nearby to help out with the children, the need for these services will continue to grow. There is a fine line between what should be called a nursery and what is really a day-care center that will accept drop-ins. We have listed some of both types. In Tokyo as well as outlying areas, nursery services are often available at department stores (see chap. 2) and at churches. Also check the information bulletin boards at community centers and grocery stores to find out about day care in your area.

Child Care International

Minami Azabu A Bldg., 1-6-36 Minami Azabu, Minato-ku, Tokyo
☎ (03) 5484-8381　東京都港区南麻布 1–6–36 南麻布 A ビル

Run by the U.S. Bright Horizons child care centers and a Japanese company, this center accepts children age six months to six years for a minimum of two hours from 8:30 A.M. TO 8:30 P.M. A one-time fee of ¥50,000 is charged, plus an annual fee of ¥12,000 for facilities and an hourly rate of ¥2,250. One day's notice necessary; English and Japanese-speaking staff available.

Little Mate

ANA Hotel, 1-12-33 Akasaka, Minato-ku, Tokyo
☎ (03) 3589-0887　東京都港区赤坂 1–12–33

At the ANA Hotel nursery, reservations must be made prior to 7:00 P.M. of the previous day. They are open from noon to 8:00 P.M. Prices are reasonable: ¥4,000 for one hour, ¥5,000 for two hours, after which the fee is ¥3,000 per hour. They accept children up to school age (about age five).

Little Mate

Okura Hotel, 2-10-4 Toranomon, Minato-ku, Tokyo
☎ (03) 3582-0111 ext. 3838　東京都港区虎の門 2–10–4

This nursery is run by the same company that operates the service in the ANA Hotel, and the terms are the same (see above). Hours are from 10:00 A.M. to 8:00 P.M.

"D" Kids Studio

Laforet 4F, 1-8-10 Jingumae, Shibuya-ku, Tokyo
☎ (03) 3408-0194 fax (03) 3408-0125　東京都渋谷区神宮前 1–8–10 ラフォーレ 4F

"D" (for "Dear") Kids Studio is a "nursery" for two- to six-year-olds. It is located in the Dear Kids Laforet Building on the top floor in a single room. It is an ideal place to drop children for a few hours while you shop or go out to dinner in the Omote Sando/Harajuku area (see chap. 2). They welcome both Japanese and foreign children, and they have native English speakers on their staff. The schedule of classes from 11:00 A.M. to 7:50 P.M. includes music, art, stories, and entertainment. Lunch is offered for an extra charge from 1:00 P.M. to 1:50 P.M. There is a membership fee and then a charge per 50-minute "class." Call for reservations in either English or Japanese.

EOS Social Service Club (ESSC)

1-34-6 Kita Senzoku, Ota-ku, Tokyo
☎ (03) 3723-7608　東京都大田区北千束 1–34–6

ESSC is available for use on a regular basis only. You must become a member and pay a registration fee, then an annual fee on top of the hourly wage. All of their employees are trained, and they educate the children as well as baby-sit them. They do not come to your home; instead, the children are cared for in volunteers' homes throughout greater Tokyo. They try to find a home as near to your house as possible. You may use them on a regular day each week, or you may change the days and times from week to week. Only Japanese is spoken.

Fairy Tale

TDF Bldg., 3-20-5 Shimo Ochiai, Shinjuku-ku, Tokyo
☎ (03) 5996-9937 東京都新宿区下落合 3–20–5 TDF ビール

This baby-sitting service, or "Baby and Kid's Farm" as they call their operation, will look after children from newborn to the age of ten at any time of day or night. Reservations must be made three days in advance. For non-members the price is ¥2,000 per hour (¥2,200 from 9 P.M. to 9 A.M.). Those mothers intending to make regular use of the service can become a Fairy Tale member by paying a ¥20,000 registration fee and a ¥10,000 annual fee, after which the hourly rate is ¥1,600.

New Otani Hotel

4-1 Kioi-cho, Chiyoda-ku, Tokyo
☎ (03) 3265-1111 ext. 351 東京都千代田区紀尾井町 4–1

The hours at this nursery are 9:00 A.M. to 10:00 P.M. Reservations and membership are not required. There is a minimum of two hours and a charge for every thirty minutes after that. They accept children up to school age (about five years of age).

Potpourri

2-10-1 Botan 201, Koto-ku, Tokyo ☎ (03) 3630-1828 (office) 東京都江東区牡丹
1-8 Maihama, Urayasu-shi, Chiba-ken ☎ (0473) 55-5000 (nursery) 2–10–1–201

Potpourri is a nursery with a licensed professional staff who will take care of children under age nine. The nursery is fully equipped with food, diapers, and toys. A doctor is on call in case of emergency. They are open twenty-four hours a day with overnight service. Advance reservation and prepayment is required, and you must have some proof of insurance with you before you leave your child. Only Japanese is spoken.

A LITTLE ROMANCE

Many parents of young children would rather have a good night's sleep than a romantic evening out. Sleep is important, but we all know that a little romance is good for parents, too. For those times when you long for a refreshing break from parenthood, we have some ideas.

Everyone dreams of a remote island getaway with his or her spouse, but many children, especially a tiny baby, cannot go for a long period of time without Mom and Dad. Fortunately, we have found that a restaurant with the right atmosphere can create almost as much romance without the risk of sunburn.

Our first suggestion would be to find a favorite spot in the neighborhood for what we call a "quick getaway." These are the nights when you can put the kids to bed early and get the baby-sitter to stay late, or have a neighbor watch the children. No hassle with reservations, picking up an evening sitter, or traveling in rush hour. All you have to do is to sneak away for a quiet dinner together. We located an inexpensive restaurant with a great house wine, just fifteen minutes from home: A couple of hours spent dining there by candlelight is just as romantic as a weekend in Kyoto—without the expense or trauma of leaving the children behind.

For foreigners, Japan is the land of earthquakes and no grandparents. This and the price of travel in Japan often make it difficult to leave the children behind for long adult vacations. If you and your spouse are desperate for some time alone, consider a trip to one of Japan's infamous "love hotels," where you can rent a room for a secluded husband and wife tryst. As outrageous as the idea may seem, the best of these hotels are clean, and they cater to married couples as well as to young lovers. In certain areas, such as Shibuya, you will find a variety of "theme" hotels. If you can stop laughing long enough to check in, you can choose between a "French chateau" or a "Scarlet and Rhett" decor, for instance. In researching this chapter, we discovered that the hourly rates are quite reasonable, and the peace and quiet make love hotels worth a visit. Try bringing a bottle of wine and some bread and cheese for a relaxing afternoon or evening. Most of the basic hotel amenities, such as robes, slippers, shampoo, and toothbrushes, are available. One word of warning: The weekends are usually quite crowded, so you may not get your first choice of room, or perhaps you will have to wait for a vacancy. To find a nearby love hotel, ask one of your good Japanese friends or just keep your eyes open for an unusual-looking building with a silly name in English. Chances are that it is a love hotel.

For another getaway option without leaving town, you can splurge on a night at one of the luxury hotels. The price for one night's stay is about the same as dinner at a fancy restaurant. We have found that room service and a night of uninterrupted sleep can do wonders to rejuvenate a relationship. Traditional Japanese inns, or *ryokan*, offer a change of pace that we find romantic. Call the Tourist Information Center for a list of *ryokan* in your area. The Japanese Inn Group, (03) 3822-2251, and the Minshuku (family-run inn) Association, (03) 3216-6556, have lots of suggestions and also will make reservations. Asaba Ryokan in Shuzenji is one of our favorites, and it is only a couple of hours out of Tokyo. Write to Asaba Ryokan, Tagata-gun, Shuzenji-cho, Shuzenji, Shizuoka-ken, or call (0558) 72-0700 to make a reservation; don't forget to ask for a peaceful room overlooking the pond at the foot of the mountains. The best part is their *rotenburo*, or outdoor hot springs bath. If you visit a *ryokan* in Japan that has only segregated *rotenburo* or *ofuro* (indoor bath), do not be afraid to ask permission to bathe together. We have always been accommodated, especially if the inn is not too full or if we wait until late at night to enjoy the bath.

One drawback to staying at a *ryokan* is their policy of an early breakfast, after which they roll up your futon. Since we prefer to cuddle in our futon until a civilized hour, we try to make this clear the night before. We have even gone so far as to say that we were honeymooners in order to get special consideration. Another tactic is to skip breakfast, but again, try to discuss this the night before with your hosts since Japanese breakfasts involve a lot of preparation. The only other problems we have encountered at *ryokan* are the thin walls and no locks on the doors. We usually bring a small radio or tape player with our favorite music. We also suggest packing a bottle of your favorite beverage—do not forget an opener. Most *ryokan* food is delicious, but beer and orange juice are the standard drinks available.

We were always anxious about being away from our children when they were very young, and fortunately we happened to stumble upon a *ryokan* right in our neighborhood. It is not as exotic as some of the out-of-town places, but we felt relieved that we could enjoy a cheap vacation for one night (only ¥5,000) and still be within walking distance of our house. Ask around your area about local *ryokan*; you may be surprised at what you find.

As parents, we all face burnout from time to time. Taking a break from the routine is a good idea. However, when an opportunity arises to visit other parts of Japan or Asia, consider taking the kids along. Jet lag is not much of a problem, and people in this part of the world welcome children at hotels and restaurants. Children are an integral and special part of society in Asia. We have usually found it much simpler to take our kids along than to leave them behind.

13 Bicultural Parenting Resources

DAD. YOU TAKE YOUR SHOES OFF IN THIS COUNTRY.

As Japan moves toward internationalization, more respect is being shown for the advantages of bilingualism and biculturalism. An understanding of the Japanese language and Japanese customs is an advantage that you may want for your child.

Some parents are content for their children to learn a smattering of Japanese and to enjoy bits of culture at festivals or other events. Other families make a more determined effort to see that their children absorb the Japanese culture and their own in equal amounts. This approach is especially important to the growing number of bicultural families with members of different nationalities.

Many expatriates assume that by living in a foreign country their children will automatically pick up the language. However, it is not quite that simple. Especially with a language as difficult as Japanese, commitment and extra effort on the parents' part is crucial.

While interviewing successful bilingual families for this book, it became obvious that a tried and tested formula that works for everyone does not exist. The parents' native language, the schools available, even the child's personality, all play an important part. We hope that some of our insights and suggestions will be helpful in creating a bilingual environment for your child.

Foreign families living in areas of Japan where there are no international schools or few foreign families may find that their children pick up the Japanese language fairly easily. The parents can continue to reinforce their native language, such as English, at home, in order for the child to be exposed to both languages. However, once the child becomes older and attends Japanese school and spends free time playing with Japanese friends, it then becomes more of an effort to keep up the English. Most parents in this situation mentioned several ways to reinforce the native language, such as visiting their home country at least once a year, sending the older children to summer school there, teaching English to Japanese friends from the child's class, limiting viewing of Japanese TV and watching videos in English instead, having English-speaking visitors or relatives in the house, and reading daily to the children in English.

As you can see, such solutions demand a lot of time and effort from the parents. In a few cases, parents mentioned that it was sometimes difficult to push the children to keep up with their English for two reasons: Their children were too tired after their Japanese studies at school, and they didn't like to use English because it made them stand out as "different" from their peers. We all know how important peer pressure is to kids, but especially in Japan where "the nail that stands up gets hammered down," being different can be painful and undesirable.

For families living among the international community, it can be a struggle for the children to learn Japanese. If the parents speak English at home and the children attend international schools, then there is very little opportunity for interaction with other Japanese children. These days there are areas of Tokyo where one can go for days without speaking Japanese. More and more Japanese speak English well enough to hold basic conversations. One American mother who frequented her neighborhood playground in the hopes of finding Japanese playmates for her son was surprised to find that the vast majority of Japanese mothers she met spoke English. They were delighted that their children would have a chance to learn English from the American child, and English became the basic language used in their gatherings, much to the frustration of the foreigner.

If you find yourself living in a "*gaijin* gulch" in Japan, there are a few things you can do to expose your children to the Japanese language. First, it is a good idea to study the language yourself and practice using basic expressions with the children. If your children are preschool age, then you may want to get involved in a neighborhood playgroup, or *yochien*. There are some Japanese preschools that accept children as young as eighteen months of age, but the average *yochien* accepts children from the age of three or four.

For Tokyoites, an ideal balance in language may be achieved by sending a child to a Japanese *yochien* five days a week until age five or six, and then on to an international school such as Nishimachi International. This school emphasizes Japanese in its curriculum, although the basic instruction is in English. By attending a *yochien*, a child's Japanese-language skills may be advanced enough to participate in the "F" program at Nishimachi. These are students who are studying Japanese as a first language in a very intense program similar to the Japanese school system, in addition to their international education. Of the expatriates we interviewed, quite a few claimed that their children were completely bilingual thanks to this system.

In an English-speaking family environment, another option is to send a child to Japanese school from *yochien* on through high school. There is no doubt that the Japanese school system offers a thorough education, and more and more foreign families are taking this route. However, depending on the child's personality, this can be a stressful and demanding choice. Mothers play an important supporting role in the Japanese educational system, and a foreigner should be aware of the time and commitment involved. One British mother said the hardest part of having a child in the Japanese school system was the reams of paper sent home with her child each day. Because she couldn't read *kanji*, she had to depend on a neighbor or her husband's secretary to translate some of the information. This is a problem in the lower grades, but fortunately the older students can read the material themselves.

If you are concerned that your child is not hearing enough Japanese, try limiting English videos in favor of Japanese TV shows. You could enroll your child in a tutoring program, such as Kumon, where he or she can get extra help in a variety of subjects, from *hiragana* to math, usually with Japanese students. Take advantage of extracurricular activities or summer camps where your child can meet other Japanese children. One family invited a Japanese college student to stay with them for the summer. She was asked to speak Japanese to the children in exchange for English lessons with the mother.

In Japan, there are several organizations with a vested interest in bilingualism. The Japan Association of Language Teachers (JALT) has established a National Special Interest Group on bilingualism. At the annual national JALT conference a symposium on bilingualism has been held for the past seven years. Masayo Yamamoto, an assistant professor at Ashiya University, and her husband, Jim Swan, were instrumental in organizing the special interest group. The group regularly publishes a newsletter entitled N-Significance. For more information about the newsletter, write to John Dean, Language Center, 1-3-18 Wakinohamacho, Chuo-ku, Kobe-shi, Hyogo-ken 651, or call (078) 261-4316.

Bicultural Families, which was founded in 1986, is an organization that strives to help families whose lives straddle two cultures, one of which is Japanese. The group seeks to pool information on educational options, bilingualism, and other issues associated with raising children in dual cultures. In the future they hope to organize seminars and family activities and to resume publication of their newsletter. In September 1990, a library was established to provide bilingual children with easy access to English-language books. For more information, contact Pam Noda, Pia Inokashira Koen #102, 4-7-12 Inokashira, Mitaka-shi, Tokyo 181.

The Association of Foreign Wives of Japanese (AFWJ) is an organization familiar with the challenges of bilingual and bicultural development in children. Although membership is open only to foreigners married to Japanese men, the journal published by this group contains many interesting articles and resources about bilingualism. For contact numbers and information about groups in your area, phone Beverly Nakamura (045) 742-6979, fax (045) 721-1315 in Yokohama or Rose Iwata in Tokyo (03) 3397-1007.

The association Kokusai Kekkon o Kangaeru Kai, which was formed as a support group for Japanese women married to foreign men, offers a wealth of information and advice on all matters pertaining to bilingualism and biculturalism. Whether you need information on dual nationality or just somebody to share your problems with, the association is an important source of information. For more information about groups in your area write to Yoshiko Delehouze, 1-15-9 Inokashira, Mitaka-shi, Tokyo, or call (0422) 46-6535.

The International Children's Bunko Association (ICBA) was formed in 1980 by a British educator living in Tokyo to address the needs of Japanese returnee children who had acquired fluency in other languages. There are branches of ICBA all over Japan and in some foreign countries as well.

The founder of ICBA, Opal Dunn, believed that reading was the key to retaining proficiency in a second language. Therefore, each ICBA branch maintains a library of children's books, as well as cassette tapes and video-tapes. In addition, at each branch, volunteer native speakers read to the children and conduct games and activities in English.

Not only returnees but all English-speaking children are welcome to join ICBA. This program enables foreign children whose stronger language is Japanese to interact in English. Several foreign mothers volunteer their time at ICBA so that their children can have access to the educational services there. To find out about the ICBA branch nearest you, call (03) 3496-8688.

A highly recommended newsletter on bilingualism in general is *The Bilingual Family Newsletter*, published by Multilingual Matters. A subscription to Japan is U.S. $12.00. For further information, write Multilingual Matters Ltd., Bank House, 8a Hill Rd., Clevedon, Avon BS21 7HH, England or call (272) 876519.

For families who are attempting to maintain proficiency in a language other than English, the Early Advantage Programs for Children offers help. This company sells the BBC course for children wishing to study French, Spanish, or Italian. Using a character called Muzzy, the programs consist of fun-filled videos with songs and animation. For more information, contact Early Advantage, 47 Richards Avenue, Norwalk, Connecticut 06857, USA.

Teach Me Tapes is the name of a company that carries instructional cassette tapes and books for young children in several foreign languages, including Japanese. For more information, write to Teach Me Tapes, 10500 Bren Road E., Minneapolis, Minnesota 55343, USA.

The Intercultural Press is a bookshop in the United States that specializes in books and videos relating to intercultural issues and experiences. They carry several of the books on our suggested reading list. For further information, write to The Intercultural Press Inc., P.O. Box 768, Yarmouth, Maine 04096, USA, or call (207) 846-5168.

Suggested titles in English for parents who are interested in a bilingual education for their children include:

Bilingual Children: Guidance for the Family, by George Saunders (Multilingual Matters, 1982).

The Bilingual Family: A Handbook for Parents, by Edith Harding and Philip Riley (Cambridge University Press, 1986).

Language Acquisition of a Bilingual Child: A Sociolinguistic Perspective, by Alvino E. Fantini (Multilingual Matters, 1985).

The Bilingual Experience: A Book for Parents, by Eveline de Jong (Cambridge University Press, 1986).

Life with Two Languages: An Introduction to Bilingualism, by Francois Grosjean (Harvard University Press, 1982).

Raising Children Bilingually: The Pre-school Years, by Lenore Arnberg (Multilingual Matters, 1987).

Recommended books in Japanese include:

Bilingual, by Masayo Yamamoto (Taishukan, 1991).

Nihon ni Okeru Bilingualism, by Yamamoto, Maher, Yashiro, and Kim (Kenkyusha, 1991).

14
Tips for
Residents-
to-be

JAPAN......

So you are off to Japan! Whether you are planning a brief vacation or are about to leave on a new overseas posting, your entire family is very lucky. There are many positive aspects about life in Japan with children. Incredibly low crime rates and subways safe enough for first-graders mean a lot to parents. Perhaps the most endearing aspect of Japan is the nature of the Japanese themselves. Children are greatly respected, and they play an integral part in Japanese society. To the parent, that can mean anything from feeling welcome with your children at any restaurant or concert to knowing that the whole neighborhood will help keep an eye on your children.

We have lived in Japan a combined total of thirteen years. It may be interesting to note that one of us was dragged to this country kicking and screaming while the other embarked upon the adventure with great enthusiasm. Anyway, after having babies and educating children here, we both agree that Japan is one of the best places in the world for parents and their kids to live.

BEFORE YOU MOVE

Try not to be daunted by the sheer logistics of transporting your family and household goods to Japan in one piece. Moving to Japan and settling in is not so difficult if you know what to expect and make plans before you go.

If you live in the United States, you may want to obtain a copy of *The Summary of Information for Shippers of Household Goods*, published by the Interstate Commerce Commission, Washington, D.C. 20423, USA. This booklet gives a step-by-step plan for moving, including definitions of terms and helpful suggestions for packing and hiring a moving company. You can order a copy by writing to the above address.

SETTING UP A SUPPORT NETWORK

There are many details to attend to before moving overseas. One of the most important is setting up bank accounts, post office boxes, or other means of taking care of bills and mail that will come to your home address. One of the easiest ways to do this is to recruit a close friend or relative to receive mail and even pay small bills on your behalf. We call this person our "contact." There will also be times when you will need something from home or want flowers or gifts sent to someone in your home country.

To make this easy for your contact to do, you may want to give them access to a small amount of money for this type of gift and for postage. If you will need things sent to you overseas, leave your contact person with a supply of address labels and envelopes. We have one friend who asks her contact to videotape television programs for her children. Each year when she is on home leave, she buys a supply of videotapes and envelopes, which she stamps with the correct postage. All her contact has to do is tape the show and drop it in the mail.

If you are unable to set up this sort of system with someone from your home country, there are also companies in the United States and Great Britain that provide such a service. Airend is an errand service that is based in Los Angeles, California. For a small fee, the company's owners will make purchases at a number of well-known stores, send flowers to someone in the United States, tape television programs, set up a post office box in the United States and forward your mail to Japan, or search out information you may be needing from your home country. You may pay for the services in U.S. dollars or in yen through a Japanese bank account. For more information, contact Marilyn O'Toole, Airend, 867 Roxbury Drive, Pasadena, California 91104, USA. Call or fax (818) 797-0326.

For those whose home base is Great Britain, a company called Linkup London will provide similar services for you. For a brochure that outlines all their services, write to Rebecca Wells and Jacqueline Cooke, Linkup London, 86 Tachbrook St., London SW1V 2NB, England. Call (71) 8282602.

DON'T LEAVE HOME WITHOUT . . .

You may find that many products that you can buy regularly in your home country are not available in Japan. Stock up on these! It is especially important to buy products for babies and children in large quantities before moving, not just to save money, but to save time and energy as well.

There are many listings throughout the book of mail-order sources in the United States for children's items that are not available in Japan. There are also a number of co-ops in Japan that sell imported goods and cater to foreigners (see the listing in chap. 10). Of course, you can always ask your contact to send "care packages," but if you have the chance before you move—buy the store out!

What to stock up on? Seasonal costumes and decorations for the kids and the house; vitamins; books, videos, and games in English; Western-sized bedding; indoor shoes and slippers for the entire family; and all of the special food and toiletry items you cannot live without! There are also some medicines you will need to buy abroad if you have young children in the house. For this information, as well as mail-order sources that will ship these items overseas, see chapters 3, 4, 8, 9, and 10.

Before leaving home, you may also want to buy a large supply of Western-sized envelopes, address labels, airmail stationery, and any other personalized stationery you may want with your new address on it. Not only are these items difficult to find in Japan, but they are also expensive. A comprehensive mail-order source for all sorts of personalized stationery goods at reasonable prices is the Writewell Co. You can write them at 215 W. Michigan Street, Post Office Box 6112, Indianapolis, Indiana 46206-6112, USA. Call (317) 264-3730 or fax (317) 264-3733 for faster service. They will mail overseas, and they accept U.S. checks or money orders and VISA, MasterCard, and American Express credit cards.

MAIL ORDER FROM ABROAD

Shopping by mail-order catalog has become a way of life for many parents in the United States and other countries. Not only do we save the time and anxiety involved in dragging our children through the stores but we also find that the financial savings can be quite substantial.

In Japan we are faced with the unusually high cost of outfitting our babies and children, plus the unavailability of certain products that we know and trust. Fortunately, many catalog companies now ship overseas and throughout the book we have compiled some of the best.

Before you leave home, you may want to write these mail-order companies and ask them for a copy of their latest catalog and overseas shipping instructions. By doing this, you will have the catalogs as a resource as soon as you step off the plane, instead of waiting weeks for the company to send you one.

To receive a copy of any of the catalogs listed in this book, contact the company by mail, telephone, or fax. Many companies will send you a catalog free of charge; others may charge a small fee to cover mailing costs. Payment may be made by US check or money order and most major credit cards are accepted, although there is often a minimum purchase for credit card orders. When placing an order with a credit card by fax, be sure to include the expiration date, shipping address, and item number or description along with your signature. For overseas shipments, there is either a set rate or a charge based on the weight of the package. Many companies use Federal Express or United Postal Service for delivery within a week. If you are not in a hurry, sea-mail orders are much cheaper.

These catalogs are also handy for ordering gifts for friends and relatives in other countries. The company will usually gift-wrap and mail the package directly to the recipient. We have contacted all the catalog companies listed in this book, and have ourselves ordered from most of them and found them committed to offering you the best available clothes, books, tapes, games, toys, and baby equipment on the market.

ORIENTATION PROGRAMS

It is helpful if your family can attend an orientation program, if possible, prior to your departure. Even if you are not able to take part in one of these seminars, the company or institution that runs them may be willing to send you orientation information through the mail.

If you live in a major city, you can contact the local Japan Society for information on lectures, language studies, or orientation programs. Learning the Japanese language is a real challenge, so you may want to take either a crash course or a few basic lessons before you leave for Japan. As in any country, a basic vocabulary will make life much easier. The Berlitz School offers some excellent programs, from a traveler's guide complete with phrase book and cassette, to intensive private language courses. We have found that cassette language tapes played in the car and around the house get the children excited about the move and help them to feel comfortable trying out a new language.

ORIENTATIONS AT HOME

Business Council for International Understanding Institute

The American University, 3301 New Mexico Avenue, N.W., Washington, D.C. 20016, USA

☎ (202) 686-2771

The BCIU Institute is over thirty years old and is the most comprehensive

and elite of all the U.S. orientation programs. They train families and businessmen for life in 147 countries, and they have excellent programs on Japan. In exploring the role and function of families overseas, BCIU offers learning sessions for the whole family, from four-year-olds to teenagers to parents. An intensive language program is often incorporated in the workshops.

Clarke Consulting Group

3 Lagoon Drive, Suite 230, Redwood City, California 94065, USA
☎ (415) 591-8100
Clarke Consulting Group specializes in intercultural consulting and training for Japanese and American companies. Besides their consulting services for corporations, they provide training for managers and their families. Training offered includes immersion programs for those on extended assignments overseas, seminars for those who travel overseas, and language training in both English and Japanese.

Moran, Stahl, and Boyer (MS&B)

355 Lexington Ave., New York, New York 10017, USA
☎ (212) 661-4878 fax (212) 949-1693
Office locations in the USA in Boulder, Colorado, and Los Angeles, California. Overseas offices in London and Tokyo.
MS&B is one of the top cross-cultural training and consulting firms in the United States. They have been conducting training seminars and workshops covering over eighty countries for more than twenty-seven years. MS&B seminars are also conducted in Japan through INTEC Japan Inc. located in Tokyo (see the Orientations in Japan section of this chapter).

Among the services MS&B offers are cross-cultural training for executives, repatriation training, and seminars on working with the Japanese. In conjunction with family or group orientations, there is a program for teenagers and children who are making an overseas move with their family.

ORIENTATIONS IN JAPAN

If you did not have time to take part in an orientation program back home, there are some services in Tokyo that can help you adapt to life in Japan. The following companies have been established to help foreigners cope with the adjustments. They can assist you in every detail of settling in Japan, from getting a driver's license to finding the right school for your children. Elsewhere in Japan, the various government and community centers (see chap. 12) sometimes offer orientation classes for foreign residents.

Intec Japan Inc.

7-5-27 Akasaka 618, Minato-ku, Tokyo
☎ (03) 3224-1812 fax (03) 3224-1822　東京都港区赤坂 7-5-27-618

This company offers services for both foreigners and Japanese who are moving to a new country. Among the programs available in Japan are language training (both English and Japanese), intercultural business training, and cross-cultural adaptation training.

Oak Associates and Welcome Furoshiki

Riviera 3B, 1-21-22 Higashiyama, Meguro-ku, Tokyo
☎ (03) 3760-8558 fax (03) 3760-8411　東京都目黒区東山 1-21-22 ルビエラ 3B

Oak Associates is a company that has been assisting newly arrived expatriates in Tokyo for more than ten years. The company offers a variety of orientation programs, from a one-time orientation on business practices for the executive to a complete life-style orientation for the whole family. The services can be customized to meet your individual needs. Oak Associates' personnel can help with all the practicalities of setting up house in Japan, and they remain available for consultation anytime during the client's stay. For more information, contact Oak Associates.

Welcome Furoshiki is a division of Oak Associates and serves as a sort of welcome wagon for foreigners. This service is sponsored by businesses and is free of charge. A Welcome Furoshiki representative will come and visit your hotel or home and give you an information packet about life in Tokyo, all wrapped in a *furoshiki* (a traditional Japanese cloth used for carrying things). The representative can also assist you with any other questions you may have. To set up an appointment for a visit or for more information, call (03) 3352-0765.

Tokyo General Agency (TGA)

Sonic Bldg., 3-2-12 Nishi Azabu, Minato-ku, Tokyo
☎ (03) 3408-5331 fax (03) 3408-5505　東京都港区西麻布 3-2-12 ソニックビル

TGA provides a complete range of services for business people and their families moving to Japan from overseas. TGA has three types of services. For overseas companies opening offices in Japan and for companies already established here, TGA offers a complete range of one-time and ongoing services tailored to the specific needs of each particular company. TGA also offers the Family Support Service, which is designed to facilitate a quick and easy transition to life in Japan for the entire family. Foreign residents are also given a chance to participate in activities and outings to help them to understand and relate to Japanese society through TGA Club.

Membership fees are quite reasonable and include an excellent monthly newsletter and opportunities to take trips and participate in Japanese cultural activities.

Tokyo Orientations

4-2-41 Roppongi 304, Tokyo　東京都港区六本木 4-2-41-304
☎ (03) 3746-0566

Tokyo Orientations, a relocation service serving Tokyo and Yokohama, provides newly arrived expatriates with practical information to enable them to function in their new home as quickly and as smoothly as possible. Cultural insights supplement topics pertinent to everyday household operation. Staff members headed by Nikki Thompson assist clients in obtaining necessary documents, familiarize them with their neighborhood, and address the individual needs and concern of each family. Follow-up telephone assistance is available throughout the client's stay in Tokyo.

REFERENCE BOOKS

There are a number of useful and comprehensive books that you should read about living in Japan. They will help you to understand the insurance system, emergency procedures at hospitals, what to do in case of a major earthquake—just about everything you may need to know while living as a foreigner in Japan. There are also books that will give you information on food, shopping, and cultural attractions. Some of these books may be found in your home country, and most are available at the major English-language bookstores listed in chapter 4 or through the foreign-resident service organizations throughout the country. The following is a short list of books to which you should have access during your stay in Japan (medical books are listed in chap. 10).

A Guide to Food Buying in Japan, by Carolyn R. Krouse (Charles E. Tuttle, 1986). This is an invaluable sourcebook for solving some of the mysteries of grocery shopping in Japan.

Born to Shop, Tokyo, by Suzy Gershman and Judith Thomas (Bantam Books Inc., 1987).

For insights on buying everything from oriental antiques to pearls, this book gives a shopper's view of Tokyo.

Living in Japan (American Chamber of Commerce in Japan).

This book offers tips on coping with the everyday aspects of life in Japan, from arriving here, to immigration, to your departure. The chapter on legal matters is especially helpful. To order, write to the chamber of commerce at 7F, Fukide Bldg. No. 2, 4-1-21 Toranomon, Minato-ku, Tokyo 105. Or phone (03) 3433-5381. In Kansai, write c/o Searle, Osaka Higashi P.O. Box 698, Osaka 540-91. Or call (06) 222-6251.

Living in Kobe (Community House Information Service, 1989).
See chapter 12 for listing under Community House.

Tokyo, A Bilingual Atlas (Kodansha International, 1987).
You will need a good map while you are living in Tokyo, and this is one of the best. In book form, the roads and landmarks are in both English and Japanese.

Tokyo City Guide, by Connors and Yoshida (Ryuko Tsushin Co., Ltd., 1984).
This is a guidebook popular with tourists and residents alike. It is easy to read and full of helpful tips.

Your Life in Tokyo, A Manual for Foreign Residents. vol. 1 and vol. 2 (Japan Times, 1987).
Volume 1 of this series is devoted to daily life in Tokyo, whereas volume 2 covers leisure. Both volumes are comprehensive and up-to-date.

This book is dedicated to our daddies who always encouraged us to look farther than our own backyards: R. Curtis Huey (in memoriam 1931– 1988), and William A. Wiltshire.

We would like to thank the following people for their advice, time, and support:

Dr. Ryoko Dozono
Dr. Gabriel Symonds
Louise Shimizu
Etsuko Sekine
Mercy Wijesiri
Kumiko Nishimura
Cecile Click
Janet Ohuchi
Beckie Johnson
Mary Nino
Stephanie Cook
Kathy Yamane
Mary Noguchi
Kay Ueno
Noriko Faust
Sumiko Kataoka
Barry Lancet
Hilary Sagar
Pam Noda
Beverly Huey
Ann B. Wiltshire
The Minato Ward office
Mike and Ray at the McComb Post Office
Members of AFWJ
Members and friends of Tokyo Union Church
Sabine Schmid
Rial Ellsworth
and Jean Pearce

Special thanks and appreciation go to our husbands, Mike and Craig, and to our children: Kennedy and Kane Kanagawa, and Michelena, Nathan, and Gabriella Erickson.

INDEX

For ease of reference, all names of stores, parks, zoos, etc., appear in italics.

The authors, Diane and Jeanne, write a weekly column, "Kidscene," for the *Asahi Evening News*. They have lived in Japan for a combined total of fourteen years. Diane and Jeanne are shown above with their "research assistants."

日本子育て便利帳
Japan for Kids

1992年 3 月15日　第 1 刷発行
1999年 4 月16日　第 6 刷発行

著　者　ジーン・エリクソン／ダイアン・カナガワ

発行者　野間佐和子

発行所　講談社インターナショナル株式会社
　　　　　〒112-8652 東京都文京区音羽 1-17-14
　　　　　電話：03-3944-6493

印刷所　株式会社　平河工業社

製本所　株式会社　堅省堂

Emergency Calls	24-hour Police Service	110
	24-hour Ambulance and Firefighting Service	119
General Information	NTT Directory Assistance in English	
	Kanto area	(03) 3277-1010
	Kansai area	(06) 313-1010
	NTT Town Network Service	(03) 3201-1010
	Japan Hotline	(03) 3586-0110
	Foreign Residents' Advisory Center	(03) 5320-7744
	Hospital Information	(03) 5272-0303
		(03) 3212-2323
Travel Information	Japan Travel Bureau (JTB)	(03) 3276-7777
	Tourist Information Center	
	Tokyo	(03) 3502-1461
	Kyoto	(075) 371-5649
	Toll free (Kansai area)	0120-444800
	Toll free (Kanto area)	0120-222800
	Teletourist Info (recorded info)	(03) 3503-2911
	Japanese Inn Group	(03) 3822-2251
	JR Infoline	(03) 3423-0111
	Narita Airport Flight Information	(0476) 32-2800
	Airport Baggage Service Company (abc)	(03) 3545-1131
Counseling Services	Tokyo English Life Line (TELL)	(03) 5481-4347
	Japan Helpline	0120-461997
	International Counseling Center	(078) 856-2201
	Tokyo Center for Foreigners'	
	Human Rights	(03) 3581-2302
Community Information outside Tokyo	Osaka International House	(06) 772-5931
	Nagoya International Association	(052) 581-5678
	Kobe Community House and Info Center	(078) 857-6540
	Kyoto International Community House	(075) 752-3010
	Kobe International Community Center	(078) 322-0030
Immigration	Tokyo Immigration Office, Otemachi	(03) 3213-8111
	Hakozaki Branch Immigration Office	(03) 3664-3046
	Meguro Branch Immigration Office	(03) 5704-1081
Tokyo Ward Offices	Adachi Ward	(03) 3882-1111
	Arakawa Ward	(03) 3802-3111
	Bunkyo Ward	(03) 3812-7111
	Chiyoda Ward	(03) 3264-0151
	Chuo Ward	(03) 3543-0211
	Edogawa Ward	(03) 3652-1151
	Itabashi Ward	(03) 3964-1111
	Katsushika Ward	(03) 3695-1111
	Kita Ward	(03) 3908-1111
	Information for Foreign Residents	(03) 3908-1111
	Koto Ward	(03) 3647-9111
	Meguro Ward	(03) 3715-1111
	Information for Foreign Residents	(03) 3792-2113
	Minato Ward	(03) 3578-2111
	Information for Foreign Residents	(03) 3578-2053

hello?